THE UPPER ROOM

Disciplines
1993

Coordinating Editor
Glenda Webb

Consulting Editors
Robert Benson
Lynne M. Deming
Lynn W. Gilliam
Charla H. Honea
Janet R. McNish
John S. Mogabgab
Robin Philpo Pippin
Mary Lou Redding
Mary Lou Santillán Baert

UPPER
ROOM BOOKS
NASHVILLE

The Upper Room Disciplines 1993

© 1992 by The Upper Room. All rights reserved.

No part of this book may be used or reproduced in any manner whatsoever without permission except in the case of brief quotations embodied in critical articles or reviews. For information address The Upper Room, P.O. Box 189, 1908 Grand Avenue, Nashville, Tennessee 37202-0189.

Cover photo © John Netherton
Cover design by Jim Bateman

Meditations for the week of October 4-10 originally appeared in *The Upper Room Disciplines 1987,* copyright © 1986 by The Upper Room. Those for the week of April 26–May 2 originally appeared in *The Upper Room Disciplines 1990,* copyright © 1989 by The Upper Room.

Page 387 constitutes an extension of this copyright page.

ISBN 0-8358-0651-0
Printed in the United States of America

CONTENTS

FOREWORD

Somewhere I read a theory about what is wrong with Western society—we no longer sit on our front porches. In days past, the writer explained, we greeted our neighbors from our front porches, and our neighbors returned our greetings. We saw children ride by on bikes or tricycles, or skate by on roller skates. We saw ambulances, police cars, and fire engines as they passed; and if they stopped, we knew one of our neighbors needed help. We heard the sounds of children laughing or crying and people working and perhaps even the angry sounds of people arguing. But we did see, and we did hear; and we were in touch with a world outside ourselves.

This picture of front-porch-sitting probably idealizes what has been (we tend to do that), and it surely oversimplifies what would need to be a many-faceted solution to our tendency to isolate ourselves. Even so, it does give us a glimpse into the continuing individualism of Western society—a society where people often move numerous times over the course of a lifetime, where many of our institutions have become impersonal, where extended family no longer functions as support, where family members work long hours and have little time or energy for outside commitments, where our contact with the world comes from a small box with a picture tube, which we stare at from our isolation behind locked doors and the soft hum of a climate-control system. Indeed, this isolated lifestyle has become recognizable enough that it now has its own coined term, *cocooning*—a sure sign that it has come into its own.

Yet, in the midst of this tendency to isolate ourselves from each other, either individually or as families, God is calling us into community—indeed, the life that God calls us to lead, the witness that God calls us to give makes community imperative. Who of us, acting out of an isolated existence, has the faith and ethical resources enough to live according to Jesus' teachings in a world that sees nonviolence as weakness, personal wealth and accumulation of things as primary goals, the happiness of the individual more important than a family's welfare, getting even rather than forgiveness as the norm? Who of us, indeed? And so we as Christians base ourselves in that supportive community which is the church—a community formed around Jesus Christ, who showed us the very nature of God and the truth about who we are called to be.

Through *Disciplines,* that community comes to us and nourishes us in our daily devotional time. In dealing with the weekly lectionary passages, the writers of *Disciplines* share their own insights and experiences of meeting God in scripture. Their expressions of faith pull and tug us a little further along on our spiritual journey, help us to find our own meeting place with God in scripture, and call us out into the community of Christians. It is there that we witness to the life Jesus modeled for us and there that we ourselves, however imperfectly, live our lives based on that model, confident that in so living we are the recipients of God's grace. And it is there that we invite others into community with us.

As you use *Disciplines* during your devotional time this year, may you heed God's call to Christian community and live your life with courage and with certainty that God is with you.

Jan McNish
Editor, *Pockets*

Editor's note: With this edition of Disciplines *we begin using the Revised Common Lectionary, which is a revision of the Common Lectionary. Use of the Revised Lectionary began with Advent 1992. The listings for the 1993 scripture readings start on page 379.*

JOY TO THE WORLD

January 1-3, 1993 **Myron F. Wicke**✣

Friday, January 1 Read John 1:1-8.

It is more than a happy coincidence that we begin the New Year with the majestic words of the prologue to the Gospel of John. The author of this matchless Gospel plunges immediately into a hymn of praise for the coming of Jesus. The Incarnation is the culmination of our understanding of God's direct activity among persons. Here the words of John rush out, almost as a flood of light: "At the beginning God expressed himself. That personal expression, that word, was with God, and was God, and he existed with God from the beginning."* Words are among the chief means of expression. So John goes back to Genesis (the beginning) but places the coming of Jesus as a "personal expression" of God.

John the Baptist is vigorously described in John's Gospel as a messenger of the Christ who was already in the world, and nothing could be quite the same again. There was powerful light that even the darkness could not overcome.

This is the glorious New Year's experience, always new, always healing, always saving. Joy to the world!

Prayer: *Gracious Lord, help me to walk in the light that I may know the fellowship of love, Christ's spirit only can bestow, who reigns in light above.** . Amen.*

✣Retired as General Secretary, Board of Higher Education and Ministry, The United Methodist Church; Nashville, Tennessee.

*Reprinted with permission of Macmillan Publishing Company (U.S. publisher) and HarperCollins Publishers Ltd. (world publisher) from THE NEW TESTAMENT IN MODERN ENLGISH (Revised Edition) by J.B. Phillips. Copyright © 1958, 1960, 1972 by J.B. Phillips.

** Paraphrased from the hymn "Walk in the Light."

Saturday, January 2   Read John 1:9-16.

The Incarnation, the presence of Christ in the world, is the momentous center of the Christian faith. Hans Küng, distinguished Catholic theologian, states it clearly: "No one is a Christian because he or she tries to live in a human, or in a social, or even in a religious way. That person alone is a Christian who tries to live his or her human, social, and religious life in the light of Jesus Christ."[*]

What Jesus meant to John was life and light. The image of light was very important to early Christians. Anyone who moves quickly from a lighted space to one of sheer darkness understands the symbolism. In sudden darkness we are disoriented and confused. Only in the light can we tell what lies ahead. As John writes, many reject the light, for reasons of their own, but many seek the light; and, finding it, they become new persons.

Many who have accepted this truth have become heroes of the world. And countless ordinary people have taught us that when we, too, become committed, we can do things that surprise even ourselves. After a profound religious experience, Mother Teresa heard a call to minister to the "poorest of the poor." Once, when asked if she considered her life a success, she is said to have replied, "God does not ask us to be successful, only to be faithful." Her work for Christ among the poor worldwide has meant joy to the world.

Prayer: *Take my life, and let it be consecrated, Lord, to thee. Take my moments and my days; let them flow in ceaseless praise.*[**]

---

[*] Hans Küng, *The Christian Challenge,* trans © 1976 by William Collins, Sons & Co Ltd. and Doubleday. Used by permission.
[**]From the hymn by Frances R. Havergal.

Sunday, January 3   Read John 1:17-18.

In a sense, the conclusion to the Gospel's magnificent prologue capsulizes the Christian faith.

John notes that the law was given by Moses, and he understands that the prophets vividly experienced God's working through them. Still, while the prophets, inspired by God, revealed God's will, Jesus brought the full revelation of God's nature and will. Perhaps the Letter to the Hebrews put the matter best: "Long ago God spoke to our ancestors in many and various ways by the prophets, but in these last days he has spoken to us by a Son....He is the reflection of God's glory and the exact imprint of God's very being" (1:1-3).

The Old Testament exhibits an awesome awareness of God; yet, it is in the life and ministry of Jesus that we see most clearly what God is like. "No one has ever seen God," but in Christ we grasp the eternal love of God. Philip says to Jesus, "Lord, show us the Father, and we will be satisfied." Patiently Jesus responds, "Have I been with you all this time, Philip, and you still do not know me? Whoever has seen me has seen the Father" (John 14:8-9).

Noted British writer Malcolm Muggeridge concludes his book *Jesus, the Man Who Lives* with: "If the story of Jesus had ended on Golgotha, it would be of a Man Who Died, but as two thousand years later that man's promise that *where two or three are gathered together in my name, there am I in the midst of them* manifestly still holds, it is actually the story of a Man Who Lives."[*] Joy to the world!

Prayer: *Sing, as a prayer of praise, the carol "Joy to the World."*

---

[*] Excerpt from *Jesus: The Man Who Lives* by Malcolm Muggeridge. Copyright © 1975 by Malcolm Muggeridge. Reprinted by permission of HarperCollins Publishers.

MYSTERY AND MINISTRY

January 4-10, 1993   **Dorothy J. Mosher**✠
Monday, January 4   Read Psalm 29:1-4.

Reading the first four lines of this thunderstorm psalm, one can imagine a group of trumpets playing their clear liquid sound above the crashing of thunder. Thunder touches our hearts with the awe and majesty and mystery of God.

> Ascribe to the LORD, O heavenly beings,
> ascribe to the LORD glory and strength.

Surely giving God what is due is an awesome experience. As we reflect on God's provision, we know that God's hand is in the events of our lives that seemed so coincidental at the time and yet can only be explained as God's action. We cannot help but be struck by how small our sphere is and how large is God's. We will never be able to know enough to control all of our life. We will never be so strong that we can go it alone.

This week we will explore both mystery and ministry. Mystery seems so foreign to much of our everyday life. We often pass up the chance to respond deeply to God's mystery. But our ministry, when enriched with the awareness of mystery breaking through, allows us to serve people in new ways, such as being silent instead of talking, looking for the mystery in other people's lives, seeing the world in wonder.

Suggestion for meditation: *Sit quietly and focus on ways God's mystery has been revealed in your life. Give thanks to God for those soul-stretching experiences.*

✠Free-lance writer; Volunteer in Mission, Scarritt-Bennett Center, Nashville, Tennessee.

Tuesday, January 5   Read Psalm 29:5-11.

When our youngest son was little, he was terrified of storms. At the first flash of lightning he would dive for cover under his bed. Remembering a game my husband and I used to play with the older children, I took him on my lap one day as a storm began brewing. At the first flash of lighting I began to count the seconds that elapsed before the following clap of thunder: "One thousand, two thousand,..." The time between the lightning and the thunder told us the flash occurred two miles away. At length my son entered into the game, becoming so engrossed in counting the time that elapsed between the lightning flash and the thunderclap that he forgot to be afraid.

The mystery of a storm still fills me with awe. The color of the sky changes. The birds quiet their songs. A hush falls; then the wind picks up, ruffling the leaves and bushes. The lightning cuts its jagged mark across the sky, followed by the deep bass of thunder.

The psalmist writes about a storm near Mount Hermon (Sirion is the Sidonian name for Mount Hermon). He uses the storm to sing praise to God, thanking God for the abundant rain that prepares the soil for new seed.

There are times in our lives when we need to know God as a comforter. At other times, we need to experience God as mystery, far beyond our knowing. Such numinous experiences bring us close to worship. We cannot speak; we can only experience wonder at the power and majesty of God. It is then, with all the angels and spiritual beings who continually worship God, that we cry out, "Glory!"

Prayer: *God of mystery, touch us with your presence. May we reverence your name and respect all that you have created. Amen.*

Wednesday, January 6 (Epiphany)

Read Isaiah 42:1-4.

This passage from Isaiah describes the qualities God's servant embodies. These qualities in the minds of Christians embody Jesus and his ministry. They are a standard for our ministry also, even though we know it is impossible to embody these qualities constantly.

Speaking God's truth, the servant works quietly: exhibiting the gentle touch, speaking the loving word in soothing the hurts of a troubled world.

Humility characterizes the servant. Our egos often get in the way of effective ministry; but the servant, seeking neither power nor position, remains in a lowly and often lonely job.

Coercion is not one of the servant's tools. Neither physical nor psychological force ever accomplish a purpose in the long run. The servant respects others too much to be manipulative.

The servant must be prepared for the long haul. What the servant works for may take a long time, but working as God's servant does not become tiresome.

Does all this sound like a recipe for burnout? Speaking God's word is never easy. That is why a caring community is so important. Members of the church community, as servants, need to sustain and care for one another. With friends in Christ we learn to share, to weep, and to laugh with each other; to uphold one another in the hard times; and to empower one another for the lifelong mission to which we have been called. The servant speaks God's word to the people. We can speak God's word through our lives.

Prayer: *Sustaining God, keep me humble. Let me work quietly, always giving praise to you in all things. Amen.*

Thursday, January 7   Read Isaiah 42:5-9.

The prophet spoke in a time of national exile. The Israelites had been conquered and forced to leave their homeland. Isaiah's message for the Israelites told of a Creator God who shaped the earth, the heavens, and the seas. The spirit of God dwelt in God's people, even though they remained far from home, swept away by pagan forces and held captive in a strange land.

Isaiah's task is to address an apathetic people who feel themselves abandoned, who have forgotten a great deal of their early history, and who serve the Babylonians because they have no choice.

Isaiah reminds them of God as Creator of the world. They owe God their very lives. He tells them that God was not left behind just because they were carried away as captives. It is possible for God to be among them even in a strange land. God does not honor the gods of this nation. But God can use forces of history to bring good news to God's people. "Though you do not perceive it," Isaiah tells them, "God is preparing a way for you to return to our home once again. Earlier prophets testified to these events. Now the release is about to happen. You will be set free in a way you least expect. I want you to have hope. So I am telling you these things even before they happen, so that you will be prepared" (AP).

Suggestion for meditation: *Think of the "new things" happening in your life of which you may be only dimly aware. Reflect on the mysterious way God opens our minds to growth and joy.*

Friday, January 8 Read Matthew 3:13-17.

John the Baptist made a great stir in the wilderness of Judea. No prophet like John had appeared in Palestine for hundreds of years. His fierce preaching shook up the established religious authorities, giving hope to ordinary people who wanted to worship God but were prohibited because of their failure to observe the many laws required for the faithful.

One day a young man came to John to be baptized. John sensed something extraordinary in him and at first objected; he did not feel worthy to baptize this man. But he sensed that the young man had an intense purpose and that baptism was the doorway to a life ministry.

When the young man, Jesus, came out of the water, he entered into mystery. It was a moment filled with the weight of a people's searching for the Messiah as well as Jesus' hopes and doubts about his ministry. But in that moment, mystery and ministry touched.

What lay ahead in Jesus' ministry was unclear. In order to sort out his thoughts, he escaped into the wilderness to be with his Father. Jesus' questions at that time could have been like the thoughts of any young person entering the ministry: *What will be the thrust of my preaching and teaching? If I need to take stands on difficult issues, will I be able to remain true to God? How do I speak the truth in love?*

For forty days Jesus thought, struggled, and prayed. When he returned after listening to God's voice, he was prepared for his life's work.

Prayer: *Help us be aware of the times you encounter us, O God. May we know you in the mystery of our lives and through our ministry. Amen.*

Saturday, January 9   Read Acts 10:9-23.

There is a tale about an effective preacher who, when asked the secret of his preaching, replied that he told the congregation what he was going to say, then he said it, and then he told them what he had said. Repetition is used in this story in Acts 10. Cornelius has a vision to call Peter and have him explain his belief in Jesus. Peter has a vision that alters his views about Gentiles. These stories interweave and repeat. Luke wants to be sure his readers get the point!

Cornelius, though a Roman, had rejected the many Roman gods in favor of one God. Through his acts of charity Cornelius became beloved by his community. All his life Peter had prided himself on being a Jew. When he had the vision on the rooftop, Peter was confronted with new truth. He had to make a choice. He could retreat into his Jewish heritage, or he could change his point of view and open the church to gentile Christians.

M. Scott Peck in his book *The Road Less Traveled* describes as a map the information we receive as children. In the beginning of our lives we have a small map, circumscribed by family and friends. As we grow, new information forces us to change our maps in order to conform to reality. Peter, when confronted with God's new truth, set aside the nationalistic and religious proscriptions of the Jews and opened the church to gentile converts. Peter, in other words, was able to change his map. The converts from Cornelius's house became part of an army of Christians.

Suggestion for meditation: *What needed change in my life am I wrestling with? How shall I change my view of reality so I can be open to new truth?*

Sunday, January 10   Read Acts 10:34-43.

The Book of Acts has countless stories of dreams and visions. People believed that God talked to humans through dreams. So Cornelius sent for Peter as he was requested to do by the angel of God. Peter also had a vision, and as he was reflecting on its meaning, men came to his house and asked him to accompany them to meet Cornelius.

Can you imagine the scene in Cornelius's house in Caesarea? Peter assures everyone that God shows no partiality to any people who fear God and follow God's commandments. Peter speaks with authority and tells them a strange story. He tells of Jesus' baptism by John. He does not understand how the Holy Spirit came upon Jesus, but he knows what happened after that time. Jesus was given the power to heal the sick, to feed the multitudes, even to raise Lazarus from the dead. Those in Cornelius's household nod their heads in approval.

A fine story so far, but Peter's words grow grim. Jesus was captured and tried as a common criminal. He is killed on a cross, the cruelest form of death the Roman government could devise. But scarcely does the gasp go around the group when the good news comes: Jesus rose from the dead and was seen by his disciples. "How can that be?" they ask. "I don't know how," Peter replies, "but I know it is true. Jesus rose, and he lives forever." Eyes fill with tears and smiles of joy appear. This mysterious news changed their lives forever.

Prayer: *We do not understand the mystery of the Resurrection, O God, yet let us live with that mystery flooding our hearts and minds. Amen.*

EFFECTIVE SERVANTHOOD

January 11-17, 1993 **Robert Dungy✛**
Monday, January 11 Read Isaiah 49:1-7.

In today's scripture we read one of Isaiah's "Servant of the Lord" hymns. These hymns express the will of the Lord performed by a person faithful to God's calling, and who is a vehicle of the divine will. The title may refer to the nation of Israel, to a king, or to that greater servant, the Messiah.

God's purpose for choosing the Servant is twofold. First, Israel needed to be restored. Israel had strayed far from her high calling and needed to be brought back in line with the will of God. The second purpose was universal in scope, that the Servant would be a light to the nations.

Bethlehem's star heralded that greater light, Christ. In him was life, and the life was the light of every person. Christ, the ideal servant of the Lord, offered God's grace and salvation.

Spiritual darkness prevails throughout the world in many forms. Internationally, the self-serving actions of governments block the path leading to a just peace and the safeguarding of human rights. Outbursts of racism, the plight of the homeless, and child abuse are but a few examples of the spiritual darkness that seems to enshroud every nation. Individually, we are confronted with our inability to become the persons we were created to be. We often find that we are alienated from ourselves and from each other.

We, the church, are called to be light bearers whom God uses to pierce the spiritual darkness of this age.

Prayer: *Let us be open, O God, to your will. Let your light shine in us that your salvation may dawn in human hearts. Amen.*

✛Pastor, St. Paul's Memorial United Methodist Church, South Bend, Indiana.

Tuesday, January 12   Read Psalm 40:1-6.

These six verses could be entitled "The Song of the Soul Set Free." Evidently the psalmist experienced a life-threatening situation from which God had rescued him.

We deal with numerous mini deaths, not solely the physical. We experience a death of the spirit when we realize that we have fallen short of becoming all that we are created to be. This condition is self-alienation, which intrudes into our relationships so that we feel alienated from others, too.

Over against our sense of alienation stands our Creator, who responds to us in love and grace. God is involved personally in our struggle to be free from the many deaths that we face. Note the active verbs in our reading for today. God always takes the initiative in freeing us from that which impedes our quest for wholeness.

We discover a twofold manifestation of the will of God in our quest for deliverance. First, God rewrites the song of our lives. A hymn of praise rises from the depth of our being. Chords that were broken vibrate again in clear, ringing tones when we experience anew the grace of God.

Second, "Many shall look on in awe and trust in the LORD" (NAB). This is news to be shared, not stored up. As we witness to what God has done in our lives, the light of hope and faith begins to dawn in the hearts of others.

God places a song within each of us. The old Afro-American spiritual says it well: "If you can't preach like Peter / If you can't pray like Paul / tell the love of Jesus / and say he died for all."

Prayer: *Help us, Lord, to sing vibrantly the new song that you have placed in our mouths, that others may look on in awe and place their trust in you. Amen.*

Wednesday, January 13   Read Psalm 40:7-11.

The Gospel message is that Christ is the Servant of the Lord *par excellence,* through whom the world can experience the love of God that brings salvation and liberation. We note that Christ modeled a life of obedience: "Sacrifice or oblation you wished not, but ears open to obedience you gave me" (v. 7).

What is the relationship between hearing and obedience? In the Hebrew scriptures the word for *obey* comes from a root that means "to hear." One listens carefully, weighs what is demanded, and conducts oneself accordingly. Thus, obedience is not to follow orders blindly; it is an inward, active listening so as to conduct oneself in accord with God's will.

Christ modeled this process through his practice of solitude and prayer. On many occasions he withdrew to a solitary place to listen inwardly to his Father in heaven. Obedience, in the biblical sense, flows out of a process of being. We need to make ourselves available to God with a listening heart before we *do* anything. When we listen in this fashion, our doing will flow out of our being.

Our text indicates the results that come from the active listening process of following the divine will: "I announced your justice in the vast assembly.... Your faithfulness and your salvation I have spoken of" (vv. 10-11, NAB). In obedience to God's call, the church is to address the social, political, and moral ills of the world by proclaiming God's justice and faithfulness. In light of scripture, can we be an obedient church if we fail to challenge the forces that abridge the rights of children, the poor, and the dispossessed?

Prayer: *May your will, O God, be done on earth as it is in heaven. May it begin with me. Amen.*

Thursday, January 14   Read 1 Corinthians 1:1-3.

The world is not governed by a passionless, impersonal force, but by God, whose nature is to relate lovingly to the world. God always takes the initiative; people turn to God after having been acted on by God. The readings for the week point to this reality. God chose Israel as God's servant. God commissioned the Suffering Servant to be a light to the nations. The psalmist was moved to sing a new song after having experienced God's healing grace. By an act of God, both Paul and the church were chosen to do the will of God.

Both were called to the vocation of servanthood. Paul was obedient to the call issued by the risen Christ on the road to Damascus. The Christians at Corinth were called out of their worldliness to be servants. This fact is essential to the self-understanding of the church. In Jesus Christ we are sanctified (set aside for a holy purpose). The church is called to be holy in Christ.

Each of us is called to be holy together with all those who in every place call on the name of Jesus Christ. The church is called to be an inclusive church, the common denominator being the grace of God.

The church, faithful to its calling, is a conduit of God's grace. That grace is like a light penetrating the darkness of racism, sexism, ageism, and any other "ism" that rears its ugly head. Just as Christ was commissioned by God to be a light to the nations, so the church is commissioned to bear witness to that Light. When the church is obedient to its calling, it preaches good news to the poor, release to the captives, recovery of sight to the blind, and liberty to the oppressed (see Isaiah 61:1-7; Luke 4:16-19).

Prayer: *God of grace and glory, make us vessels of your grace, not wanting to be served, but to serve you and humanity. Amen.*

Friday, January 15   Read 1 Corinthians 1:4-9.

A well-known story tells about a farmer who found a wounded eaglet and put it in the barnyard with the chickens to be nursed back to health. It was not long before the eaglet began to act like a chicken, daily scratching for food.

When the eaglet had healed, the farmer took it up a tall ladder and gently tossed it into the air. Unaware of its full potential, the eaglet promptly fluttered its wings and landed back in the barnyard. The farmer then took it to the rooftop and gently tossed it into the air. This time the eaglet flapped its wings and began to climb higher and higher, discovering a world and a destiny greater than the barnyard.

Some of us, not realizing who we are and all that we have in Christ, act like the little eaglet scratching with the chickens. Our text for today declares that "because of the grace of God that has been given you in Christ Jesus, in every way you...have been enriched in him...so that you are not lacking in any spiritual gift." Why do so many of us content ourselves with scratching in the barnyard of life when we were created to be and to do so much more? How is it that so many of us seem unaware of the riches of God's grace that are freely given to all?

God has equipped us with all that we need to be effective servants. As we practice the disciplines of spirituality we discover the immensity of God's grace. Centered in ourselves, we find our resources quickly depleted. We slip into patterning ourselves after the values of our culture rather than the example Christ gave us. But focused on Christ, we discover unlimited resources to help us live the life of servanthood to which Christ calls us.

Prayer: *God, for the limitless resources of grace, we give thanks. Grant us the desire to follow you in a disciplined manner. Amen.*

Saturday, January 16   Read John 1:29-34.

A centuries old Middle-Eastern custom is the dedication of sheep to God. Because God has a claim on all possessions, lambs are dedicated to God even before they are born. In early spring the choicest lamb, chosen and called "God's lamb," receives loving care. During late summer or early autumn, the lamb is sacrificed. The blood of the lamb is applied to the head of the person presenting it. The meat is shared with the people at the place of sacrifice.

John's audience would have realized the import of this metaphor used by John the Baptist: "Behold the Lamb of God." This fits well with Isaiah's portrayal of the Suffering Servant. "Like a lamb that is led to the slaughter or a sheep before the shearers, he was silent and opened not his mouth" (Isa. 53:7, NAB). Christ, the obedient servant, would follow his destiny even to the cross.

Paul, in Philippians 2, encourages us to have the mind that was in Christ that accepted death on the cross as his destiny. We cannot carry Christ's cross; however, he demands that we take up our cross and follow him. We need to die daily to our self-centeredness so that greater life might come through Christ. Do we shield our eyes from seeing the homeless and the poor among us? Do the stained glass windows of our churches isolate us from encountering abused children and victims of AIDS in our communities?

We need to ask ourselves prayerfully what we need to die to, so that Christ might impart greater life to us. Christ, the Lamb of God, bore the sins, the diseases and sorrows of us all. The call to Christian servanthood is to be Christ to those who are despised and rejected in our society.

Prayer: *Risen Christ, you were God's Lamb sacrificed at Calvary. Make us worthy to become your lambs in the world. Amen.*

28

Sunday, January 17   Read John 1:35-43.

Two of John's disciples were attracted to Jesus as he passed by and followed him. Turning, Jesus asked, "What are you looking for?" He received a strange response: "Where are you staying?" They were intrigued with this one whom John called God's lamb. Perhaps their question was a request to become more intimately acquainted with Jesus. At his invitation, they spent the day where Jesus was lodging.

What happened to the disciples in those hours with Jesus was transforming. Andrew sought out Peter with the declaration that he had found the Messiah. We do not know the nature of the conversation that Jesus had with these disciples. We do know they felt a pressing need to share with others what they had found.

What is it that *we* are looking for when we attend our services of worship or when we engage in our private devotions? Are we motivated to tell others of our discovery? If it is little that we expect will happen, that is exactly what we will get. Our religious exercises will be a dull habit or an acute fever. Do we as Christians have a mutual, reciprocal relationship with Christ? Morton Kelsey once remarked, "People need to get out of nominal Christianity...." and experience "the real thing."

A servant church witnesses to the world that we have found the Messiah and invites persons to become acquainted with Christ on a personal basis. Then they, too, can be transformed and empowered to tell others what they will have found in the risen Christ.

Prayer: *Lord, we do not always know what we seek or what we need. Grant that we may find anew the one called the Lamb of God. Amen.*

THE WAY FROM DARKNESS TO LIGHT

January 18-24, 1993   **Donald E. Kohlstaedt**✚
Monday, January 18   Read Isaiah 9:1-4.

"The rod of their oppressor, you have broken as on the day of Midian." What a strange allusion, this recollection of a time centuries earlier when Gideon routed the Midianites! But it must have been intended as a boost to the morale of the people of Israel now at the mercy of a new oppressor. It was no happy ending when the king of Assyria made Hoshea, Israel's king, his vassal and afterward at the end of a long siege captured Samaria and took many of the Israelites away to Assyria (2 Kings 15:29; 17:1-8).

Even in the face of enslavement by a powerful eastern king, the prophet could promise, "There will be no gloom for those who were in anguish....but in the latter time he will make glorious the way of the sea, the land beyond the Jordan, Galilee of the nations." But in the same chapter Isaiah charges Ephraim and Samaria with pride and arrogance of heart (v. 9). In the time of the judges, when the Israelites drifted away from worship of the true God, they fell into the power of their enemies until in fear and desperation they cried to the Lord. Our study this week may suggest the proper course for nations in times of perplexity and fear.

Prayer: *Lord, help us to know where we are in relation to you. Forgive our pride, our insincerity, our lack of trust. Teach us to depend on you for everything good. Amen.*

✚Active layperson in the United Methodist Church; adult Sunday school teacher; retired lay speaker; Spokane, Washington.

Tuesday, January 19
Read Judges 6:1-2, 7-10;
Psalm 27:1, 4-9.

"But you have not given heed to my voice." So proclaims the prophet in Judges 6:10. This is the unqualified conviction of the writer of Judges that Israel's oppression under the Midianites was the outcome of their unfaithfulness to God. So in contrast to the psalmist's exultantantion "He will hide me in his shelter in the day of trouble," under the Midianite oppression the Israelites "provided for themselves hiding places in the mountains, caves, and strongholds."

What are our caves and strongholds when our spiritual vision becomes dim? Unless we turn to the Lord in contrition and humility, don't we fall back on the false hopes of returning prosperity, the seductions of the plenty money can offer, or just the hope that things will remain the same? Or perhaps we listen to the prophets of an imagined new age where no repentance toward God is called for, and material values and self-glorification submerge the grace of God. Then, coming to ourselves and seeing reality, it is time to seek God's face and affirm from our hearts that we do indeed want to come back into God's favor.

From our perspective millenniums after the New Testament fulfillment of the promised Messiah, where are we placing our hopes and expectations?

Prayer: *God, our Father, help us to recover the prophet's vision that "there will be no gloom for those who were in anguish" (Isa. 9:1). May your power bring peace at last to the people who are in anguish in nations at conflict within their borders and to those who are fearful of hostility from without. We pray through Christ our Lord. Amen.*

31

Wednesday, January 20   Read Judges 8:22-23; 33-35;
                                              Isaiah 9:11-23.

When Gideon became their hero, the people of Israel wished him to rule over them, but Gideon rightly directed their thoughts to God, through whom he had obtained his great victory. But no sooner had Gideon died than the Israelites regressed again into idolatry. The writer used no soft-spoken words about the people of Israel, "who relapsed and prostituted themselves with the Baals, making Baal-berith their god." They forgot that because of their unfaithfulness to the God of their fathers and Moses, their enemy had defeated them earlier. How similar Isaiah's reference to the Syrians and Philistines about to devour Israel is to Judges 6, where the Midianites prevailed over the tribes.

Now, late in this twentieth century, we "Christian nations" seem to be forgetting our Judeo-Christian heritage. Why are the witness and testimony of the committed too weak to withstand powerful forces of secularism? While new freedom in Eastern Europe seems to offer hope for a new and better world order, are high aspirations expressed for these nations to become nations "under God"? And after a moment of euphoria when the Allied military forces defeated a Middle-East dictator, new boundary disputes arose in central Europe while Middle East tensions continue.

Prayer: *Help us, Lord, not to judge lest we be judged. We know that we can make no claim to righteousness acceptable in your sight. Only with humble and contrite hearts do we still dare to pray for ultimate triumph against evil and wrong. Through Christ we pray. Amen.*

Thursday, January 21   Read Matthew 4:12-17.

From the gloom of military defeats and subsequent oppressions the Israelites suffered through their history, we come to Matthew's quotation in a new setting for Isaiah's prophecy. At last the true light has dawned! The oppressed tribal lands of Zebulun and Naphtali are blessed by the long-awaited Messiah's proclamation of God's new day. But little did the people realize that they were seeing the beginnings of God's new acts not only for the Jews but for all subsequent humanity. How dim was their perception of the one who was proclaiming to them, "Repent, for the kingdom of heaven has come near." Who could have imagined that an obscure prophetic voice in their very midst was nothing less than the voice of God announcing peace to them and to countless generations after them?

A long look at this point is reassuring even though tumultuous times seem never to end. God's faithful and holy people composing the church are the proof that the Kingdom has indeed come. They (we) experience God with us and can no longer doubt the final outcome—the triumph of righteousness and victory over all the forces of darkness.

God's new covenant is for all nations, not just Israel. But like the faith heroes of Hebrews 11, we still must receive the kingdom by faith. God has indeed "provided something better" (Heb. 11:40) for us, and that something better is as sure as creation!

Prayer: *O God of all assurance and comfort, we affirm with joy our confidence in your triumph at last. May your time and our time finally merge until we see the promised glory of our risen Lord. Amen.*

Friday, January 22   Read Matthew 4:18-23.

God gives the kingdom to people, but the implementation comes through chosen instruments. Proclamation alone would have been mere rhetoric; even the Son of God must call ordinary people like ourselves to his service. It has always been so; Gideon was thunderstruck that he was notified by an angel that he would become Israel's deliverer. It was equally so with Moses and Jeremiah; both had to be convinced that God was really calling them to give out the divine message and to become leaders—even God's voice—in perilous times.

Now the time had come at last for the kingdom to be proclaimed, and who were first called but laborers and tradesmen going about their business and earning their living? Not people in positions of authority, not the interpreters of the Law, not the priests or members of the Sanhedrin, but Galilean fishermen were appointed emissaries of the one who would become King of kings! No wonder the upper-class leaders and dictators of the Law were scandalized when rumors circulated that this might be their messiah.

Can we feel with these first disciples some of their excitement and the thrill of being with Jesus? Already they had encountered him; Andrew had impulsively come to Peter exclaiming, "We have found the Messiah," and brought him to Jesus (John 1:41).

Prayer: *Blessed Lord, if your voice clearly comes to us, how can we be less stirred and aroused than those who joyfully answered your call at the beginning of your ministry? Our answer must indeed be our grateful "Yes, Lord." Amen.*

Saturday, January 23   Read 1 Corinthians 1:10-18.

What Paul is contending for here, unity among God's people, could be viewed as a microcosm of the church to be.

Since that first century of Christian witness and outreach, there have been misguided leaders, countless divisions, and destructive heresies that reduced the impact of the gospel. But throughout Old and New Testament times, and the whole history of the church, outstanding figures have emerged who were examples of God at work in human lives. As in apostolic times, Christians moved by the Holy Spirit have shown in their generations and centuries what God can do.

Our century, foreboding as events may be, is no exception. Along with evils too evident to be overlooked, there are the companies of God's own people in every nation and on every continent still bearing witness to the sovereign authority of God. These faithful persons and communities of faith witness to the supreme revelation of God with us in the person of the Lord Jesus Christ. The Holy Spirit has not been withdrawn, even in our day. And it is in the power of the Spirit that God's good news to confused and troubled nations continues to be proclaimed.

Prayer: *God of all nations, give your messengers good success in proclaiming the gospel of Jesus Christ, the gospel of deliverance. May we faithfully sound your invitation to life through the powers of the Spirit until there is true repentance among all the people. Through Christ our Lord. Amen.*

Sunday, January 24   Read 1 Corinthians 1:26-31.

Paul's faith in God's power offsets whatever disappointment he felt over disunity among the Corinthian converts. Quite realistically he admitted the ordinariness of the people who responded to the gospel. Far from being of the elite or being people with secret knowledge through esoteric revelation as in the mystery religions, these were people accounted on the bottom rung of society. They were the slaves, the uneducated, the despised by those who considered the cultured and privileged their equals, not the lowly Christians. And, lest the converts take credit for themselves, Paul echoes Jeremiah 9:24: "Let the one who boasts, boast in the Lord." It was God's choice to invite the low and despised in the world, not their own wisdom that encouraged them to choose God's way for their lives. Where is there any place for our self-glorification when God is the very source of our new life in Christ?

The apparently humanly insoluble problems of our times dismay and frustrate us. A century of "wars and rumors of wars" (Matt. 24:6), when one point of tension is resolved only to be followed by new ones, scarcely gives us time even to dream up solutions. The biblical answers are for us to search out and take to heart. And candor must admit that the biblical answers don't play up to human pride and self-esteem; rather, they throw us squarely on God's willingness to see our need and come to meet us in it.

Prayer: *Our Father, as with Job of old your voice comes to us, cutting through all our protestations. Teach us to listen, to believe in your mighty revelation through Christ, to submit and to obey your will. Amen.*

THOSE WHO . . .

January 25-31, 1993   **Donald E. Collins**✢
Monday, January 25   Read Micah 6:1-5.

Like all biblical prophets, Micah preaches that it is not God but the people of Israel who have broken the covenant. In this passage Micah uses the image of a court trial to accuse the people of not remembering what God has done for them. The mountains and foundations of the earth serve as the jury as the people are cross-examined by God, who is the prosecutor. We are reminded of God's asking Job,

> "Where were you when I laid the
> foundation of the earth?"
> Job 38:4

How easy it is, when things are going well, to forget what God has done for us and take the credit for ourselves. The ritual of the Jewish Passover meal provides a wonderful corrective for this very human tendency. Repeated examples of God's care and guidance for the Israelites during the Exodus are recalled and celebrated, saying, *"Dayeinu!"* ("It would have been enough.") For example, "Had God brought us to Mount Sinai and not given us the Torah, it would have been enough! Had God given us the Torah...and not sent us prophets of truth, it would have been enough!"

How blessed are *those who remember what the Lord has done.*

Suggestion for prayer: *Pray for the grace to be one of those who never forgets what God has done for us.*

✢Author; United Methodist pastor, Church of the Good Hope, Milwaukee, Wisconsin.

Tuesday, January 26   Read Micah 6:6-8.

As our biblical ancestors grew in their understanding of and relationship to God, they struggled with the ancient practice of sacrificial offerings. Amos and Isaiah proclaimed that grain, animal, and other ritual offerings were unacceptable, calling instead for justice and righteousness. Psalm 51 calls for a humble heart and a repentant spirit. And Micah says, "What does the Lord require of you but to do justice, and to love kindness, and to walk humbly with your God?"

It is easy to read this passage and think of justice, mercy (KJV), and humility as three separate "items." But in the biblical view they are so closely related as to be almost inseparable. As Frederick Buechner has said, "Justice is the pitch of the roof and the structure of the walls. Mercy is the patter of rain on the roof and the life sheltered by the walls. Justice is the grammar of things. Mercy is the poetry of things.* Likewise, humility is our proper stance before God and our proper stance in relationship to other people and to the earth, points us in the direction of justice and mercy.

However, we should not oversimplify the requirements of justice, mercy, and humility by thinking of them as easy to fulfill. We live in a time when many of the decisions we make have implications which reverberate around the world, affecting the lives of countless others, not to mention the planet itself.

Blessed are *those who do what the Lord requires.*

Suggestion for prayer: *Pray that all you do may be done with justice, mercy, and humility.*

---

*Excerpt from *Whistling in the Dark* by Frederick Buechner. Copyright © 1983 by Frederick Buechner. Reprinted by permission of HarperCollins Publishers.

Wednesday, January 27   Read Psalm 15.

The opening question of this psalm, "O LORD, who may abide in your tent?" reflects a time when the people lived in tents and were always on the move. Psalm 15 was probably part of a ritual involving those who came to Jerusalem to worship in the Temple. As such, the psalm might be thought of as an examination of conscience for those coming to the Temple.

The answer to the opening question begins with, "Those who walk blamelessly...." The psalmist then lists ten characteristics of those who are considered worthy, undoubtedly a reminder of the Ten Commandments. It may be that pilgrims were required to memorize these answers or were asked for them by a priest.

The Bible contains other similar lists which are intended to help the people better understand their faith. We read in Isaiah 33:15-16 the offerering of six precepts followed by a similar assurance to those who follow them. Micah, as we have seen in verses 6:8, offers three; and Jesus summarized in two commandments what was required (see Luke 10:27). These lists of requirements reflect the needs and conditions of the time in which they were written. If someone asked you to produce such a list for today, what would you put on it?

Suggestion for meditation: *The psalm concludes with "Those who do these things shall never be moved." Spend a few minutes taking inventory of your own life to see how you measure up to these requirements or, if you prefer, how you measure up to those of Isaiah, Micah, or Jesus.*

Suggestion for prayer: *In your prayer ask God to open your heart and mind to those virtues which need to grow in order for you to be counted among "those who...shall never be moved."*

Those Who . . .

Thursday, January 28   Read 1 Corinthians 1:18-25.

Years ago the Army Corps of Engineers decided to dig a huge canal to drain the Florida Everglades. At the time, it was considered a wise thing to do. But the result was an ecological disaster. Now we are spending billions of dollars to restore the area to its original condition!

"God's foolishness is wiser than human wisdom," Paul says; "and God's weakness is stronger than human strength." The truth of Paul's words is confirmed by endless examples in our personal and corporate lives, yet how we continue to live as if it were the other way around!

After all these centuries, something in us still questions God's wisdom: A savior born out of wedlock and in a stable? A messiah who refuses to defend himself at his own trial? A bunch of clumsy disciples who can't seem to get it straight no matter how many times Jesus tells them? Losing one's life in order to find it? Becoming a servant in order to be great? Loving your enemies? Becoming like a little child in order to understand? What kind of wisdom is this that sounds more like foolishness?

Ask Saint Francis of Assisi, who gave up a rich inheritance and even the clothes off his back to seek it. Ask the people of Eastern Europe, who discovered that carrying candles in the street was more powerful than tanks and guns. Ask Mother Teresa, who sleeps on the floor and devotes her life to those who are dying. Then ask yourself, because you have also experienced God's foolishness and have found it wiser than human wisdom. May we be among *those who believe in God's foolishness.*

Prayer: *God of wisdom, teach us to think more like Jesus, whose words were often filled with surprises and whose actions often took unexpected turns. Amen.*

Friday, January 29   Read 1 Corinthians 1:26-31.

Having written philosophically about wisdom and foolishness, Paul now asks the Corinthians to reflect on their own personal experience. "Now remember what you were... when God called you" (TEV). Most of those in the church at Corinth were very ordinary people. Indeed, some of them were or had been slaves. Paul goes on to say, "God purposely chose what the world considers nonsense in order to shame the wise, and...what the world considers weak in order to shame the powerful."

It has been said that among the members of almost any church there is one person who is looked upon as the congregation's "holy person." Usually such a person is one without worldly recognition or high social standing. What draws others to this person is not what we would expect in a community leader but rather what we expect to find in Jesus.

Even in a time when the church is accused of conforming itself too much to the values of the world, the church is still a place where we see each other not in terms of our worldly image but in terms of how we reflect the image of God. Who we are as Christians depends not on what we have done but on what God has done in us and for us.

How do you respond to Paul's "remember what you were ...when God called you" (TEV)? Unlike those to whom Paul wrote at Corinth, many of us either grew up in the church or have been a part of it for so long that we have difficulty remembering "who we were." Perhaps we ought to ask: What is the relationship between who we are in the world and who we are in the community of God's people?

Prayer: *God, help us to understand, especially in our own lives, the difference between wisdom and foolishness. Amen.*

Saturday, January 30   Read Matthew 5:1-9.

The Beautitudes reflect some differences in the two Gospels that record them, although both writers probably used the same source. Matthew has nine "blessings," while Luke (6:20-26) has a set of four "blessings" followed by four "woes." In Luke, the Beatitudes are addressed directly to Jesus' disciples. Matthew's version is less personal.

Neither version is intended to suggest ways to attain happiness. Rather, they are meant to illustrate the difference between life inside the kingdom of God and life outside it.

The Greek *makarios* is "blessed" or "happy" in most English translations. Neither communicates the rich meaning of a joy which cannot be taken away. Robert H. Gundry suggests that the meaning is clearer if we substitute the word *congratulations!** This carries a feeling of sympathetic rejoicing with someone.

In God's kingdom the ordinary values of the world are turned upside down. Thus, those who are poor are to be congratulated because they, rather than the rich, are in a position to hear and receive what God offers them.

The final beatitude summarizes the others, calling for rejoicing because "your reward is great in heaven." ("Be cheerful and good-humored, because your spiritual advantage is great."**) For Jesus those who live by his upside-down values will experience the Kingdom here and now.

Suggestion for Prayer: *Ask God to help you experience more fully the joy of living into the kingdom of God.*

---

*Robert H. Gundry, *Matthew: A Commentary on His Literary and Theological Art* (Grand Rapids: Eerdmans, 1982), p. 68.
**Clarence Jordan, *The Cotton Patch Version of Matthew and John* (New York: Association Press, 1970), p. 22.

Sunday, January 31   Read Matthew 5:10-12.

If someone has ever made fun of you because of your belief in God or your going to church, you have some idea of what these final verses of the Beatitudes are all about. Yet, unlike those who were in the first generation to read Matthew's Gospel, few of us have experienced true persecution.

Those who take the gospel seriously and seek to live out its implications—particularly its social implications—may well find themselves insulted, looked down upon, ostracized or even subjected to personal violence. Most who witnessed to their convictions during the civil rights movement or took a stand against the war in Vietnam know all too well what persecution feels like, twentieth-century style.

When Jesus says, "This is how the prophets who lived before you were persecuted," he is not talking just to those who feel a special call to prophetic ministry. He is talking to ordinary people like us! After all, how can one be serious about Jesus' teachings without speaking and acting prophetically?

If you have ever spoken up about environmental issues, you have spoken as a prophet. That may or may not have resulted in your being persecuted. But what about more controversial issues? How do you feel about the rapid rise of poverty in an affluent society? How do you feel about equal justice for women? How do you feel about some of the double standards in our nation's foreign policy? How do the values of Jesus apply to these issues? How much can one speak out about such things before a degree of harrassment or persecution begins?

If you are one of *"those who are persecuted for righteousness sake"*...congratulations!

Suggestion for meditation: *Think about where God is calling you to be in prophetic ministry today.*

February 1-7, 1993   **Elizabeth Nordquist**✝
Monday, February 1   Read Isaiah 58:1-5.

Futile fasts

The Hebrews who had returned to Jerusalem after the Babylonian captivity had much work to do to reclaim their identity as God's chosen people. They knew that they were to express their spiritual faith, and they attempted to do that by going through the rituals that had once been central to their lives. But the prophet confronted them with a deeper reality: "Look, you serve your own interest on your fast day, and oppress all your workers." They had confused familiar forms of worship with genuine expressions of faith in God. Their fasting and appearances of humility were superficial, not offered from a heart full of love for God and God's justice.

For those of us with a heritage of faith and community, we may often find that our bodies and souls move into familiar faith practices—hymns, prayers of confession, even the Lord's Supper—without engaging our hearts. The prophet calls us beyond the comfort zone of our practiced piety to look at the way we live out the mercy and justice of God with those around us. How do we treat our employees, our families, our volunteers, our neighbors? Are there ways in which we use our personal power to oppress those with whom we come in contact? The prophet tells us that our expressions of faith are futile without acts of justice.

Suggestion for meditation: *Ask the Spirit to bring to your mind those in your sphere of influence and care whom you need to treat more fairly.*

✝Associate pastor, St. Peter's By The Sea Presbyterian Church, Rancho Palos Verdes, California.

Tuesday, February 2   Read Isaiah 58:6-12.

Graceful gardens

A thriving garden, lush and blooming, is the sign of home for many; it is a sign that we have been there long enough for things to grow, that we have created a space for things to take root and to flower, that a cycle of life in seasons is happening. What a nourishing image for the re-entering Hebrew who has been away for such a long time! How will their lives reflect this image?

The prophet calls the people to some very pragmatic behaviors as a way of blooming: loosing bonds of injustice, sharing bread and room with the hungry and homeless, removing accusation and blame. If the Hebrews do these things, the prophet says, "the LORD will...satisfy your needs and make your bones strong" and "make you like a watered garden...whose waters never fail."

To be a well-watered garden of the Spirit is to be an activist not of religious rites but of deeds and words of justice and mercy. To have our parched places watered is to look around our workplace and to make a change in the system that discriminates on the basis of age, gender, or race. To feel our bones made strong is to sense the atmosphere in our homes and to refuse to assign blame. To be called the repairer of the breach and restorer of the streets is to nourish and make comfortable those in our circle of vision and opportunity who are starving and miserable, whether out of physical need or spiritual need.

Suggestion for meditation: *Imagine yourself as a watered garden; what actions must you take today to tend that garden?*

Wednesday, February 3   Read 1 Corinthians 2:1-5.

Persuasive power

Words of wisdom! Logic, credibility, plausibility, reason! Those are the criteria we are trained to look for when making a decision, charting a course, or casting our lot with someone or something. Yet, the apostle Paul tells us that none of those things were characteristic of his message from the Spirit when he brought the gospel to the Corinthians; instead, he came in weakness, fear, and trembling. Neither we nor the Corinthians recognize those as the attributes of a powerful persuader. Paul knew that the power he had came from the crucified Christ.

As with the prophetic words of Isaiah, the power of the spirit of God comes in paradoxical, unexpected, almost irrational form. A crucified Christ? What power can be seen and experienced from him? Paul says that the power we see in Christ is God's power. It is God's continual option to use poor, broken, frail, vulnerable demonstrations of the One who is not limited to predictable and habitual ways of working; who is not bound by human systems of thinking; who is able to take that which is hopeless and bring newness of life from it. To trust that kind of power is to have faith.

To trust the paradoxical power of the crucified Christ, instead of all of our developed cognitive skills, may be our largest step of faith.

Suggestion for meditation: *Think of a situation where your logic has left you stuck; ask for the power and Spirit of the crucified Christ to enlighten you.*

Thursday, February 4   Read 1 Corinthians 2:6-12.

Unexpected understanding

Living by faith means being open to the surprises of the mystery of God. Our texts this week have spoken to the facts of God's mysterious appearances in our lives. And now we are told that we will never fully understand the ways in which God might work. There is more available to see, to hear, to imagine than any of us have experienced yet.

We have been given the spirit of God which acts as an interpretive mentor when we begin to look for signs of God's presence and activity in the world. God's wisdom is not academic or political wisdom, sketched out for us in popular analyses or critiques. God's wisdom is something deep, something given, something surprising. It reveals to us the way God resources us, the way God speaks to us, the way God comes to us, and the good plans that God has for us.

Along with all the disciplines of mind and body we need for functioning and thriving as human beings, we need to develop those senses that are in tune with the spirit of God that has been given to us. We need to ask for eyes to see the face of God when it appears to us in someone we meet. We must ask for ears to hear the voice of Christ saying "follow me" into places we might not dare to go. We are called to ask for hearts that can encompass the hurts and slights of the world in which the Spirit dwells.

Suggestion for meditation: *Walk through a day, attending to the wisdom of the Spirit through your eyes, ears, and heart. What becomes clear to you?*

Friday, February 5   Read Matthew 5:13.

Useless salt

According to these words from the Sermon on the Mount, we who are followers of Jesus are salt. That's who we are in our essence: that substance which, for Jesus' listeners, was necessary for life, for preserving food, for giving flavor. Jesus says that in our very being we have life-enhancing power, not just for ourselves, not just for our own community, but for the whole world.

I rarely think of myself as salt of the earth, a source of preserving power, of tastiness, of influence in the world around me. The world is so vast and diverse; how could I, one follower of Jesus, be of some use in the restoration and to the delight of the world? Yet the designation is clear—I, along with other Christians—am "salt."

The challenge is for me to be who I am—for us to be who we are—as followers of Christ. To be "salt," as in the parable, to truly be an influence of healing, of life-enhancement in the world, we must be in touch with the source of our power as Christians and be in touch with the people and situations that need the healing and salvation that is offered by Christ.

Suggestion for meditation: *Think of the ways in which you are in contact with God's spirit (prayer, scripture study, and other ways). Think of ways in which you make yourself available to those in need of healing, in need of the life that Christ has to offer.*

Suggestion for prayer: *Pray for God's spirit to show you other ways you can be available to persons in need.*

48

Saturday, February 6   Read Matthew 5:14-16.

Limited light

To have light, to be in the light, to work in the light, feels very hopeful and cheerful. We have a sense that we can see clearly, that we have all the information we need, that we don't have to strain to do what we need to do. Jesus says that we are light.

We may be tempted to keep light to ourselves; we like to feel as if we have insight, illumination by which we can govern our own destinies, warmth that fills our own nesting places. But Jesus says that we are to let our light shine before others. It is not just for our personal warmth and comfort; it is to be shared with a world that has very little light. There is part of the rhythm of our lives as Christians that is private and personal; but what we are given in private that heals and enlightens us is given to us to assimilate and to share with others.

Jesus says that the medium through which our light shines is our good works—the attractive acts of mercy and justice that let people know that the Light has shone within us. To keep our warm experiences of the Light (Christ) to ourselves creates a spiritual smugness; it may feel jolly and comfortable to us, but it is unhealthy. To be whole in our spirits, we must express the effects of that which we have received.

We do not lack for opportunities to do good works. Wherever there is a human being or a system with need, there is an opportunity for good work—of affirmation, of listening, of suffering with, of healing, of giving money and time, of speaking the truth.

Suggestion for meditation: *Let the Light show you where your light must shine.*

49

Sunday, February 7   Read Psalm 112:1-10.

Models of the Spirit

"Happy are those who fear the Lord....They are gracious, merciful, and righteous" (AP). To demonstrate the Spirit in our lives is to be active. The life of the Spirit is not exclusively passive, private, and personal. Graciousness, mercy, and righteousness are activities of the Spirit.

The psalmist sums up with joy the effects of those who are responsive and responsible persons of the Spirit: they are blessed; they leave an enduring heritage; they are fair; they are secure; they are expansive; they are not afraid. The activities in which they engage are an exterior expression of the nourishment and enrichment they have received from God, and they are not reluctant or fearful to share it.

These models of the Spirit, models which we are called to be, are givers of hope to those in need of hope. Not only are physical needs met but needs of encouragement and emotion are also met. Furthermore, these models of hope have joy in being all they are meant to be. They are happy and content with the contribution that they make out of who they are.

To be who we are meant to be and to make a contribution to the ongoing work of God in the world is to live in grace. It is the grace of God that we are who we are. It is the grace of God that who we are is sufficient for God to use in the ongoing salvation of the earth. It is the grace of God to do more abundant things in us and through us than we can ask or think. Praise the Lord!

Prayer: *Spirit of God, empower me to be what I am and to do what you want me to do, for Jesus' sake. Amen.*

GOD'S GIFT OF CHOICE

February 8-14, 1992   **Charles B. Simmons✠**
Monday, February 8   Read Psalm 119:1-8.

Our scripture readings this week reveal that God gives people a choice. Moses chose the way of Lord. That choice had certain consequences—living and multiplying and being blessed in the land which God would give the Israelites. For Jesus the choices led to being either "the least" in the Kingdom or "the greatest." Paul argues that the decisions result in "spiritual people" or "people of the flesh." A common theme emerges: God's people are called to hard choices.

We begin this week's lections with a poem in praise of Torah and of the freedom to choose which the Law affords God's people. These verses are a remarkable example of acrostic poetry in which the form reinforces the message: Life is reliable and utterly symmetrical when Torah is honored.

To the psalmist the commandments are not restrictive or burdensome. Instead, God's law shows what it takes to be happy. The holy statutes prioritize, give life focus, saving us from an exhausting daily re-deciding of right and wrong.

What a helpful corrective to our modern resentment of moral rules and spiritual disciplines! Never forget, reminds the psalmist, when we are blessed to learn "righteous ordinances," genuine obedience becomes an option. Praise God, then, all of us privileged to fix our eyes on God's commandments and to choose to walk in God's ways!

Prayer: *Teach us, O Lord, to recognize and receive the choices your commands confront us with as gifts. Amen.*

✠Senior pastor, Broadmoor United Methodist Church, Baton Rouge, Louisiana.

Tuesday, February 9   Read Deuteronomy 30:15-20.

These words from Deuteronomy, ostensibly delivered by Moses to the Israelites just prior to their entering Canaan, define what God demands from those who desire to be God's people. A choice must be made. If Israel will love God and obey God's voice, life will be found. If, instead, people refuse to walk in God's way, death will abound.

These verses reveal the most common Old Testament understanding of God's righteousness: When the people turned away from God, they were punished, not so much *for* their sins, as *by* them. So the choice is clear, as are the consequences. To not be "good" at keeping promises made to God breaks the covenant and costs dearly.

Although we may no longer share the Deuteronomic view that good people always get good and bad folks are sure to suffer during this earthly life, discipleship still requires a right relationship with the Divine. God commands us to follow God's way, the "loving path" designed into creation. The choice is still ours to make: life or death, good or evil?

Suggestion for meditation: *What choices have I been faced with this past month? this past week? How have I felt God's guidance in recently made decisions? In what ways can I be more attuned to God's way, the "loving path"?*

Prayer: *Lead us, O Lord, to consider carefully the choices you are calling us to make right now. Amen.*

Wednesday, February 10   Read 1 Corinthians 3:1-3.

The church at Corinth was beset with problems. The congregation was split into factions (1:12) and puffed up with pride (4:8). The members tolerated gross immorality (5:1), sued each other in the courts (6:1), patronized prostitutes (6:15), toyed with idolatry (10:14), and got drunk at the Lord's Supper (11:21). Times of worship were times of confusion (14:33). Some even denied the resurrection (15:12).

Concerned, Paul writes a letter that, in these verses, confronts the Corinthians with the double demand of discipleship: Not only must choices be made, they must be visible. Church members can decide to live as "spiritual people" or as "people of the flesh."

Spiritual people is a term that may have been used by those opposing Paul as they boasted of their superior "wisdom" and, as a consequence, quarreled among themselves. Paul uses the term in an ethical sense to argue, with a touch of irony, that his opponents are really the very opposite. They are "people of the flesh" because of their quarreling. The fractured church is Exhibit A to confirm Paul's charge. As long as there is jealousy and strife, the people are not "spiritual" but are behaving according to "human inclinations."

Note that Paul is not saying the Corinthians do not have the Spirit. They do, and that's the problem. They are thinking and acting in a manner contrary to the claim. His plea is, "Stop it. Spiritual people simply must not behave the way you are behaving. Your choice for Christ must be made obvious in thought and deed. The choice must show."

Prayer: *Help us to grow us in grace, O Lord, that we may bear witness. Amen.*

Thursday, February 11   Read 1 Corinthians 3:4-8.

As seen in the preceding verses, Paul has no patience for belief that does not result in proper behavior. He finds it immature and intolerable to have received the Spirit, which makes a person more than "merely human," and to continue to live as though one were nothing more.

The apostle therefore launches a frontal attack on the problem of "jealousy and strife" in the church at Corinth. At issue, however, is not simply quarreling. It is their erroneous perception of what has real value for "spiritual people." Some in the church are bestowing importance on unimportant matters—namely, the human leaders through whom they had come to know Christ. They are viewing things from below, again as "mere humans," and thus think altogether too highly of their teachers. To say, "I belong to Paul," or "I belong to Apollos," misses the point.

In response, the questions "What then is Apollos? What is Paul?" are answered with a resounding "Nothing!" Verse 8 clarifies that this is not the only thing to be said. Paul and Apollos do have essential tasks to perform, for which they will receive their own rewards. But they have no independent importance.

Put simply, Paul and Apollos matter as persons but count for nothing ultimately. Without God's prior activity bringing the Corinthians to faith and causing them to grow, there would be no church. This is the message that still addresses Christians everywhere: "Stop taking sides in trivial disputes. Quit quarreling over those whose tasks are nothing in comparison with the activity of God. Choose what matters."

Prayer: *Dear God, may our prayers, thoughts, and deeds find their center in you that we may lead lives that matter. Amen.*

Friday, February 12   Read 1 Corinthians 3:9.

In his letters, Paul commonly refers to himself and his co-workers as "servants." The image portrays his understanding of the relationship both to his Lord and to the gospel. He is God's servant and, as such, is a servant of the gospel. Such terminology came from the teaching of Jesus himself. Jesus was among them as one who served and, in the ultimate expression of servanthood, "gave his life a ransom for many." This differed radically from the Greek attitude toward leadership. Thus, in Paul's claim, "We are God's servants," the community at Corinth hears a call to decide.

God's way stands in contradiction to human ways. A decision must be made, then, even about one's model for ministry. The choice is between servanthood and a merely human understanding of the role of leaders, such as the Corinthians were exhibiting. Says Paul, Choose to serve.

Too often clergy and laity alike act as if the church is "ours." We pay lip service to its being "Christ's Body," then proceed to operate on the basis of secular structures. But the church does not belong to its leaders, anymore than it belongs to those who have attended all their lives or supported it with money. The church belongs to its Lord, and all else should flow out of that single realization.

Those "in charge" must be ever mindful of who is really in charge. To be a servant does not mean the abdication of leadership; nor does it mean being willing to run everyone's errands. It has to do with our *attitude*, not our *altitude*, on the organizational chart. Christians choose to be fellow laborers under God. "We are God's servants."

Prayer: *Master, make us this day more mindful of your Lordship and our servanthood. Amen.*

Saturday, February 13   Read Matthew 5:17-20.

The Sermon on the Mount does not teach a common morality. Jesus suggests to his hearers something more. He is no ordinary teacher of goodness, even among Jews. He has come to reveal, as Paul put it, "a more excellent way." He is looking for followers who will choose to exceed the usual expectations for an ethical life, disciples who know what it costs to live God's way and are willing to pay for it.

This leads to conflict with the scribes and Pharisees who were recognized for their righteous living based on the law of Moses. Theirs was a rational model of morality, wherein life was broken down into basic units and rules applied, so that each had laws governing it. That meant a person could approach any situation in life and know exactly how to behave morally. Society looked upon the scribes and Pharisees as "experts" who understood precisely what was expected of them and did it to the letter of the Law. Yet, that is why Jesus rejected their example. They did not aim for excellence. They aimed for what was required and were content with themselves for having reached that goal.

Simply put, our Lord's criticism of the Jewish leaders was not that they were evil, but that they were merely good. They were only as good as they had to be. Jesus taught that God has created us to be as good as we can be, to strive for the excellence made possible by the Holy Spirit. That is his point when he says, "Unless your righteousness exceeds that of the scribes and Pharisees, you will never enter the kingdom of heaven." In the Kingdom the goal is excellence. Do not sell discipleship short. Choose to be all you can be, by God's grace.

Prayer: *Lord, help us strive to be more than merely good people. For Christ's sake, let us excel at loving. Amen.*

Sunday, February 14   Read Matthew 5:21-26.

Our week began with the choice set before the Israelites of life and death, of obeying the commandments of the Lord or turning their hearts away. It concludes with Jesus setting before his followers a similar choice. Decide this day to keep to the righteousness of the scribes and Pharisees or choose the "more excellent way" that leads to the Kingdom.

The Sermon on the Mount presents these new expectations for God's people as new commandments. Each is introduced by way of contrast with the old. "You have heard ...But I say." Each teaching has to do with a "righteousness of the heart" that fulfills the ultimate aim of the imposed righteousness in the code of Moses. Jesus' call is to carry out God's law in attitude as well as action. Thus the new righteousness supersedes the old, making it more a matter of inner character than outward behavior.

The first example is a reinterpretation of the commandment, "You shall not kill." In prohibiting anger, insult, and disdain toward a brother or sister, Jesus' extension of the Law says no to every form of unloving behavior.

Next Jesus requires that we move beyond the prick of our own conscience to satisfy other people's sensibilities as well. The command to be reconciled with a brother who feels offended before we worship God suggests that no rite is right if relationships are wrong. If we wish to be at one with God, we need to be at one with each other.

Clearly the new righteousness demands a deepened obedience to a higher standard. Yet, when Jesus says, "Follow me," the meaning is, "Come be with me!"

Grace is sufficient. Choose the Kingdom.

Prayer: *Dear God, keep calling us to embrace your loving ways until we obey and become all you created us to be. Amen.*

A MOUNTAINTOP EXPERIENCE

February 15-21, 1993   **John A. Stroman**✞
Monday, February 15   Read Exodus 24:12-14.

God commands Moses to come to the mountain to receive the Decalogue. Here for the first time God explicitly states the purpose of the law, "for their instruction."

On the mountain God's will is revealed to Moses. It was God's purpose to bring this wandering group of nomads into a community bound together by law that was preceded by grace—the grace experienced in the Exodus.

Essential for human life are externally defined boundaries and internal disciplines. Living together in community requires agreeing on and adhering to certain laws. Without civil and criminal laws enforced fairly and promptly, the community's power to protect human life would collapse. The Decalogue reveals to us the practical value of the law in regard to our corporate and social life together. It provides the cohesiveness necessary to form the community of all God's people. This ancient law revealed to Moses on the mountaintop continues to provide fundamental guidelines for living, even in our technological, highly sophisticated world.

Moses discovered, what we also discover, that the mountaintop experience of God's self disclosure would forever affect his life as well as the life of the Israelite community. Once he had been to the mountaintop and experienced a revelation of God, his life was forever changed.

Suggestion for prayer: *Pray Psalm 119:10-11.*

✞Pastor, Pasadena Community Church (United Methodist Church), St. Petersburg, Florida.

Tuesday, February 16   Read Exodus 24:15-18.

In that mountaintop experience, Moses learned a great deal about God. This God who was so remote and distant, whose presence was made known only through fire and smoke, became near and personal. God became so personal that God's will and purpose were made known to Moses.

Moses was able to bridge the gap between the fire, the smoke, and the clouds of Sinai and the people. Moses discovered that God was not a God on a distant mountain, but a God whose presence was to be made known to the people at the foot of the mountain.

During this Epiphany season, the emphasis has been on the manifestation of God's presence among us in Jesus. To the first century world it was an incredible, startling fact, that the Word—that power, that dynamic, that reason that controls and orders the world—had become a Person, and, "we have seen his glory" (John 1:14).

Moses discovered on the mountain which became a central theme of the Christian gospel, that this God who was so remote had now come near. As Moses bridged the gap between God on the mountaintop and the people in the valley, so did Jesus bridge the gap between God and the world.

The discovery that Moses made on Sinai came to its fruition in John 1:14, "And the Word became flesh and lived among us." John is saying, "If you want to see what this creating Word, this dynamic power, this controlling reason looks like, then look at Jesus of Nazareth." In other words, in Christ, God is down to earth.

Prayer: *Thank you, Lord, for coming into the midst of our lives. In Christ you are not distant but near. Amid all our pain, suffering, setbacks and heartaches, you have made your presence and power known. For that we are grateful. Amen.*

Wednesday, February 17   Read Psalm 99.

"The LORD is great in Zion...exalted over all the peoples." This psalm of the Lord's enthronement rather remarkably draws together two key factors in Israel's faith tradition: God's holy presence and God's righteous will.

Even though there is a strong emphasis on the Lord's transcendence, the psalmist points out that this "Mighty King, lover of justice," has established equity and has executed justice and righteousness. Even amid the Lord's transcendence is immanence! Even in the Lord's enthronement is nearness. In verses 4 and 5 we discover the Mosaic tradition of liberation, expressed in the words "the lover of justice," who has "established equity" and "executed justice and righteousness."

From the bondage of Egypt we still hear the cry, "Let my people go." These are the words that the God of the Bible increasingly directs against every aggression or system that threatens to enslave or impoverish. The psalmist points out that "equity," "justice," and "righteousness" are the characteristics of the Lord. Therefore, the final issue of human history is in the hands of the Lord, whose unwavering nature is to deliver the helpless.

The whole movement from Advent to Christmas to these closing days of Epiphany reveals to us a God of hope and freedom. What started as freedom for a small nomadic tribe in the Sinai desert is now, through Christ, freedom and hope for all people. Thus the final word in the liberation God offers is *joy*. Out of the joy of God is Christ born, and light forever shines in this dark world.

Prayer: *Help us, O Lord, to walk in the light as you are in the light, that we may have fellowship one with another. Amen.*

Thursday, February 18   Read 2 Peter 1:16-18.

The author seeks to convince us that he was not following some mystical, nebulous, or vague myth. Rather, the basis of his hope was his own eyewitness account of being with Jesus upon the mountain. He states emphatically that he had heard the words spoken to Jesus: "This is my Son, my Beloved, with whom I am well pleased." He heard this voice while he was on the mountaintop along with James and John.

It is difficult to refute an eyewitness account. The author was convinced by what he had seen and heard. It was upon this personal encounter that he establishes his hope.

The mountaintop experience is a religious experience, one that holds mystique, awe, and glory. It is difficult to express adequately what such experience means. If you have ever had such an experience it remains part of your life having breath-taking significance. Such a vision of God transforms life irrevocably. This was true for the author of our text.

The mountaintop experience wears well in the valley. The authenticity of that experience helps give guidance and hope when the mountain is obscured by the clouds and the heavenly voices can no longer be heard.

We must not confuse hope with optimism. To do so leads to disappointment. Hope, for the author, is based on personal experience of a genuine encounter with Christ. If our hope lacks such objectivity and remains merely optimism, it will eventually wane and perhaps even fade away.

The problems that the author faces are real, but so was his personal encounter with Christ. The previous reality of the mountaintop experience makes it possible to cope with present reality. Optimism means faith in people; whereas, hope means faith in God.

Prayer: *Pray Psalm 39:7.*

Friday, February 19   Read 2 Peter 1:19-21.

The second part of the Epistle text is concerned with the reliability of the prophetic witness. The author points out that "no prophecy ever came by human will, but men and women moved by the Holy Spirit spoke from God."

The Christian community constantly is faced with the task of "testing the spirits" to see if they are of God. The Christian community cannot escape the responsibility of evaluating the source and relevance of what is offered today as truth, or whatever claims to be the will of God for the present. Are there certain criteria given to us by the scriptures or by the Christian community that can be used to discern what appears to be of God? As history reveals, the church has made some good, as well as some very poor, decisions. The apostle Paul had one basic test—the test of love as expressed in 1 Corinthians 13.

The apostle's emphasis on love was directed to those in the Corinthian church who were inspired with their own contribution and importance. Paul does not doubt their devotion or question their commitment and insight. Simply put, if their accomplishments and achievements do not reflect the character of Christ-like love, then such experiences are valueless. Can truth ever be separated from love? The apostle's answer is an emphatic, "No!" Is it fair, then, to say that whatever violates Christian love is not of the Holy Spirit?

The Holy Spirit creates community—and Christian love holds that community together.

Prayer: *O Lord, in our world of divisiveness and conflict, make us instruments of your love and reconciliation. Amen.*

Saturday, February 20   Read Matthew 17:1-4.

Jesus prayed at the most significant times in his life. He prayed prior to his baptism. He withdrew to pray in the wilderness prior to beginning his public ministry. He prayed prior to Peter's confession. He prayed in Gethsemane prior to Calvary. Here on the mountaintop as he was in an attitude of prayer "the appearance of his countenance was altered," and suddenly Moses and Elijah appeared with him.

When Jesus took Peter, James, and John to the mountaintop, it was a time to better understand God's will and purpose. Here Jesus gained perspective on his life. Prayer can give us perspective, too.

It seems that Jesus' first thought when facing a decision was to pray. He would ask to know what God would have him do. Jesus put his plans and intentions before God. He prayed at each critical moment of his life, wanting to be certain that he was following God's will for his life.

How necessary it is for us to pray! There is an assurance and direction that only prayer can bring to our lives. Jesus was not only assured that he had chosen the right way, but more importantly, he now saw the role that Jerusalem and the cross would play in his life. Prayer can help us see the role, the place, that significant events in our lives play.

What are those things that you are wrestling with today? For some it may be the loss of a job or a job change; the decision to get married, moral or financial matters; or what course of action to follow. If these factors are important enough to worry about, then surely they are important enough to pray about.

Prayer: *Help me, Lord, to speak first with you before I speak to others. Amen.*

A Mountaintop Experience

Sunday, February 21　　　　Read Matthew 17:5-9.

Peter was overwhelmed by this mountaintop experience. How was he going to tell the folks back home about this? He wanted to stay there, to forget the world below. Peter was convinced that life couldn't get any better than this.

How many of us would have said and done the same things as did Peter? He vainly tried to hold on to this moment, to capture it and solidify it. But the mountaintop is not an end in itself.

We are often tempted to withdraw and live on the fringe of life. Do we send our dollars to missions and avoid personal involvement? When Christians are ready to go "out on location" they find an authentic setting for their story.

The gospel story travels well. There are those who are waiting to hear the story. We need to take it to the marketplace, the highways and byways, the psychiatric wards, the hospitals, the jails, the streets, the penthouses, the state houses, the offices, and the conference rooms.

The Transfiguration is meaningful to us because represents the conscientious anguish of human beings attempting desperately to comprehend the will of God for their lives. We are part of this story. We do not know in advance where the truth of God will send us or what we will find when we get there. But we have been to the mountaintop and experienced the spirit of God's presence and beheld the divine glory. There is a radiance and glow that will remain with us even in the valley.

Prayer: *O Lord, as we descend from the mountaintop let us remember your promise, "I am with you always, to the end of the age." Amen.*

RETURNING TO GOD

February 22-28, 1993   **Jean M. Blomquist✠**
Monday, February 22   Read Genesis 2:15-17; 3:1-7.

I have difficulty reading the temptation story, because for centuries it has been used as a weapon against women. Yet, when cultural biases are laid aside, the heart of the story emerges and exposes a part of our humanity that we would surely prefer remain hidden.

Some interpret knowing good and evil as the ability to make moral judgments or as a loss of primal innocence. But knowing good and evil also connotes knowing *everything*— knowing as only God can know. Our desire to stand in God's place—and by extension our unwillingness to recognize our dependence on God—forms the core of sin.

Today this sin often exhibits itself in our need to control. That which we see as good—just as Eve saw the good fruit, the delightful tree, and the desirability of wisdom—sometimes hides reality. Efficiency, expediency, or autocratic leadership, for example, can sometimes be symptoms of what, in recent years, has been termed "functional atheism"; our belief that nothing will happen if we don't do it; our compulsion to fill lulls and silent spaces rather than allowing the Spirit to move in its own time; or our need to "create the appearance of results rather than waiting for reality to emerge."* When our sin is exposed, we cover up with reasons and excuses which only move us further away from God.

Suggestion for meditation: *Reflect on your own desire to be "like God." How does this distance you from others, God, and yourself?*

✠Writer; Berkeley, California.
*Parker J. Palmer, Earl Lectures (Berkeley, California), Jan. 30, 1992.

Tuesday, February 23   Read Psalm 32.

While Adam and Eve try to cover up their transgression with fig leaves and, later, excuses, the psalmist keeps silence, holding his iniquity within. Verses 3-7 have been variously interpreted as describing physical illness that the psalmist thought was punishment for his sin or physical distress due to his sense of God's displeasure. Could it also be that the psalmist wallows a bit in his sin as he groans "all day long"? Perhaps obsession with his sin helps him avoid the more daunting task of changing attitudes and ways.

Yet the keeping of silence, the holding within, the moaning and groaning do not ameliorate his feelings of guilt. God's presence weighs heavily on him, and his strength evaporates. But what might this "strength" be, that evaporates in the tension between the reality of sin and the presence of God? Is it, perhaps, the illusion of power, of being "like God"?

The tension and anguish inherent in the psalm are broken open with the psalmist's acknowledgment and confession of his sin. Only when we acknowledge our sins and "open" them through confession, bringing them into the gracious and healing light of God, can we experience the release, relief, and joy of forgiveness.

Suggestion for meditation: *Reflect on the ways you avoid acknowledging your sin.*

Prayer: *Gracious God, at times I do not know my own sin; at others, under the guise of sorrow, I wallow in it. Open my eyes and my heart to my own brokenness. Free me from all that keeps me from confession and all that keeps me from living my life fully in you. Grant me, I pray, the freedom and joy of your forgiveness. Amen.*

Wednesday, February 24 (Ash Wednesday)
Read Isaiah 58:1-12.

Ash Wednesday challenges our illusions. We are reminded of our mortality and of the many ways, individually and collectively, that we have fallen short of the glory of God.

Similarly, the writer of today's passage from Isaiah exposes and challenges Israel's illusions of faithfulness, their surface observances that substitute for faithful living. Caught in their own inability to see clearly, Israel complains that they fast and humble themselves, but God doesn't see or notice. God's response is sharp: You call this a "fast," observing practices that make you look good while you quarrel, oppress, and abuse others? No! A true fast integrates faith and life by ending injustice, relieving oppression, caring for the afflicted. When you observe this fast, I will guide you, strengthen you, and satisfy your needs.

The faithful will be "like a spring of water, whose waters never fail," a powerful image of the life-giving quality of faithfulness. Lent calls us to be that spring, to be a source of life-giving faithfulness. To do that, we must remove, give up, or turn away from that which blocks the freeing presence of God in our lives. How, we must honestly ask ourselves, are we like Israel? How do we quarrel with, oppress, or abuse others? How do we refuse to "loose the bonds of injustice" and neglect to care for the afflicted? How can we turn again to God, to a life of faithfulness?

Prayer: *Loving God, it is often hard for me to recognize and face my own sin, especially my pious substitutes for faithfulness. Grant me the strength, courage, and vision to "break every yoke." Open my heart in compassion to those who are in need, that I may be "a spring of water, whose waters never fail." Amen.*

67

Thursday, February 25   Read Matthew 4:1-11.

The temptation of Jesus immediately follows his baptism, where God announces, "This is my Son, the Beloved..." (3:17). Jesus now faces temptation, or testing, concerning the expression of his Sonship. Will he obey God's call to be a servant-messiah, or will he embrace a more worldly manifestation of power over nature, God, and the world?

Jesus is famished when the tempter asks, "What could be wrong with using a bit of your Son-of-God power to feed yourself?" No, Jesus answers; and the tempter tries again, probing a bit deeper: "You have been so good and faithful in this God-forsaken wilderness. Has God forsaken you as well? Why not see if God still cares for you?" Jesus refuses to test or manipulate God, so the tempter tries a third time: "Worship me and I will give you everything you could ever want or need." Jesus refuses temptation a final time.

Each time Jesus is tempted, he rejects the temptation with words from Deuteronomy (8:3; 6:16; 6:13). Here Matthew contrasts the faithlessness of the Israelites in the wilderness with the faithfulness of Jesus, who is the new revelation, the new Torah, which the Jews are to follow.

Can we follow Jesus today when we are needy and tempted to fill our needs in inappropriate ways? when we are weary and desire spectacular proof of God's care or magical solutions to our problems? when we feel powerless and are offered false promises of power over others?

Prayer: *O God, when I am tempted to misuse power, strengthen and guide me. When I feel needy, weary, or powerless, guard me against temptation and fill me with the power of your presence, that I may keep my life centered in you. Amen.*

Friday, February 26　　　　Read Romans 5:12-19.

These few verses are thick with Paul's theology and rich with his sense of God's abounding grace. Here are the two poles of existence: Adam and Christ, sin and forgiveness, death and life. Adam's transgression brought sin, condemnation, and death; Christ's righteousness brings forgiveness, "justification" (or acquittal), and life.

Paul's language and tone shift as he moves from the opening section on sin and death (vv. 12-14) to the verses that follow. The ledger of life, with its column for us and its column for God, is not balanced. Despite our inheritance of sin, despite our own sins and our responsibility for them, Paul reminds us that "the free gift is not like the trespass." Adam's trespass brought death, an appropriate punishment for his transgression; but God's free gift of life is generous and undeserved. We are made "righteous" (given freedom and life in the Spirit) through Christ. God's movement toward us and God's gracious, free gift of forgiveness permeate life.

When I read this passage, my head is filled with the chorus "Since by Man Came Death" from Handel's *Messiah.* Based on 1 Corinthians 15:21-22, this brief piece echoes Paul musically. Slowly, ponderously sin and death come into the world—but then brightly, joyously, Christ brings resurrection and life. Handel uses repetition for emphasis, but again the ledger is not even. The phrases of death repeat twice, but the phrases of life resound three and four times.

God's grace, vital and freeing, abounds.

Suggestion for meditation: *Listen to a recording of "Since by Man Came Death," if it is easily available to you. Carry the melody and the words with you throughout the day.*

Prayer: *Each hour, each moment of this day, enliven me in Christ, O God, I pray. Amen.*

Saturday, February 27   Read 2 Corinthians 5:20b–6:10.

Be part, Paul urges the Corinthians, of a world and a people restored to God through Christ. Become the new creation where Christ's love governs all perceptions and actions (see 5:17-19). "Be," Paul writes, "reconciled to God."

Reconciliation certainly is needed. Things are not going well for Paul in Corinth. Opponents, whom Paul refers to earlier as "peddlers of God's word" (2:17), have stirred up the community against him by asserting that he possesses neither the appearance, skills, and social status nor the correct achievements and religious experiences to be a true apostle. Yet Paul maintains that he and his associates are "ambassadors for Christ" (v. 20a), those through whom God appeals for reconciliation.

In this appeal, Paul weaves together his call to carry Christ's message to the Corinthians, his theological understanding of reconciliation, and his desire for personal reconciliation. He weaves together his relationships with God, the Corinthians, and himself. Can these be joined in Christ?

Paul reminds the Corinthians of the opportunity to become more than who they are. By drawing themselves more fully into Christ by their deeds, they may become "the righteousness" of God in the world.

The passage closes with a cataloguing of the events and qualities of Paul's ministry, which echo the life of Christ. The anguish of his lived experience makes Paul's appeal all the more eloquent. Perhaps through his own pain, he has come to a deeper and broader, more vital understanding of reconciliation in and with God. Is this possible for us as well?

Prayer: *Soften my heart, O God, that I may be reconciled to you and to all. Amen.*

Sunday, February 28   Read Psalm 51.

Today's reading is one of the most eloquent and moving of the penitential psalms. David's sin with Bathsheba sets a powerful metaphorical frame for this confession: sin violates God's love. Through confession and forgiveness, we are reconciled with God.

An underlying current affirming God's "steadfast love," or covenant faithfulness, flows through the entire psalm. Perhaps it is the psalmist's trust in God's faithfulness that enables him not only to confess his sinful actions but also to acknowledge his ongoing propensity toward sin.

God's desire for "truth in the inward being" sparks the psalmist's own desire for wisdom and cleansing. With cleansing comes not only release from the crushing load of guilt but also joyous thanksgiving and a commitment to sharing the news of God's graciousness.

The psalmist's assertion that "the sacrifice acceptable to God is a broken spirit" is countered by a later addition (vv. 18-19), designed to allow for liturgical use of the psalm in the Temple and to diffuse what might be perceived as the anti-sacrificial spirit of verses 16-17. (In our own time, ironically, this addition may reveal the temptation of institutions to perpetuate themselves in ways that are no longer necessary.) It reminds us also of the need for healthy interaction between individuals and institutions, of our need to call each other to repentance and mutual accountability.

On this first Sunday in Lent, let us hold in heart and mind this week's readings on sin and forgiveness, temptation and reconciliation. Then, let us turn toward God—repentant, reconciled, and rejoicing in the graciousness of God.

Suggestion for prayer: *Pray Psalm 51:10-12.*

THE BLESSINGS OF THE FAITHFUL

March 1-7, 1993   **Robert P. Gardner**✝
Monday, March 1   Read Genesis 12:1-4a.

When God called Abraham (Abram) out of his homeland to journey into a new country, the Lord's only directions were "I will show you." The people of Ur practiced idolatry. Abram dared to worship God despite temptations to serve pagan gods. When God called, Abram heard and followed. Through his obedience, God established an eternal covenant of love with humankind. By faith, we obtain the blessings of this covenant.

Faith is an action. God is more concerned about how we live the Christian life than what we say about Christianity. The test of our faith in Christ is seen by our willingness to obey God's commandments. Jesus told the disciples, "If you love me, you will obey what I command" (John 14:15 NIV).

When the Lord calls there is a promise to lead and guide. God promised Abraham that he would inherit a great land, become a great nation, and be blessed among all people. Through the eyes of faith, he would obtain the promises of God. As sons and daughters of Abraham, we are children of God's promise who share in the inheritance of abundant life through Jesus Christ. We are blessed to be a blessing.

God calls us to Christian mission and responsibility. Sometimes the Lord speaks to us through the advice of friends; sometimes, through scripture; still other times, through a quiet voice of "inner knowing." Is God speaking to you today? What is God calling you to do?

Prayer: *Lord, when you call us to mission and service, help us to hear, obey, and walk by faith. In Jesus' name. Amen*

✝United Methodist clergy, Memphis Annual Conference; pastor, Jackson Parish, Jackson, Tennessee.

Tuesday, March 2   Read Psalm 121.

God honors those who trust and obey the commandments. In this passage, the author assures the weary traveler that when we trust God, help is on the way. God is always near and ready to respond to our needs. For the trusting soul, help is but a heartfelt cry away.

The psalmist puts trust in the sure and mighty hand of God, the ultimate source of help. There is no doubt about who and where this believer seeks help. "I will lift up mine eyes unto the hills, from whence cometh my help" (KJV). Whether we read this last part as a question (from whence does my help come?) or as a statement, this believer knows that God is the supreme keeper and deliverer: "My help comes from the LORD, who made heaven and earth."

In time of trouble, we may put our hope and trust in human ability or strength. But God is the sure source of strength and help. Without God, we become like ships without a sail or rudder—powerless, with no sense of direction. Life presents us with perplexities in which only God can bring about a solution. The psalmist encourages us not to look outward at circumstances or inward to our own human strength but "upward" in expectancy towards God for help.

Like the psalmist, when we look with eyes of faith, we see God, who watches over and keeps us. The Lord, who neither sleeps nor slumbers, preserves us from evil. Like a child who runs to mother or father for protection and comfort, we are to run to God for help in times of need.

Prayer: *Dear God, in the midst of life's perplexities and uncertainties, help us to look "upward" in faith and trust you to guide our every step. Amen.*

Wednesday, March 3   Read Psalm 33:18-22.

The eyes of the Lord are on the faithful. Again, the psalmist describes the love of God towards the believer. This does not mean that God shuns the sinner. The Lord's love reaches out to us regardless of our shortcomings. When we humbly submit to the will of God, the promises of God avail themselves to us.

The psalmist uses the word *fear* to explain how we are to serve God. Many Christians understand the word *fear* literally. In the biblical sense, this word means to revere and adore the Lord as Giver and Sustainer of life. God is good and worthy to be praised. Adoration unto the Lord begins with a grateful heart in response to God's love towards us.

Next, the psalmist offers adoration and reverence unto God as the one who would deliver his soul from death and keep him alive in famine. The psalmist's faith in God was founded on past blessings and the hope of future blessings. Faith rises within us when we reflect on God's love for us. When we count our blessings, the reality of God's goodness is impressed upon us. We adore and worship God out of the understanding that the Lord is divine Protector and Keeper of our souls.

Finally, the psalmist tells the faithful to wait, rejoice, and trust in God. Waiting is an act of faith in which we show our confidence in God's timing to bring forth the best solution. By faith, we know that the Lord will bring to pass that which is best for us. Waiting is trusting God to meet us at the point of our need at the right time and with the right answer. The faithful are to rejoice in this surety of God.

Prayer: *Heavenly Father, thank you for watching over us. Help us to be faithful Christians in word and deed. Amen.*

Thursday, March 4 Read Romans 4:1-5.

Christians touch God through their faith. Through faith we obtain the blessings and promises of God. Paul shows us this truth in today's passage. First, the believer is "justified" by faith, made right with God. Through faith in God, we enter into a new relationship of grace and love. As in the case of a marriage, the husband and wife create a new union based on trust and belief in each other. Through faith we enter into this holy and right relationship with God.

Peace of mind and heart is a result of this new faith relationship with God. Through faith in the redemptive work of Jesus Christ, we have entered into the sphere of God's grace and love. God's love through Christ is not something that we have to work for, to earn. Our goodness does not buy it. The divine parent-child relationship is not built on works but on our freewill response to God's goodness towards us. This unearned favor is a gift from God. God's only request is that we accept what has been provided. By faith, we say yes to God's offer of salvation through Christ.

Finally, faith brings us into the reality of hope and certainty. When we know that God is in control, hope comes alive in us. Through faith we know that the Lord will ultimately bring us through the storms and uncertainties of life. Faith does not have to see the solution to know that there is an answer. When we look beyond the outer appearance, we see the glory of God. Thus, as Paul taught, Christians can weather trials and tribulations to the glory of God. Through faith in God, our mountains and walls of difficulties can become opportunities for God to be glorified.

Prayer: *Gracious Lord, thank you for bringing us into a right relation with you. Through Christ we pray. Amen.*

Friday, March 5   Read Romans 4:13-17.

Paul helps us to understand that sin and evil cannot prevail over God's grace. Grace was present before sin came into the world. John Wesley used the term *prevenient grace* to describe this unconditional love that goes before us. Although we approach God in faith, grace is the gateway by which we enter into the kingdom of heaven. Faith takes us to the door of the kingdom; grace allows us to enter.

Sin is missing the mark, is failure to live up to God's divine standard. Before the Law, people did not know how to define sin. Yet sin has always been present. Although Adam did not live under the Law, his disobedience to God resulted in death. The refusal to obey God's commandments results in alienation from God. Nevertheless, the Lord loves us despite our shortcomings and even our disobedience.

Adam represents the means through which the consequences of sin came to humans; Christ, the means by which the grace of God flows to humankind. Through Adam's and Eve's disobedience, the penalty of death has been imposed upon humankind. Through Christ, new life is offered.

Christ came as the righteousness of God to lost humanity. Adam brought sin and death while Christ brought grace and hope. God's grace is abounding and overflowing love towards us. Through the sacrificial and meritorious work of Christ on the cross, we are made right with God. What God did shows the level of divine love towards us. By faith in Christ, the believer now stands in a divine-human love relationship with God. Through this gift of righteousness to us, we have entered into newness of life.

Prayer: *Thank you, Lord, for sending Christ into the world. Through him we now move from darkness into your marvelous light. Amen.*

Saturday, March 6   Read John 3:1-8.

Nicodemus was fascinated by the signs and wonders that followed Jesus' ministry. This curiosity led Nicodemus to go to Jesus in search of more information about this Galilean minister.

Jesus said to Nicodemus that a person must be "born again" ("born from above") in order to enter into the kingdom of God. The Christian journey begins when a person receives the spiritual birth that can only come from God.

One of John Wesley's great discoveries was that when he crossed the ocean to offer salvation to the Native Americans and the colonists in Georgia, he himself was in need of this salvation. Only those who have been born from above through God's grace can genuinely bring others to Christ. Spiritual rebirth is based not on church membership or position but on an openness to receiving the free gift of God.

What did it mean to be "born anew" or "born from above"? Nicodemus did not know. Can a person "enter a second time into the mother's womb and be born"? Some Christians see rebirth as an ecstatic and emotional expression, while others understand rebirth as a warm and quiet experience of the heart. Jesus gives no answer but only describes this work of the Spirit. The Spirit is like a wind that blows where it chooses. No one knows where it comes from or where it goes. So is that person who is born anew from God. Jesus' only absolute command here is that the Christian's life must begin with spiritual rebirth. If our faith is to be alive and effective in touching others, the new birth must be a reality in our lives.

Prayer: *Lord Jesus, help us to experience and live the life of one who has been born from above. Amen.*

Sunday, March 7   Read John 3:14-17.

Jesus Christ was the fulfillment of God's promise made to the faithful. John uses the story of the bronze serpent in the wilderness to explain God's plan of salvation. When the Israelites murmured against God and Moses for bringing them out into the wilderness, the Lord sent fiery serpents to plague the people. Many of the people were bitten and later died. The Israelites repented of their ungrateful attitude and asked Moses to pray that God would take the serpents away.

After Moses prayed for the people, God instructed him to make a bronze serpent and place it on a pole. The serpent was lifted high so that all the people could see it. If a serpent bit a person, he or she would only have to look at the bronze serpent and live. Through the lifted-up serpent, the pain of suffering and death would be conquered.

Jesus was lifted up on Calvary's cross for the world to see. When we look at Christ on the cross, we see God's unconditional and universal love for the world. God saw the pains of sins and death plaguing the people. Yet, God's love reached out to hurting humanity. "For God so loved the world that he gave his only Son, so that everyone who believes in him may not perish but have eternal life." Christ is the visible proof that God heard and responded to the cries of suffering humanity.

Are you lifting up Jesus today? Does the world see the Savior in you? God calls us to lift Christ through our prayers, presence, gifts and service. Do people see Christ in how we go about our daily living? Are we examples of God's love for others to see?

Prayer: *Dear God, help us to live each day so that others might see the raised Christ who comes to take away the sins of the world. Amen.*

FREEDOM FROM BARRIERS

March 8-14, 1993   **David Maldonado, Jr.✢**
Monday, March 8   Read Exodus 17:1-3.

The Hebrews had lived in oppression in Egypt for generations. Harsh and ruthless treatment had been their daily
bread. Their survival was a continual challenge, and plans to
destroy them were drawn up. Yet, it seems that in the midst
of their oppression, God was with them and heard their cry!
God's response was to seek their liberation.

After four hundred years, most of that time under oppression, the Israelites were eager for their freedom. When they
were offered liberation, they accepted. However, accepting
God's action required faith and obedience. Israel was called
to follow God's road to liberation, which is not an easy
journey. It meant the challenges of the desert and moving
into an unknown world. Israel's commitment to complete
God's task of liberation and their faithfulness were tested,
not by God, but by their own need for security and assurance. Was God really with them? Were they doing the right
thing? Was it not easier to live within the status quo? Was
liberation worth their pain?

To accept God's revealing and liberating action is an act
of faith. To live one's life in faith calls for obedience, that is,
a sense of faithfulness and trust. To accept God's invitation
is to enter God's journey and to trust that God is indeed with
us as we travel the difficult road to liberation.

Prayer: *God, grant us the patience and power of faith, that as we
travel the road you have chosen for us, we may learn to trust in
you. Amen.*

✢Associate Professor of Church and Society at the Perkins School of
Theology, SMU, Dallas, Texas.

Tuesday, March 9 Read Exodus 17:4-7.

The Israelites could not wait to leave Egypt and its centuries of enslavement. They were eager to get to the promised land—the land of freedom and plenty. It sounded so good and so easily obtainable. Had God not promised it to them? Arriving seemed be a simple matter of following Moses. However, the road toward liberation was a long and a hard road. While liberation had been a gift from God, a human response was required if it were to be reached.

By the time they had reached Rephidim, the Israelites had already known hunger and thirst. But they had also witnessed God's promise to provide. God had sweetened the water at Marah (Exod. 15:23-25) and had provided shade and springs of water at Elim (15:27). Yet, as they faced thirst again, they quarreled and complained again. How short was their memory, how limited their faith! In the midst of an immediate human need they quickly forgot God's action and God's promise. The Israelites were ready to sacrifice the ultimate promise for an immediate desire. They were more concerned with water that would only temporarily satisfy their thirst than with being faithful to God's call and promise. They had drunk the water that God had provided, but had they tasted the vision that God had offered?

God has presented us a glimpse of the Kingdom through the life and ministry of Jesus Christ. God has called us to enter that road toward the Kingdom. It is not an easy journey. There will be distractions and competing desires. Yet, God's presence and vision reinforce our commitment to continue in our faithful journey.

Prayer: *God, grant us the perseverance of faith and the strength to seek first your kingdom. Amen.*

Wednesday, March 10   Read Psalm 95.

As the people of God, Israel was called to worship God and to celebrate God's greatness. As the people fled Egypt, they witnessed God's dominion over the physical and natural world. The plagues in Egypt and the miraculous provisions in the desert had affirmed that, indeed, God is the One who is above all things and worthy of praise!

In recognizing this, however, the people of God immediately were called to recognize that they also were a part of God's creation. God was known as their Maker. They were called to understand themselves as God's creatures. But they were also the people of the Lord's pasture. The all powerful God is also the God of mercy who had provided pasture for them.

To be in God's presence is to be totally opened and exposed to God—the One who knows our hearts and our history, as well as our potential. The people of God were reminded that they stood before God who provided for them in the desert, who was with them, and who was tested and put to the proof. To affirm that they were the people of God's pasture was also to recognize that they had questioned God's promise to provide for them. To question God's promise was also to question whether they were truly the people of God's pasture—the people of God.

We are called to know God as our Maker, who in mercy and love created us as the people of God's pasture, the ones for whom God cares. To be the people of God's pasture is to be the people of faith and trust in God's grace.

Prayer: *God, we confess that we have tested you and have taken your grace for granted. Be merciful to us and grant that we might be faithful and trusting in you. Amen.*

Thursday, March 11 Read Romans 5:1-5.

Like the freed Israelites, Christians are the people of God who have heard God's call to join in the journey toward liberation. God has heard our cry in the midst of our human turmoil and social oppression and has offered nothing less than his Son that we might be free. God has chosen to be with us and to lead us from our oppression. God's action through Jesus Christ reflects the very nature of divine love and desire for us to enjoy his peace. Thus we stand in God's grace through Jesus Christ and enjoy God's peace.

However, to accept God's invitation to join in the journey is not to enter an easy walk. Saul's encounter with Jesus Christ on the road to Damascus radically changed his course. Once Jesus Christ had entered his life, Paul's task was to travel a totally new road, to take the liberating news to others, and thus to free them as well. It was to be a difficult road filled with personal challenges, hardships, and even suffering. In his letter to the Romans, Paul shares that such experiences do test us. However, instead of weakening or distracting us, they can serve to strengthen our commitment and result in a stronger faithfulness.

It is a road that we are also called to travel, that will challenge our faithfulness and commitment. We will be tested. We might even try to test God, as the Israelites did in the desert. However, we are now assured of God's love and promise, for we have known Christ. And God's spirit has already been given unto us, not as a reward at the end of the road but as a source of strength to endure the journey.

Prayer: *God, grant us your grace, and pour into our hearts your Spirit, that as we journey upon your road we may find the strength to be faithful to your call. Amen.*

Friday, March 12   Read Romans 5:6-11.

Paul could well recall his own ungodliness, his act of turning his back upon God's will for the future. Hadn't Paul persecuted the church in Jerusalem and approved the killing of Stephen? His persecution had brought fear to God's people! He had challenged and tested God's purpose. He had stood in opposition to God's liberating action. If ever there were an enemy of God, Paul saw himself as such. If ever there were reconciliation with God, Paul had known it.

Paul's religious heritage was of the Law. Right relationship with God was through obedience to the Law. In fact, much of the early persecution was because the early Christians were teaching things that went beyond the Law—a new and strange message of grace. The people of God who lived under the Law understood their relationship with God to be a matter of righteousness through obedience to the Law. But those who lived under the Law angered God when their hearts had gone astray.

Paul had experienced a great transformation. He had met Christ and experienced God's grace! Jesus Christ had come to Saul, the persecutor and enemy of God. Grace had come to him even while he was in the midst of persecuting the church. Paul, who had been blind to God's purpose, could then see that Christ had died for him, a sinner. God does love us even while we are sinners and makes reconciliation a new reality!

To be loved while we are sinners is to know God's grace undeservedly. It is truly a gift from God. Like Paul, we can also recall our own ungodliness. Like Paul, God's grace is offered to us in spite of ourselves.

Prayer: *God, grant us your grace that we might be transformed and reconciled, to you and to our neighbor. Amen.*

Saturday, March 13   Read John 4:3-30.

Jesus was keenly aware of the disdain the Jews had for the Samaritans and of the distrust the Samaritans had toward the Jews. Jesus was equally aware of the position of women. It was not acceptable for a man to speak with a woman in public! Indeed, the world in which Jesus lived was a world of divisions and rigid lines between people based on their gender and their race or ethnicity. Tradition and status quo were powerful forces which imprisoned people within rigid social structures and practices.

Jesus broke through social and ethnic barriers by asking the Samaritan woman for water. He surprised the woman as well as his disciples. The disciples had witnessed his miracles and acts of ministry, had heard his words of revelation. Yet, they were shocked as Jesus moved freely and lovingly in his simple act of talking to a Samaritan woman. It was as if they did not expect him to do such a thing, nor did they understand the significance of his actions. Jesus often did the unexpected. He crossed lines and overcame barriers that humans had built. However, it was more than simply a daring act; it was an act of revelation, a revelation of God's desire for the world.

Our world is just as divided and separated by gender, race, and ethnicity, by economic class, religious traditions, and other bases for discrimination. However, today we do know who Jesus is, and we know the nature of the gift he offers to all. The gift of living water is offered unto us that we might be free from those prisons which oppress our lives and the lives of our neighbor.

Prayer: *God, grant us your gift of living water and the faith to drink of it, that we may be freed to love our neighbor. Amen.*

Sunday, March 14   Read John 4:31-42.

In the context of hearing of her hope in the coming of the messiah, Jesus revealed himself to the Samaritan woman. "I am he, the one who is speaking to you" (v. 26). She left her jar and went back to the city to tell the people what she had seen and heard. Jesus had spoken to her faith in such a way that it freed her to share the good news with the people of her city. And many believed because of her testimony. She became a spring of water to her friends and neighbors.

Jesus reached out to her across all the social and ethnic barriers. His act of reaching out to her and his words of God's gift freed her from the confining roles of her world. Because of her experience at the well, she dared to speak to all the townspeople—men and women—and led them to where Jesus was. Just as Jesus had reached out across rigid barriers and traditions, the Samaritan woman herself became a bridge between this Jew and her Samaritan neighbors. And the Jew who had once been denied hospitality in Samaria was asked to stay—and he did, for two days.

We live in a world of both overt and invisible barriers. Whether these be racial, ethnic, national, class, or even religious, they work to divide God's creation. As Christians, we are called to let our faith and hope be known in such a way that God's creation might be in peace within itself, as well as with God.

Prayer: *God, grant us your grace that we may find the courage to reach out to those from whom we have been separated, and that we may extend your love to all your creation. Amen.*

LIGHTER PATHS FOR TREADING

March 15-21, 1993   **Henry F. Woodruff✠**
Monday, March 15   Read 1 Samuel 16:1, 6-13.

Those called to walk the path

The story of biblical faith is the story of a transcendent God who chooses to become immanent in historical existence. God interrupts human life for a purpose, calls persons to be a part of the purpose, and works through persons to accomplish the purpose. We might not grasp fully the entire scope of God's purposes, but our lack of understanding does not preclude our participation in God's redemptive work.

Such is the superstructure for the biblical narrative of the anointing of David as king. The story reminds us not only of whose agenda is ultimately to be served but also that God can and does penetrate our hearts and minds, seeing what we often cannot: a human life as an instrument for God's redemptive purposes. Surprised by the choice of David, Samuel heard the Lord say, "The LORD sees not as mortals do; they look on the outward appearance, but the LORD looks on the heart.." God calls persons—even unlikely persons—to walk the path of God's purposes.

It is a lesson for us to learn as we consider what path God has for us. We may not see the potential we have for God's purposes; our inadequacy, our brokenness may move us to exclaim to the One who calls, "Look elsewhere!" In such moments God can and does speak with clarity, surprising even us, beckoning even us to step where God chooses and uses.

Suggestion for meditation: *What—for God's purposes—has God seen in me?*

✠Senior minister, Hudson United Methodist Church, Hudson, Ohio.

Tuesday, March 16   Read 1 Samuel 16:4*a*.

Preparing to tread the path

James Russell Lowell was right: "Time makes ancient good uncouth." It is out of fashion, even insulting, to call "professionals" those called by God to tread the path of God's redemptive purposes. Henri J. M. Nouwen's model of the "wounded healer" will gain assenting nods, but heads hang when priests and prophets are labeled "professional."

Today's text invites us to reclaim the label, even dare to wear it as our own. One nuance of meaning the word *professional* carries is extensive preparation for a specific task. We admire professionals in medicine and law who have endured the rigors of extensive preparation. Should God's world, in desperate need of healing and justice, not be entitled to the same kind of prepared, thoughtful, and dedicated care?

God's word through the writer of 1 Samuel says yes. Trembling before the one who will be part of God's redemptive purposes, the elders of the city wonder what lies ahead for them. Samuel announces that his intention is for good, that he has come intending to enter into the presence of God. He invites them to join him on the way, but before it can all happen "preparation" must take place: Consecration must precede the sacrifice. God's world waits for those prepared through consecration and sacrifice. Whether laypersons or clergy, we are called to be ministers who are prepared for a ministry of caring by scripture study, by prayer and listening to God, and by a commitment to walk God's path of redemptive purpose.

Suggestion for meditation: *What preparation for God's purposes is mine to make today? What consecration of my life will prepare me for the self-sacrifice God calls me to make?*

Wednesday, March 17   Read Psalm 23:1-4.

The experienced guide

Today's text places in sharp relief the difference between mental abstractions and experienced reality. As any path, any calling, and every purpose are only extensions of the mind until they are lived, obeyed, and walked, so is the shepherding of God a mental "might be" until it is experienced. Love in action, real caring, is like this: We know it is real when we have experienced its creative and re-creative power in our lives.

God's guiding into right paths near peaceful streams of refreshment and to rich places of nourishment is always like this. We know the Guide to be good and caring, strong and protecting because we experience such grace-full caring in treading the path. It is the lived experience of love experienced, not a fantasy of wishful thinking but a reality solid and true. The psalmist's words draw their power from such lived experience: God's guiding light of care shined even into the places of deep darkness, and what had been a "might be" became reality—"The Lord *is* my shepherd."

Our experience confirms that reality for us and is the reservoir from which we draw our courage to tread the path of God's redemptive purpose. Only then do we fear no evil, for then what has been an extension of the mind becomes the out-eached staff of the experienced Guide.

Suggest for meditation: *In what moments of my living has God's guiding and protecting care become real for me? Into what paths of rightness and nourishment have I been led, that I might find courage and strength for the journey?*

88

Thursday, March 18   Read Psalm 23:5-6.

Strength for the middle miles

Hikers refer to them as the "middle miles." These are the most exhausting, challenging miles on the path, when the exhilaration of beginning the journey has evaporated into drudgery and the promise of the path's end has not yet given new energy for the stepping. Experienced hikers know how to triumph over the middle miles; they carry with them high energy foods and plan for moments of rest. Then with a burst of energy and a refreshed mind, the heart is lifted and the steps become lighter.

The psalmist proclaims that God has prepared a table for us, where rest, refreshment, and new energy for the journey can be found. The table is prepared in the midst of all that is an enemy to faithful following: vanished excitement, depleted energy, a fatigued spirit, heavy steps which find the path too long, too hard. In the middle miles God is our host, giving us a super-abundance of all we need to triumph over fatigue and despair. Anointed with a new Spirit, steps become lighter. Not only can the journey continue, but the path becomes a joy to tread, a thing of celebration.

Such is the hope for all who have chosen—and *been* chosen—to tread the path of God's redemptive purpose. Regardless of the length of the journey, the power for the treading comes not only from the promised end or from the joy of beginning; the power is from the Host, who gives strength in the middle miles.

Suggestion for meditation: *What nourishment for treading the middle miles has God given me? Over what enemies to faithful following has God given me victory through the anointing and sustenance of the Holy Spirit?*

Friday, March 19   Read Ephesians 5:8-14.

Stepping in the light

Even smooth, straight, and easy paths become treacherous to tread in the darkness; how much more so when the path is crooked and rough, when the way is shrouded in darkness as deep as death itself! For those called to tread the path of God's redemptive purpose the hope of a shining light illuminating unsteady steps is the hope that gives courage.

Light does this. Shadows are driven back; illusion is exposed for what it is; truth stands in clear relief, and new confidence for the journey becomes the fruit light produces.

This is the word of hope and courage which the writer of today's text shines on our path. In a society antithetical to the way of Christ, the exhortation is not one of cloistered withdrawal but rather the challenge is to "live as children of light" *in* the darkness. Such is the way of authentic witness, for when those who tread God's path step in the light, more than firm footing is found. The text says the "works of darkness" are exposed. Witness to truth is made.

Is there a more urgent challenge or a more courageous word for us? It is not difficult to see the darkness; we, too, are surrounded by values and their lived expression antithetical to the way of Christ. The difficulty is seeing with clarity the path God offers us and then stepping into it with courage. So it is with hope and joy *we* sing the Epistle's hymn: "Sleeper, awake! Rise from the dead, and Christ will shine on you."

Suggestion for meditation: *Where am I called to walk today, with steps illumined by Christ, for witness to Christ? What "fruit" of God's light can I produce in a world surrounded by darkness?*

Saturday, March 20   Read John 9:1-12.

Reflections on the path

Some journeys are made in solitude, while others demand—even require!—community. Today's directive from the One who leads and gives light is a corporate "we." John affirms that not only has Christ chosen to walk with us, making our steps lighter, but Christ who is the light of the world summons us to reflect the light which has called us out of the darkness.

This is to "work the works" of God, who sent the light into the world. John is clear that even as the man born blind from birth becomes a mirror of Christ's power to give authentic sight, so are the disciples—*all* disciples—instruments with Christ of this creative power: we are those sent, given the power to open the eyes of the blind.

It is in obedience to Christ's directive that light is reflected and the blind see. However, with irony that is typical of the Fourth Evangelist, the challenge of faith and obedience is a challenge for all who think they see the path, as well as for all who suffer from blindness. How, then, can we be faithful to the One who says, "Go, wash…"? The first step is to recognize our own need for corrected vision. John begins this discourse on blindness by first calling our attention to the disciples' own need: they, who think they can see, are also blind. To reflect light necessitates being washed in it. Other steps follow, but without the light of Christ having touched us, we cannot see to touch others or reflect anything other than our own blindness.

Suggestion for meditation: *What blindness in my life has the light of Christ exposed?*

Sunday, March 21   Read John 9:13-41.

Paths for choosing

No steps are forced on anyone who chooses to tread the path of God's redemptive purpose. Whether to take any step, whether to choose this or that path, is a free and individual decision; else the journey is without meaning. The terror of the choice is that in the choosing we open one possibility and close another. When one path is taken another is excluded, and this choice makes all the difference—as Robert Frost explores in his poem "The Road Not Taken."

The reality of self-judgment by means of personal choice is the reality of the Light in the world. Following the Tabernacles discourse on Jesus as the Light of the world, the Evangelist turns to demonstrating what this means. In the unfolding of the narrative in today's scripture our minds are illumined: The light of Christ makes clear the choice of faith or rejection, seeing or blindness. When Jesus announces, "I came into this world for judgment, that those who do not see may see...," we are being confronted with the inescapable decision of obedience or faithlessness. The word John uses for "judgment" can also be translated "crisis," and the crisis is the crisis of choice: Either for or against Jesus, either the path of faith illumined by the Light of the world, or the way of blind darkness. John's word is one of sober reality: By our choosing we judge ourselves.

God's gracious word is that we have before us lighter paths for treading! The poet is quite right: the path taken—or not taken—*will* make all the difference.

Suggestion for meditation: *What lighter path is God opening to me today for my choosing, my treading? What redemptive purpose can I choose reflecting the light of Christ?*

THE GIFT OF NEW LIFE

March 22-28, 1993   **William O. Paulsell✝**
Monday, March 22   Read Ezekiel 37:1-14.

It is a frightening experience to be alone in a desert. The land is arid and barren, and there are no signs of life. The landscape looks the same in every direction. Ezekiel's vision was particularly eerie because the area was strewn with human bones dried by the burning sun. Was this a battlefield where thousands had died?

In the midst of this scene, the prophet is told to prophesy and command the bones to come to life. They take on sinew and flesh, and life is breathed into them. The bones represent Israel, and this was the prophet's way of proclaiming that the nation would be restored. The larger meaning, however, is that God brings new life into hopeless situations.

The desert has often been used as an image of our spiritual condition. Our prayer life may be dry and barren, yet God is ever ready to breathe new life into us. Indeed, God has promised to put a new spirit within us. It may take the desert experience to make us realize the extent of our spiritual poverty. Moses, Elijah, John the Baptist, Jesus, and many others encountered God in the desert.

The prophet, free of the distractions of normal living, heard the voice of God in the desert. We can sense it too in those dry times in our own religious lives if we will put aside the distractions and listen.

Prayer: *Lord, we often find ourselves in a spiritual desert, seeking new life. Give us stillness of mind and the capacity for discernment, that we might know your life-giving presence. Amen.*

✝President, Lexington Theological Seminary, Christian Church (Disciples of Christ), Lexington, Kentucky.

Tuesday, March 23   Read Psalm 130:1-4.

The psalmist, like ourselves, wants to be heard by God. Out of what depths is God called? The depths of despair, fear, anxiety, insecurity? Here the psalmist appears to be calling to God out of the depths of guilt. Who of us, indeed, could stand if God marked our iniquities, if God held all our sins against us? In our solitary moments we know how imperfect we are, how far from the gospel ideal we live. We harbor secret fears that what God knows about us will condemn us.

The psalm, however, promises new life. We may not understand why God sometimes seems not to hear us, but one thing is sure: there is forgiveness. The fact that God forgives us, no matter what, is so hard to believe. When we meditate on the significance of reality, we are in awe of God.

This psalm is a concise summary of the whole Christian gospel: God forgives sinners. Thomas Merton once said that there are many things we want in life, but the only thing we really need is the mercy of God. If we have that, nothing can condemn us or destroy us.

It is the mercy of God that gives us new life. Paul tells us, "If anyone is in Christ, there is a new creation: everything old has passed away; see, everything has become new!" (2 Cor. 5:17).

God does not mark our iniquities but is always ready to give us new life in Christ. And for that, we stand in awe and revere God.

Prayer: *Merciful and forgiving God, it is so hard to believe that you actually forgive us. Grant us the capacity to accept the mercy you offer. Take away our feelings of guilt and bless us with new life. Amen.*

Wednesday, March 24   Read Psalm 130:5-8.

Psalm 130 ends with an emphasis on hopeful waiting. We can easily identify with the psalmist because we, too, have often waited for God to act and nothing seemed to happen. We pray for a sick child, an unemployed parent, a teenager on drugs, a marriage on the brink of disintegration. We have faith that God will act, but the waiting is so frustrating!

Likewise, the psalmist waits like the person who has the night watch, who waits for sunrise and the freedom to go home and go to bed. The night can seem so long.

We are an impatient society. We want instant gratification and instant solutions to all our problems. We do not understand why God does not eradicate evil right now so that we can live in peace and justice and freedom. Yet God makes us wait.

This waiting is not unusual in the Bible. Hebrew slaves in Egypt waited centuries for a liberator. The Hebrew people had to wait for an entire generation before they could enter the promised land. Exiles from Judah waited for decades to return to their homeland. People waited for a messiah. Early Christians waited expectantly for the kingdom of God. Biblical people spent a long time waiting.

The psalmist acknowledged waiting, but the psalmist knew what God would do. Israel would be redeemed from her iniquities and would be forgiven.

We wait for God's time, but we wait in the hope that "with the Lord there is steadfast love, and…great power to redeem." The psalmist understood the purposes of God and in that knowledge could wait with patience.

Prayer: *O God, give us patience and trust in your wisdom. Forgive our restlessness and grant us the grace to know that you know what is best for us. Amen.*

Thursday, March 25   Read Romans 8:6-8.

Paul tells us that there are two ways we can approach life. We can live by the flesh, which only leads to death; or we can live by the Spirit, which brings new life and peace. The word *flesh* has many meanings in the New Testament. It sometimes refers to a legalistic approach to religion. In other contexts it means living by natural impulses. In general it seems to refer to an understanding of life that is only temporary and will end with death. In this passage, Paul sees it as hostility to God and a refusal to submit to God. Such attitudes do not please God.

Spirit, on the other hand, represents a higher approach to life. To "set the mind on the Spirit" is to discern the work of God in human life, the movement of the Holy Spirit. It is foolish to live by temporal values when the values of the Spirit bring life, not death.

Flesh could never successfully obey the law. We cannot depend upon our own efforts or our own goodness. Paul was frustrated at his inability always to do what was right even when he wanted to do so. There is something about our human nature that leads us to death.

But the Spirit is another matter. It is the source of life. The new life that we seek comes not from an extraordinary effort of the flesh but from opening ourselves to the Spirit. "To set the mind on the flesh is death, but to set the mind on the Spirit is life and peace." It is a question of our orientation and our values. Living only by materialistic values leads to death. Discerning the work of the Spirit within us makes us aware of our new life in Christ.

Prayer: *Help us, O God, to set our minds on that which gives us new life, the presence of the Spirit within us. Amen.*

Friday, March 26   Read Romans 8:9-11.

As Christians we are not in the flesh; we are in the Spirit, according to this passage. That is, the spirit of Christ is in us, so that we have new life now and do not wait for death to find it. "If the Spirit of him who raised Jesus from the dead dwells in you, he who raised Christ from the dead will give life to your mortal bodies also through his Spirit that dwells in you."

That Spirit that dwells in us orients us to what is important. Our task is not to satisfy the demands of culture and society but to live on a higher level with Christ in us.

We have been considering the theme of the gift of new life this week. What does "new life" mean, and how is that different from any other kind of life we may be living? So far this week we have seen that new life is restoration to what we should be. Dead bones took on new life. New life is being forgiven and accepting the mercy of God. It is waiting patiently, knowing that God's purposes will ultimately be fulfilled for and in us. Today, Paul tells us that it is living by the Spirit, being motivated by something higher than our selfish desires.

This new life that the gospel promises us comes as a gift of grace. Our task is to be open and receptive, not resisting the work of the Spirit but letting the Spirit motivate and direct us. Discerning the Spirit is not easy, but its presence is a reality promised us. Listen for the working of the Spirit within you, offering new life.

Prayer: *Almighty God, we are grateful for the promise of your Spirit's presence. Give us the capacity to recognize and understand it as well as the courage to be led by it. Help us to seek always the higher things that give not death but new life. Amen.*

Saturday, March 27   Read John 11:1-27.

Jesus made some strange decisions when he heard that his friend Lazarus had died. Rather than come immediately, as we would expect, he decided to wait for two more days. The decision to go to Jerusalem involved more than just raising a friend from the grave. It meant that Jesus was putting himself in jeopardy by going to a place where people were wanting to destroy him.

The delay in Jesus' coming frustrated Mary and Martha. His decision to go to a dangerous place frustrated the disciples. Yet Thomas was ready to go with Jesus, even if it meant joining Lazarus in death.

The Gospel of Luke contains two stories of Jesus raising people from the dead. Jairus's daughter had just died (8:40-56), and the son of the widow of Nain was being carried to the grave (7:11-17). Jesus raised both. In John, however, Lazarus had been in the tomb for four days. But Jesus did not hurry, knowing that God was in control. The God who brought life to dry bones in the desert could bring to life one buried for four days. That same one would bring to life our crucified Lord. "I am the resurrection and the life. Those who believe in me, even though they die, will live, and everyone who lives and believes in me will never die."

In our anxiety to solve all problems immediately, we must remember that God is ultimately in control. That knowledge engenders patience, the kind of patience that Jesus exhibited when he remained where he was for two more days before going to Lazarus. There is no reason to be impatient. God will give us new life.

Prayer: *God of life, forgive our impatience and help us to trust in your wisdom. We believe that you are in control; help our unbelief. Amen.*

Sunday, March 28   Read John 11:28-45.

"Lord, if you had been here, my brother would not have died," said Mary. If only God had acted, we would not have had to face some of our own problems. It is tempting to blame God's slowness to act for our difficulties. When Jesus began to weep over the loss of Lazarus, some of the by-standers said, "Could not he who opened the eyes of the blind man have kept this man from dying?" Could not God have prevented evil from coming into our lives? If God loves us, why do we suffer?

For the sake of the crowd standing around, we are told, Jesus prayed and then shouted at the tomb, "Lazarus, come out!" Lazarus emerged, his hands and feet and face wrapped in cloth. He found new life with Jesus but was still bound until others, at Jesus' command, unbound him.

God acts mercifully in our lives, but our faces are often so bound by our own insensitivity that we do not see it. Removing the cloths from our eyes requires the development of a contemplative attitude, a looking for God's presence and work in the world. God is constantly working in our lives, but instead of seeing that, the temptation is to com-plain that nothing is happening.

We expect God to act in spectacular ways, but the deep-est spiritual maturity is the capacity to see God at work in the ordinary, the mundane, the routine aspects of our lives. When we can see that, we can experience the new life that Christ brings into human experience.

Prayer: *O God, forgive our impatience and our accusations that you ignore us. Remove the bandages from our eyes that we may sense your presence and see your mercy at work among us. May we fulfill Jesus' command to remove the bindings from others that they may see the possibilities of the new life that you offer. Amen.*

THE TRANSFORMING LOVE OF CHRIST

March 29–April 4, 1993   **Larry R. Kalajainen✛**
Monday, March 29   Read Matthew 21:1-11.

Everybody loves a parade! Life is so much hard work and so little fun that whenever we can find a reason to celebrate, we call out the brass bands and the fire engines, and down the street we go.

Matthew describes Jesus' entry into Jerusalem in more dramatic fashion than the other Gospel writers. We can imagine parents bringing their children to see the spectacle and elderly people bringing the first-century equivalent of folding lawn chairs so they could watch in comfort. It is a happy scene. No cloud hangs over to rain on this parade.

But as parade lovers know, the parade passes by all too quickly. The sound of the band dies in the distance, the fire engines return to the station, the mayor takes off the sash and returns to the office, the lawn chairs are folded up and put back in the garage. Parades are great fun, but they don't change anything. The problems we brought to the parade are still there. We've had our moment of celebration, but we're the same old people with the same old attitudes and the same old problems after the parade. And prophets are no more appreciated after the parade than they were before. Prophets, after all, are people who tell us how we have to change if we expect to solve our problems, and we'd much rather listen to someone who promises to solve our problems for us. If only real life could be a continual parade!

Prayer: *O God, help us to listen to the prophets who speak your word to us, not merely to wave at them as they pass by. Amen.*

✛Pastor, United Methodist Church at New Brunswick, New Jersey; adjunct faculty, Drew Theological School.

100

Tuesday, March 30   Read Psalm 118:1-2, 19-29.

An elementary school teacher, watching the vibrant young woman receive her doctorate, can't help remembering a child with a reading problem that led to a behavior problem. Who would have dreamed that child would turn out like this? Something must have happened to her.

The same incredulous surprise is voiced in Psalm 118. It is the last of the "Egyptian Hallel" or thanksgiving psalms, sung before and after the Passover Meal. This psalm was sung during the fourth cup of wine. It celebrates the covenant community's deliverance from bondage in Egypt as though it were the personal deliverance of an individual. The "I" is Israel, the delivered people. Verse 22 expresses the surprise ending. The stone that the builders thought worthless turns out to be the stone that anchors all the rest. Something must have happened.

Something did. "This is the LORD's doing; it is marvelous in our eyes." The Lord is always doing surprising things, delivering an insignificant people from slavery and making them God's own special people, raising a crucified Jewish teacher from the dead and making him Savior of the world, even transforming a behavior problem into a Ph.D. One never knows what surprising twist will come along next. But whatever it is, it will always be "the Lord's doing." That's the business God is in—transforming unlikely persons and situations. Experiencing God's surprises evokes a response of gratitude. We want to celebrate and give thanks because the unlikely has happened. Who could have dreamed it!

Suggestion for meditation: *What is there in my life that needs the transforming touch of God? Am I willing to become one of God's surprises?*
Prayer: *Pray Psalm 118:29.*

Wednesday, March 31   Read Isaiah 50:4-9.

"Some people! I really put myself out to help. I put myself to a lot of trouble and inconvenience. And do I even get so much as a 'thank you'? I don't expect a reward, but a little gratitude would be nice once in a while."

The lament of the Servant of the Lord in Isaiah 50 strikes a familiar chord with us. Who hasn't had the experience of attempting to serve others, only to find that service rewarded with ingratitude and even rejection? It's enough to make a person want to forget about extending oneself for other people. Why bother?

In some of the "Servant Songs" in Isaiah, the Servant of the Lord appears to be a personification of the faithful people within the nation of ancient Israel; in this passage, the Servant may be the prophet himself. Called to bring God's message of comfort and hope to an exiled and suffering people, he is treated shamefully rather than being greeted with welcome. It's little wonder that the early Christians seized upon this passage and others like it to help them understand the significance of Jesus' life and death. They saw the response to the Servant in Isaiah's prophecy mirrored in the response to Jesus. To them, Jesus was the Servant par excellence.

Jesus' reaction to ingratitude mirrored the Servant's reaction, and it is important as a model for us. The Servant did not allow ingratitude to make him bitter or irresolute. Rather, he recognized that his message and calling was not his own but God's, and, therefore, the outcome was in God's hands. The Servant's part was simply to be faithful. That is our part too.

Prayer: *Lord, let us serve others for your sake and not for the sake of our own egos. Make us faithful as Jesus was faithful. Amen.*

Thursday, April 1   Read Psalm 31:9-16.

She'd had a stroke and her right side was severely weakened. In addition, she had deteriorating nerves in her lower back that caused her constant, excruciating pain— "like something stabbing a hot knife into me," was the way she put it. She lived all alone, no relatives, no close friends nearby. Often her words were bitter and full of lament, like the words of the psalmist in verses 9-11. Age, debilitating weakness, pain, and loneliness were her constant companions.

One day, during a pastoral visit, her bitter lament and the reality of her suffering had reduced me to silence. What did I have to say in the face of such all-consuming pain? All I could do was offer her the bread of Christ's broken body and the wine of his own cup of suffering. As she received the elements, her eyes filled with tears, and she said, "Do you know how I find the strength to go on with all this pain? Whenever it gets so bad I can't stand it any longer, I think of Jesus on the cross, and I know that he understands what I'm going through. That gives me the strength to endure a little longer."

Suffering, in and of itself, is always evil and is never God's will. There is no truth to the notion that God sends our sufferings to us as punishment or as discipline. God is not the author of pain. God can, however, use the sufferings we undergo as instruments of grace if we remain faithful and trusting as Jesus did. When we, by faith, identify our sufferings with those of Jesus, we make them holy. What in itself is evil becomes redemptive when we trust God.

Suggestion for meditation: *What will it mean in my own times of suffering to say with Jesus, "Into thy hands, I commit my spirit?"*

Friday, April 2   Read Philippians 2:5-11.

"You're outta your mind!"

A commonly heard expression, isn't it? Sometimes we are the ones who have used it when responding to what we consider someone else's ridiculous proposal. At other times, it may be someone else saying it to us for the same reason. It is never complimentary, however, and even when said in jest, it signifies a lack of unity or agreement among the parties in question.

But Paul, writing to the Christians in Philippi, tells his readers that in their life together as the church, they should be "outta their minds." This passage is generally recognized as an early Christian hymn to Christ which Paul cites as the model for how Christians are to live together and behave toward each other in order to experience unity. The Christian community, he tells them, is a community that has lost its mind...and has gained the mind of Christ.

What does it mean to "let the same mind be in you which was in Christ Jesus?" The hymn that follows in verses 6-11 provides the clues. The mind of Christ is characterized by self-giving, humility, servanthood, and obedience to the will of God "to the point of death—even death on a cross." This is very different from the mind that drives most of the world. Competition, self-interest, greed, and intolerance are the marks of the worldly mind. If God's people are prepared to lose their minds and gain the mind of Christ, they will become a visible model of a peaceful and unified community that the whole world may see, and seeing, take hope. Peace and unity are the products of transformed minds.

Suggestion for meditation: *Am I ready to risk losing my mind in order to gain the mind of Christ? What will it mean for me to "lose my mind"?*

Saturday, April 3   Read Matthew 26:6-16.

A saying of the Chinese sage Confucius may be roughly translated, "It's hard to smell the flowers while galloping along on horseback." When the anonymous woman poured her flask of expensive perfume on Jesus' head at Simon's home in Bethany, Jesus' disciples might have reacted better had they known and heeded that ancient bit of folk wisdom.

Their irritable reaction is understandable if not laudable. Dedicated as they were to Jesus and his mission of proclaiming the kingdom of God, they had a deep sense of the seriousness and urgency of their purpose. Theirs was the high (and sometimes thankless) task of proclaiming good news to the poor, binding up the brokenhearted, and announcing liberation to the oppressed. So when this woman gate-crashed their dinner party to make an extravagant gesture of love for Jesus, they were incensed. What a waste of expensive perfume that could have been sold to raise funds for a soup kitchen or a shelter for the homeless! So zealous were they for their mission and so single-minded in their dedication that they missed the beauty of this generous act of love.

When Jesus chided his disciples for their failure to appreciate the beauty of the woman's action, Judas couldn't stomach it. He had no room left for generosity of spirit or the spontaneity of love. He was too serious, too committed to making things happen. Possibly he saw Jesus' attitude toward the woman as a fatal weakness of character and resolve. And so he betrayed the very person to whose cause he was so attached. How often do we betray the person or cause to which we're committed because we forget that the only real reason for living is love?

Prayer: *Lord, help me never to become so busy in your service that I become blind to the beauty of love. Amen.*

105

Sunday, April 4   Read Matthew 26:47-75.

When a sudden crisis confronts us and overturns all our carefully laid plans, our first reaction is often to feel afraid and to attempt to run away from the problem. It's the old "fight or flight" pattern of emotional response, which is built into us for the purpose of self-preservation. Sometimes, fear and flight are the most appropriate responses to a dangerous situation. At other times, however, the fear itself can destroy us.

We see this pattern in the lives of Jesus' disciples when he was arrested. "Then all the disciples deserted him and fled," Matthew tells us. The crisis came upon them suddenly, precipitated by Judas's betrayal. Having failed to watch with Jesus in Gethsemane, they were unprepared for the threat posed by his arrest. Fear gripped them and paralyzed their faith. It was time to cut their losses and run. And run they did.

Peter was a little braver than the others. He, at least, followed at a distance to see what would happen to Jesus. Perhaps he even entertained some desperate notion of rescue and escape. The crisis escalated when he was recognized as one of Jesus' followers. His frantic denial is pathetic to hear, "No, you've got it all wrong. I don't even know him" (AP). Fear without faith is a terrible thing. It paralyzes the will, hamstrings the judgment, and turns our knees to water.

Peter deserves our sympathy rather than our disapproval. Which of us hasn't been "eyeball to eyeball" with our own moment of truth and blinked? If the risen Christ could make a special effort to restore Peter's faith, perhaps there is hope for us too, in spite of our own fearful denials.

Prayer: *O God, when fear causes my faith to falter, seek out my hiding place and restore my courage and trust. Amen.*

| April 5-11, 1993 | **John Killinger✢** |
| **Monday, April 5** | Read Isaiah 42:1-9. |

"Behold my servant" (RSV). Isaiah was probably thinking about Israel, the nation God had intended to become a servant nation, sharing its life and knowledge of God with the entire world. But the early church understood the reference to be to Jesus, the Messiah who was crucified for the redemption of the world.

God delighted in a servant, in one who was lowly and without power. He was so gentle he would not break a "bruised reed" if he stepped on it. The breeze from his motions would not extinguish the flame of even "a dimly burning wick."

We live in a world in love with power. People are always trying to gain the upper hand with other people. Employees want more power in their companies, teachers want more power in their schools, children want more power in their families. I enjoy viewing TV programs I have already taped, because I have a feeling of power when I hit a fast-forward button and speed through the commercials.

But the good news of the Bible is that God uses people who are powerless to bring the divine love and salvation to others. God's power is sufficient without any power in the servant. The important thing for the servant is to be empty and yielded, to be open to the leadership of God's spirit. God's greatest gifts often come through the humblest channels.

Prayer: *What good news this is, O God, that you prefer servants without power or status! Take my life now, and use it in any way that will bring glory to your name. Amen.*

✢Author; Distinguished Professor of Religion and Culture, Samford University, Birmingham, Alabama.

Tuesday, April 6   Read John 12:20-36.

There were many signs by which Jesus understood that his hour of greatest servanthood had arrived, when he would die like a common criminal. One of these was the coming of some Jews from Greece who had heard of him and wanted to see him. This was an indication of the universality of his ministry and perhaps a foreshadowing of the way the gospel would spread beyond Israel.

Most of us, when told that our fame had spread abroad, would probably react by rushing to greet the people who sought us. But not Jesus. For him, it was a fitting occasion for remembering his essential powerlessness in himself. Only as his life was yielded fully to God would it become the channel of God's mighty purposes.

Therefore, he spoke about his mission in terms of a grain of wheat that doesn't exist to be held up and admired. It exists only to die and produce more wheat, an abundance of wheat. This was the way Jesus saw his purpose. He had not come to this hour in order to preen himself and say, "What an attraction I am, that even foreigners come to see me!" No, that wasn't his way at all. It was *God's* glory he was concerned with, not his own. Therefore, he was ready to die on the cross, knowing that God would use this act of supreme powerlessness to change the history of the world.

When we become mature followers of Christ, this is how we, too, will think. It is not our own fame or power we are concerned with, but God's. Then God has a chance to do everything through us.

Prayer: *Forgive me, O God, for having desired to be famous or powerful, and let me delight in being your servant; for in that I shall find eternal joy. Amen.*

Wednesday, April 7   Read John 13:21-32.

Few things ever hurt us more than betrayal. Even as children we often feel a sense of injustice and disappointment when a friend or parent takes sides against us. Betrayal makes us feel devalued and abandoned, as if all love had fled the universe.

Surely, Jesus felt hurt and demeaned by the behavior of his friend Judas, who was consorting with the enemy to betray him. It was an attack on his self-worth as a leader and teacher. It was an act of humiliation before the final humiliation of the cross itself. In some ways Judas's behavior was even worse than what the soldiers would do, for it was the almost unforgivable deed of a man he had trusted and loved.

Maybe permitting this awful act of betrayal was a part of God's way of completing Jesus' servanthood. Slaves and servants have always been betrayed. Their masters have not considered them worth keeping promises for. They are, after all, the lowliest of the low, without status or respect in the world. When Judas began dealing with the scribes and Pharisees to deliver Jesus into their hands, it was another reminder of Jesus' powerlessness.

How did Jesus take it? It is all for God's glory, he said; the worse things become for the servant, the more others will perceive the greatness of God when the divine power is demonstrated!

Prayer: *It is hard to accept the faithlessness of a friend, O God, and then speak of your glory. Yet this is just what Jesus did. Help me to accept my misfortunes and turn them into occasions for acknowledging you. Amen.*

April 8 (Maundy Thursday)
Read John 13:1-17, 34.

What a beautiful picture of Jesus' servanthood this is! Imagine the Lord of glory—for that is precisely the way John's Gospel views Jesus, as the Eternal Word who existed with God before the world was made—taking a towel and getting down on his knees to wash the feet of these ignorant, unruly disciples! It is surely one of the most startling images imaginable.

Often, when we have positions of power and influence, we do not think we should be expected to perform menial tasks. We feel that we are *above* certain things.

How instructive it is to behold the Lord of the universe washing the feet of his followers! Surely this should remind us that there is no honorable service in the world that we cannot do with a sense of dignity and self-worth, especially when it involves loving or helping others.

Ernest Gordon's *Through the Valley of the Kwai* tells the story of men who were prisoners of war during the Second World War. One of Gordon's friends, a man named Dodger Green, was bitter and unfriendly when Gordon first ran across him in the camp. But later, after the man had discovered how much his friends cared about him, he became happy and outgoing again. Gordon remembers that then Dodger Green often volunteered for the most odious task in the camp, carrying the buckets with the infection drainage from the prisoners' wounds down to the river and washing them out each day; and he always whistled and sang as he did it!

Prayer: *How wonderful it is, O God, that Jesus has shown us this beautiful picture of servanthood. Help me never to feel that I am above anything you give me to do, and let me do it cheerfully. Amen.*

April 9 (Good Friday)

Read John 19:1-30.

There it is again, this business of power. Pilate says to Jesus, "Do you not know that I have power to release you, and power to crucify you?" But notice what Jesus replies: "You would have no power over me unless it had been given you from above." Jesus knew that all power belongs to God. We only have the *illusion* of power here on earth. Therefore, to be truly powerful means to be yielded to God's spirit, so that God's power flows through us, as it did through Jesus.

Some might call Pilate a servant of the people. But his servanthood is shallow, for he is concerned about his own welfare and popularity. He is afraid of going against the will of the people. It is Jesus who is the true servant, the one ready to lay down his life for God and his friends.

Jesus' servanthood is underlined again when the soldiers cast lots for his clothes. He is treated like the total slave, the complete nonentity, with no dignity at all. And yet, irony of ironies, he rules the world from his cross! Stripped and crucified, he commands from his humble throne with true power, the power of his Father in heaven. For, as Paul will later say, because Jesus has been obedient unto death, "God also highly exalted him and gave him the name...above every name, so that at the name of Jesus every knee should bend, in heaven and on earth and under the earth, and every tongue confess that Jesus Christ is Lord, to the glory of God the Father" (Phil. 2:9-11).

Prayer: *O matchless Lord, let me, too, fall down and confess you and take upon myself your perfect servant nature, that I may be ready even to die in your name. Amen.*

111

April 10 (Holy Saturday)

Read John 19:38-42.

We are still on the theme of servanthood. Observe how these men, Joseph and Nicodemus, have feared becoming servants with Jesus. Oh, they respected him, and perhaps even loved him. But they were not emptied enough to become open followers. It would have cost too much. They might have lost their positions as rulers.

Now all that is changed. They have watched the Lord of the universe die like a common thief or murderer. It is staggering! The very Son of God has so completely emptied himself of power and glory that he has been treated like the vilest of slaves and put to death in nakedness and shame.

Enough of halfhearted discipleship! Seeing Jesus die in this manner has overcome all their hesitance. It is time to become his followers openly, to empty themselves as he was emptied, to let God be God in their lives. They approach Pilate fearlessly to request the body. They do what most self-respecting Jews would not do; they handle a dead body on the very eve of the Passover, making themselves unclean for eating the Passover meal. They share the accursedness of their Lord!

We don't know what happens to Joseph and Nicodemus after this, but we can imagine how their lives have been changed. No longer secret disciples, now they are engaged in full and open servanthood. If anyone is prepared to receive the joyous news of the Resurrection, they are. On Easter morning, they are surely two of the happiest men in the world.

Prayer: *Sometimes I, too, am inclined to follow secretly, O God; for I have not yet learned to live in total fearlessness. Lead me to new levels of servanthood, where I am willing to be exposed to anything in Jesus' name. Amen.*

April 11 (Easter)

Read John 20:1-18.

What a beautiful scene this is! And how appropriate it is that Mary thought Jesus was a gardener, for who has more of the form of a servant than a gardener?

Yet we see what being a servant of God leads to. Not even death, the most irresistible force in the universe, is finally able to bind us. When we are fully open to the power of God, it overcomes everything.

The late Urban T. Holmes, Dean of the School of Theology at the University of the South, liked to talk about the "anti-structures" of God that will one day replace all the structures of this earth. We have seen in this week's readings how the anti-structures work. When we yield ourselves to God's spirit in emptiness and love, becoming servants of the divine, all the conventional categories of our lives are upended. When we are weak, we become strong. When we abase ourselves, we share in the glory of heaven.

Many people have a hard time understanding the nature of true servanthood. They want to have power and influence and importance. But in seeking to save their lives, they lose them. Even if they get what they want, they are still dissatisfied; for the treasures of this world are only apples of dust. But those who lose their lives for Christ's sake, and the gospel's, find them. They learn what all the great saints have learned, that the best thing any of us can ever experience is to stand where Mary stood that morning and have Jesus, the Everlasting Servant, call our names.

Prayer: *I wish no greater blessing, O God, than to hear the Savior speak my name. Teach me to become so emptied of self that I can hear him at any time. Amen.*

113

CHOOSING THE PATH OF LIFE

April 12-18, 1993   **Cheri Farr Keipper✢**
Monday, April 12   Read Psalm 16.

Clearly, the psalmist teaches, there are always two choices before us as we sojourn through this world. We may choose the path of death or the path of life. David never questions his choice. For him, "the Lord is my chosen portion."

As David surveys the religious landscape of his day, he compares his own spiritual journey with that of others. His experience of God is one of a "fullness of joy." Both David's body and soul dwell secure because he has placed God first in his life. Meanwhile, the pagans only know sorrow upon sorrow.

David was on the run from Saul's threats much of his life, but he never gave in to the path of death. A televised movie special entitled "Survive the Savage Sea" illustrates the keen importance of choosing life even in the midst of death. The boat of a family on a private cruise capsizes in shark-infested waters. After drifting for a month, their raft deteriorating, the children write letters to whomever may survive them. Ther father angrily responds that he will not write his epitaph, only words of hello.

Every day we choose the path of death or the path of life. At the correctional facility where I serve, many men confess that coming to jail was not so much an arrest as a rescue. Had they stayed on the path of addiction and crime, they never would have survived. But incarceration has led them to God, who gave them a second chance. Now they walk the path of life.

Suggestion for meditation: *Consider the paths you have walked, the choices you are making. How do you choose?*

✢United Church of Christ minister, serving as a Protestant chaplain at Orleans Correctional Facility, Albion, New York; and interim pastor at East Aurora Christian Church (Disciples of Christ).

Tuesday, April 13   Read 1 Peter 1:3-5.

The post-resurrection message is clear: new life is available to us all. Peter's message is urgent, for Peter thinks time is of the essence. The early church needed to understand that the Christian received an inheritance no one else could receive. Because God, out of mercy for humanity, sacrificed God's only Son, the gift of new life suddenly became accessible to the believer. It was as if God had written a will for the whole human race. In this will, God bequeaths the single most-hoped-for gift.

Moreover, the promise of eternal life is kept safe for the future use of all generations. No one and no thing can defile or diminish the legacy. Such a guarantee can never be found on earth. Only God can set up an imperishable trust fund for our souls.

We do, in our humanness, long for certain dimensions of our life to go on and on: our love for and sense of belonging to one who loves us, the health and well-being of our children, the security of a career. Invested in each of these finite extensions of our selves is the single hope Peter addresses, the hope for the infinite. We yearn for our life to be a life without end.

David, after listing the many blessings God had given him, concludes that the ultimate gift is "the path of life" (Psalm 16:11). God makes the path of life possible through the resurrection of Jesus Christ. God adds a "new testament" and we are the heirs. No other "life insurance" can insure us of a life everlasting.

Suggestion for meditation: *Assess what you prize most in life, and reflect on how each is linked to your inheritance of new life in Christ. Amen.*

Wednesday, April 14   Read Acts 2:14*a*, 22-24, 32.

Trying to explain a miracle to a group of nonbelievers is like trying to ride a bike before learning how to walk. But Peter was determined to do just that. As an eyewitness to Jesus' resurrection, Peter was determined to convey this truth to those who were not privy to Jesus' company in the post-Easter hours (see Acts 4:1-12). In fact, these men were the very ones conspiring to deliver Jesus to death. Being convincing was one thing, but to be convicted was another. Peter knew the difference.

A witness is someone who sees firsthand, without reliance on a second- or third-party information. If we are witnesses to a car accident or a crime, we are called upon to testify about what we actually saw. A witness, in the spiritual sense, is one who has a firsthand experience of God, who sees God with the heart but not necessarily with the naked eye. When we witness a miracle, we are in a state of believing in something beyond the tangible or visible.

Peter witnessed Jesus as Jesus appeared to him in the days following the resurrection. But Peter was not at the tomb when the stone rolled away. Peter's witness is a personal belief in a risen Christ. His appeal, then, is to the inner spirit of those in attendance at the Jerusalem conference. The Jesus they had observed performing signs and wonders was the same human being they saw nailed to a cross and the same one whom God had raised up from the cross. It was not a sleight of hand or a trick of the eye. Jesus arose in the power of God.

Today we continue to be witnesses of the living Christ. We testify to nonbelievers of his deeds. We do so by choosing to live a life in faith.

Prayer: *Dear God, may our life be a valid witness to Jesus alive in us for the sake of others. Amen.*

Thursday, April 15   Read John 20:19-31.

Thomas was the kind of person who needed hard-nosed, practical facts. Throughout his discipleship, he had seen for himself the miracles Jesus performed. Now, in the absence of his Master, he needed that visible evidence all the more. Believing in the resurrection was too incredible for him.

There is a Thomas in each of us. Our human nature expects concrete, rational explanations of the spiritual realm. We doubt what our heart desires most to trust. In my very first church, a young person in the youth fellowship challenged me in front of his peers. "Prove to me there is a God," he demanded. I was tempted to share my own view of who God is in my life, but I simply replied that I could not prove anything about God to him. Yes, I could tell my own faith story, but he had to discover God for himself.

The great news is that God responds to those who doubt as well as to those who believe. Thomas was not left doubting. Eight days later, Jesus returned to the place where the disciples were staying and restored Thomas to him. Thomas's worries washed away instantly, as he reaffirmed his faith: "My Lord and my God!"

When the Thomas in us gets the upper hand, we can have faith even amid our doubts. God will enter our house of fear and restore us with a touch. We do not have the benefit of Jesus' actual post-resurrection appearance. However, the Lord does appear to us in many unexpected ways. Our faith can be reaffirmed in encounters with people whom we admire and in situations that cannot be conveniently excused, moments of "holy coincidence." God cares enough to change our doubting Thomas into a believing Thomas.

Prayer: *Merciful Lord, thank you for coming to us in the deep places of our doubt and showing us the path to belief again. Amen.*

Friday, April 16   Read 1 Peter 1:6-7.

Peter had watched his Lord being hauled off to prison and in the bleak hours following had denied Jesus three times. Months earlier, this very same Peter had been the only one bold enough to identify Jesus as the Christ. In those last days, Peter felt the knife of shame and grief go through him. He spoke from experience to the exiles of the Dispersion (that is, to the Jews scattered over the Graeco-Roman world).

Now Peter was the wiser. He understood fully the reasons why he had to suffer. Moreover, he was able to teach these new Christians about the meaning of their own trials. He placed suffering in the same context as refinement. Gold is refined in fire; it is purified. So too, faith is refined by means of suffering. Our personal tragedies are not faith-producing *per se*; however, the way we journey through our sufferings builds our character and stretches the resilience of our faith.

Every fall after the blossoms die, I cut back my roses and mulch around the roots. I know intellectually that pruning is essential to growth, but I still feel that I am hurting the plant. In the spring, I am reminded of the whole context in which pruning is a part, a necessary part, of new life as the green sprouts break free from winter's grip. So, too, when we are severed from our old habits and addictions, we suffer. Out of the woundedness emerges a brand new self and a steadier faith.

According to Peter, every time our faith is enhanced, God is glorified. So we can rejoice in our deepened faith and in the joy we have given God, all of which makes our suffering worth its weight in gold. What we endure is ingredient to the glory of a richer life in Christ.

Prayer: *Refine us, O Lord, in the crucible of suffering, that our lives may grow ever closer toward you. Amen.*

Saturday, April 17   Read 1 Peter 1:8-9.

Imagine Thomas's joy as he touched the wound marks of Jesus, dispelling his doubt that Jesus had overcome death (John 20:27-28). It was a joy born of relief and release. It was a relief for Thomas to let go of his gnawing unbelief. More significantly, it was a release from his preconceived ideas about what happens to someone we love who dies. Thomas knew beyond a shadow of a doubt that the resurrection was real and Jesus was alive!

The joy Thomas felt sprang from personal contact with the living Christ. He saw with his own eyes. However, in the weeks following Jesus' appearance, as Peter and Paul ministered to new church starts, it was vital to convey with equal conviction the realness of Jesus' resurrection. These early Christians did not have the same opportunity Thomas had. Theirs was a faith based solely on believing without seeing.

Peter could not contain his excitement over the kind of joy that a Christian inherited by believing Jesus arose from the grave. He exclaims that "although you have not seen him you...rejoice with an indescribable and glorious joy."

Most of us spend our lives trying to attain this inward joy, only to discover how elusive and fleeting it is. We search for enduring happiness in things we see: loving relationships, chemical highs, material possessions. We are disappointed at every turn. However, Peter explains that the only joy that outlives mortality is the invisible joy of salvation. Knowing that we can participate in the resurrection life of our Lord, we cherish a joy that lifts us above all earthly joys.

Prayer: *Eternal God, we thank you for the inexpressible joy you have made possible for those who believe in the risen Christ. Amen.*

Sunday, April 18   Read Acts 2:14*a*, 22-32.

The risen Christ was living proof for Peter that death did not have the final word. God, having freed Jesus from death, had more to say. It was imperative for Peter to communicate the "good news" of the Resurrection to the assembled religious leaders, as well as to the common folk, in an understandable language. Life beyond death was a brand new theology; it was a transforming belief of the inner spirit.

Peter employs David's experience of the Lord to affirm the reality of Jesus' resurrection. God will "not abandon my soul to Hades." It was God's intent all along to free humanity from the fear that death is the closure of life. Many people panic at the idea of entering the unknown, of having no control over their destiny. They live life as if they could take everything with them. But Jesus was delivered to take away the sting of death.

As Christians, we claim a resurrection life, a life that cannot be held by death's power. We can live life abundantly because we know there is more to life than mere existence and an empty, disillusioning death. I heard it said of a parishioner who had suffered for years with multiple sclerosis that "she died with grace and dignity. God freed her from that prison her body was in, and her spirit lives on."

Resurrection life is triumphant. We can sing: "Because He lives, I can face tomorrow; Because He lives, all fear is gone; Because I know he holds the future, And life is worth the living just because He lives."[*]

Prayer: *Living God, may we live every day as an Easter day!*

---

[*]From "Because He Lives" by William J. and Gloria Gaither, copyright © 1971 by William J. Gaither. Used by permission.

JESUS CHRIST—ALIVE AND TRAVELING WITH US

April 19-25, 1993   **Robert K. Smyth**[+]
Monday, April 19   Read Luke 24:13-16.

The Emmaus Road story is a singularly beautiful and inspiring post-Resurrection event. Paul Scherer describes it as "a history of God's gracious dealing with the human soul."[*] It is worth our devotional attention at Eastertide.

The two on the road in deep conversation about the past few days in Jerusalem are you and I, or any other two Christians grief-filled by the crucifixion of our Redeemer. Every person walking beyond that dread Friday and its Calvary has to talk about that nadir of righteous ignorance. The personification of God's grace and mercy stood face to face with self-aggrandizement, and God's servant spirit was nailed to a cross.

A devotional life that expects to grow will, at some moment, ponder Christ's Passion. It is a part of the wilderness that almost every Christian experiences in the quest for spiritual assurances. A thorough grounding in our Savior's suffering, as part of redemption, becomes the firm foundation upon which we build our Resurrection theology. It happened to two in Emmaus who found out that their living gained meaning through the manner of Jesus' dying; and now his being alive and traveling on the road with them.

Jesus Christ is surely the living presence of God with us in our ways of living, awakening within us a new nature to be worthy of the name that is above every name.

Prayer: *O divine Redeemer, be with us this day, to make every act of our serving worthy of your passion. Amen.*

[+]Retired pastor and district superintendent, Southern New Jersey Conference, The United Methodist Church; Riverton, New Jersey.
[*]*The Interpreter's Bible,* (Abingdon Press, N. Y., 1952), Vol. VIII, p. 422.

Tuesday, April 20　　　　　　Read Luke 24:17-27.

It is a truth that if, in walking or jogging we are only intent on avoiding the stones, we will miss the grandeur of the stars. Two men were heading toward Emmaus, their sight dimmed by despair. They were not even able to recognize the one on the road with them whose loss they mourned.

Jesus overlooked the inconsequential matters, the minor events in Jerusalem to which these two men gave major attention. "How foolish you are, how slow you are to believe everything the prophets said! Was it not necessary for the Messiah to suffer these things and then to enter his glory?" (TEV). Jesus goes on to paint a biblical panorama of the mighty hand of God which, across centuries, had prepared the way for the coming of the Messiah. Jesus awoke the vision of the immeasurable majesty of God's action to redeem God's people from sin and lostness, to redirect all human energies to obeying the divine will as well as in serving neighbors' needs.

Jesus Christ, Redeemer and Friend, is the living Word. Jesus enables us to see God as truth and light, impelling us to help bring God's kingdom to all people.

The more Martin Luther Luther immersed himself in studying scripture, the clearer became his vision of God's right way and the more grieved he became over the practices of the church of his day. On October 31, 1517, Luther carried out a most courageous act. He posted his ninety-five reasons for reforming the church into all that the apostles meant it to be—the Body of Christ. For Luther, and for the church reformed by the power of the word, it was "only scripture." The living Word is always on our road with us, guiding us with light and truth in our discipleship.

Prayer: *Loving God, let your Word dwell richly in us. Amen.*

Wednesday, April 21   Read Luke 24:28-32.

In his gentle way Jesus comes into the company of two walking to Emmaus. He presumes nothing, but simply joins them since safety in numbers was common for travelers. When occasion presents itself, Jesus shares his good news. At village edge, he hints at going on but accepts their offer of hospitality. Luke gives no indication that Jesus is yet recognized.

The economy of details leaves a lot of the story to our imagining. We depend on studying translations and commentaries for details. J. B. Phillips translates the key event by giving this emphasis in verse 31: *"Then it happened!"* * When Jesus was at table with them, he took bread, gave thanks, broke it, and handed it to them. In that most common of daily privileges—breaking bread—their eyes were opened.

Perhaps they were among the five thousand when Jesus broke bread, or perhaps they had heard him say, "I am the bread of life" (John 6:35). Whatever the reason for their recognizing that Emmaus moment, Jesus became present. Then they understood why it had been like fire burning within them as he had explained the scriptures to them.

John Wesley was listening to scripture being explained on the evening of May 24, 1738. He wrote in his Journal, "I felt my heart strangely warmed. I felt I did trust in Christ, Christ alone for salvation: And an assurance was given me, that he had taken away my sins...." The assurance of the presence of the risen Christ bonds us to Christ and inspires us to reproduce his life in our faithful living.

Prayer: *O God, enable me to remember all through the day that whatever some people see of Christ they will see in me. Amen.*

---

*From THE NEW TESTAMENT IN MODERN ENGLISH © J. B. Phillips 1958. Used by permission of Macmillan Company.

Thursday, April 22   Read Luke 24:33-35.

Every so often something exciting breaks into life's routine and daily sameness, and we are bursting with good news we want to share with someone else. The two from Emmaus lacked the modren telecommunications. They had only their feet. Not even the coming dusk could deter them from racing back to Jerusalem to tell of their encounter with Jesus. Before they could share their story, others in Jerusalem were joyously singing that Jesus, once crucified, had risen from the dead. Jesus had even sought out Simon, freeing him of the shame of his denial.

God chose to come among us incarnate in Mary's son. When none but a few prophets could speak of it, God employed a choir of angels. As Jesus entered Jerusalem, people believing in him waved palms and sang glad hosannas. If they had not, Jesus says, God would have had the very stones cry out (Luke 19:40).

The disciples' joy, revived by Jesus alive, ignited a spontaneous scattering of devoted people to share the good news to the ends of the earth. They became the voice, the hands, the feet, the compassion, and the service of Jesus risen. With a cross, a few people tried to silence him. With a resurrection, the one God set the spirit of Jesus free to come into the lives and faith of countless millions. Jesus entered Jerusalem by one road but left by every road you and I travel in our discipleship.

We have our daily agenda in the pages of the Bible, the story of redeeming grace of God. We exemplify good news when we enable the word to become flesh in us; when caring, justice, peacemaking, grace, and mercy are the evident fruit of the Spirit in our lives.

Prayer: *God of grace, enable me to become more like Jesus, in whom word and deed are always one. Amen*

Friday, April 23   Read 1 Peter 1:17-23.

One of the everlasting joys of Eastertide is celebrating our emancipation from the past. Jesus delivers believers into our new freedom through his own suffering, sacrifice, resurrection, and living presence. The risen Christ is God's pure gift of immeasurable love. Each day we need to remember what was paid to redeem us and rejoice in our freedom in Christ.

I remember hearing of the emancipation of slaves on the island of Jamaica. The British Parliament had voted in 1834 to set a day when with the rising of the sun their bondage would end. Slaves positioned themselves on the highest hill in eastern Jamaica and on other hills. When the first edge of the sun appeared on the horizon, slaves shouted to one another, "We're free! We're free! We're free!" They commenced their new life.

Jesus Christ is the truth of God who makes us free. He is God's yes, Yes, YES about the greatness and goodness of life in our companionship with him. Paul writes, "For it is [Jesus] who is the 'Yes' to all of God's promises" (2 Cor. 1:20 TEV). Jesus, our Lord and Redeemer, takes us by the hand and raises us into being the persons God has created us to be.

Jesus yearns for us to be a holy, distinctive people. The remembrance of his sacrifice evokes the fullest faithfulness from us: "But you are...the holy nation, God's own people, chosen to proclaim the wonderful acts of God, who called you out of darkness....At one time you were not God's people, but now you are." (1 Peter 2:9-10, TEV).

It is the privilege of Christians to live our gratitude in bringing Christlike care and love to all relationships with our sisters and brothers.

Prayer: *O Lord Jesus, help us find our true life by losing self for your sake. Amen.*

Saturday, April 24   Read Psalm 116:1-2, 12-19.

The texts of many of the great hymns of faith are songs of thanksgiving. Yet, even our best means of expressing gratitude to God are inadequate. The psalmist feels this incompleteness: "What shall I return to the Lord for all his bounty to me?" (TEV). We revere God as Creator and Source of every blessing. We are voicing our thankfulness in the best ways we can but are ever aware that many inner feelings are beyond expression.

In these days just after Easter, we remember the awesome act of God's grace in raising Christ to life. No one can dare claim to be worthy. Our one claim is to love God with our entire being, grateful for the hope we have through the Resurrection. From the wise and the humble we learn the valuable lesson of living our gratitude rather than just speaking it.

A couple I know toured Alaska, and while there, attended worship at a small United Methodist church in the fishing village of Ninilchik. During the prayer concerns, they learned of a work team from New Jersey who were helping construct a new sanctuary at a church in North Pole, Alaska. My friends later learned that the volunteer team was working near Fairbanks, and they drove several hundred miles to donate their time and labor with the other Jerseyites. The next year my friend returned to Alaska for another two week work project with a team. When asked why, he said that as he sat in his home church, he realized that people in another era had established the congregation, built the building, and provided a house for worship and fellowship. Helping another group of Christian people was his way of saying thanks. The spirit of the living Christ has been on this road with people such as this.

Prayer: *May the words of our hearts and the works of our hands be acceptable to you, O Lord, our Redeemer. Amen.*

Sunday, April 25   Read Acts 2:14*a*, 36-41.

Fifty days after Jesus' resurrection, Peter is his strongest advocate, donning the mantle of leadership and preaching. Peter is a cardinal example of what rising to new life in Christ means. At dawn on the day of the cross, Peter had denied his Lord three times. One day after the resurrection, Jesus comes among the disciples as they fish at the Sea of Galilee (see John 21). Three times Jesus asks Peter, "Do you love me?" Through this dialogue, Peter is redeemed.

Sooner or later, each of us who names Jesus as Lord wrestles with the concerns which Peter addresses in his Pentecost sermon. Whatever the stage of our spiritual progress, Jesus needs us to help someone else in the steps: to turn away from sin, to be baptized in the name of Jesus, to accept God's forgiveness by faith, and to receive God's confirming gift of the Holy Spirit.

Jesus asks us to be light to the world, the full light of God's right way. When this light floods the soul of a wanderer, and he or she realizes the need to do an about face, then this person is one the threshold of new life in Christ. *Conversion* (to turn around) is a beautiful word and a priceless experience. it is the fresh beginning of a closer walk with our Lord, who is alive and on our road with us.

God's new light can come to us at any age. It is part of progressing toward the perfection of spirit which Jesus wants us to pursue. The awakening intervention of God is our personal spiritual experience and occurs when our hungering spirit is fed by Christ, the bread for our life. Through the Resurrection we become the people blessed by God's grace. We have a Savior, a message, and a mission to share with the world.

Prayer: *Loving God, use us to bring the Redeemer and your redeeming grace to the world where we live. Amen.*

OF SHEEP AND SHEPHERDS

April 26–May 2, 1993   **Justo L. González✢**
Monday, April 26   Read John 10:1-10.

This week I want to invite you to think about the images of sheep and shepherds. For many of us, the first scripture passage we memorized was the shepherd psalm, Psalm 23. Then in Ezekiel we recall the powerful word of the Lord: "I myself will search for my sheep, and will seek them out. As shepherds seek out their flocks when they are among their scattered sheep" (34:11-12). Many paintings and stained glass windows have captured this image of the lost sheep and the good shepherd searching until the sheep is found.

Certainly our reading for today has spawned numerous sermons, and we remember hearing that Jesus referred to himself as the "door of the sheep" and "the good shepherd."

As we look at this text from John and other passages that deal with sheep and shepherd images, try to recall what you feel each time you hear the words "The Lord is my shepherd." What does it meant to be a sheep—alone or in a flock? As a sheep, what do you need from your shepherd? Can you be both a sheep and a shepherd at the same time? The image of sheep/shepherd is surely a comforting one. But is there also within this image an element of challenge and responsibility for us as we move ever closer to the Shepherd who gives abundant life?

Prayer: *O Lord, our Shepherd, we thank you that when we go astray you search for us until you have found us. Lead us to the abundant life you have promised. Amen.*

✢Clergy member, Rio Grande Conference, The United Methodist Church; editor of *Apuntes;* director of Hispanic Summer Seminary Program of the Fund for Theological Education, Decatur, Georgia.

Tuesday, April 27   Read John 10:1-6.

When we speak of Jesus as the Good Shepherd, what we usually think of is his love for us and the care he takes of us. But in these first six verses of the chapter the emphasis is not on the love of Jesus in leading the sheep. The contrast is rather between the true shepherd and the thief.

The crucial difference between the true shepherd and the thief is that the shepherd has a claim on the sheep, whereas the thief does not. In verse 3 we are told that the shepherd "calls his own sheep," and in verse 4 that he brings out "all his own." This emphasis was important in the early church, where there were some who claimed that this world was the creation of a god who was not the same one who sent Jesus. According to this view, Jesus came into an alien world, to call to salvation people who had been created by another. Our text says exactly the opposite. Jesus has a claim on us, not only in salvation but also in creation. We are his sheep even before we are ready to claim him as Savior. He is not a messenger from an alien world, but the true shepherd, the creator and owner, come to his own.

This true shepherd is known because he comes through the door. In the early church there were those who denied the birth of Jesus, or his flesh, or his death. But Jesus is the true shepherd in that he came to be with the sheep, entering through the door of birth, and suffering, and death, and resurrection. He is the true shepherd because, like any good shepherd, he lives with his sheep and walks the path with them.

Prayer: *We marvel, Lord, that you are both our master and our companion. We are your own, and you have come through the door to walk with us. Keep us forever awed, and yet forever at ease, in your loving presence. Amen.*

129

Wednesday, April 28   Read John 10:7-10.

Here the image changes. Now Jesus is the door. It is at this point that we grow restless and decide that what we have here must be a mixture of several different sayings. But that is probably because we insist that things be neat and rational, while the truth is that life itself is not usually all that neat and rational. In real life we are at the same time parents and children, faithful and faithless, sheep and shepherds. In real life, Jesus is both the shepherd who comes in through the door and the door through which the sheep must go.

To say that Jesus is the door is not terribly striking—at least not until we begin considering what that might mean. It certainly means, as we often hear in sermons, that it is through him that we enter into the abundant life he has promised. But it means much more than that. Just as he came through the door, we must go through the door which he is. There are no short-cuts. There is no jumping over the fence, like a thief.

We know from another text that "The gate is narrow" (Matt. 7:14). How can this be? Certainly, the love of Jesus is not narrow! If there is anything we can count on, it is the wideness of his love! What makes the door narrow is our own unreadiness to go through it, our willingness to try to find another opening that is less demanding. Jesus himself came through the gate of humiliation, obedience, and suffering. We must also be willing to go through the gate just as he went, for otherwise, as he would say, we are nothing but thieves and interlopers.

Prayer: *Lord, for our sake you became one of us and shared our life and our suffering. Help us for your sake and for the sake of the other sheep in your flock to share in their pain, so that they too may come to know the life abundant that there is in you. Amen.*

Thursday, April 29   **Read Psalm 23.**

Probably no other portion of scripture is as familiar to us as this one. Many of us learned it while sitting on our parents' laps. Ever since, whenever life's anxieties threatened to overwhelm us, we have often found solace in the well-known words, "The Lord is my shepherd, I shall not want."

Yet there is much that we miss in this image of sheep and shepherd. In his commentary on Hosea 4:16, John Calvin points out that there is a vast difference between cattle and sheep. Left alone in a field, cattle wander off, each looking for its own food. Sheep, on the contrary, tend to stay together as a flock. Cattle show no need of a shepherd and must constantly be goaded and fenced in order to stay together. Sheep are happier when the shepherd is around and they are together as a single flock.

As we look again at the Twenty-third Psalm with this insight in mind, it is clear that the psalm speaks of much more than private comfort. To be part of the Lord's flock means that the Lord takes care of us. But it also means that we are such that by nature we belong together. The Lord takes care of us in part by keeping us together, by making us a flock. To say, "The Lord is my shepherd" is also, by the very nature of what it means to be a sheep, to say, "The Lord is *our* shepherd." And it is also to say, "The Lord takes cares of me in the midst of the flock, by providing a flock, by keeping me within the flock."

No matter how often we find private solace in this psalm, through it the Shepherd Lord is also calling us to the comfort and company of the flock.

Prayer: *Shepherd of each sheep and of the entire flock, teach us to trust in you and in the support you give us through each other. Together may we faithfully serve and follow you. Amen.*

131

Friday, April 30   Read 1 Peter 2:19-25.

This text ends with words that remind us of the Twenty-third Psalm: "the shepherd and guardian of your souls." But its tone is very different from what we find in Psalm 23. There the stress was on comfort. Here it is on suffering; yet, the two are like different sides a coin. It is often in times of suffering that we find the Twenty-third Psalm most comforting.

The text in First Peter was probably addressed to a church suffering persecution, or at least severe pressure from the society around it. In that respect, it is addressed to a situation very different from ours. In our part of the world, it is not very often that Christians are called to suffer on account of their faith. Society at large either respects us or simply lets us be. The unjust suffering to which this Epistle refers may have been the lot of Christians at an earlier time. It may even refer to Christians today in others parts of the world. But it is not our common experience.

One of the reasons why such unjust suffering is not common today is that society has accepted many Christian values. For that we should be thankful. But, could it be that another reason why Christians do not suffer unjustly may be that we have ceased to oppose the injustice in our society? Perhaps society has changed, accepting much of what early Christians proclaimed, and we have also grown lax in our obedience and thus made ourselves more acceptable to society. The answers may not be simple; but the question is one that we must constantly ask if we wish to be obedient to the Shepherd and Guardian of our souls.

Prayer: *Show us, Shepherd, where we have gone astray. Where it is your will, lead us to green pastures and still waters. But also, where it is your will, lead us by your example of suffering, that we may truly follow in your steps. Amen.*

Saturday, May 1   Read Acts 2:42-45.

During this week, we have studied texts held together by the theme of sheep and shepherds. Now we come to a very different text, and we wonder if the lectionary makes sense. What does today's text have to do with sheep and shepherds?

As we look carefully at the text, we realize the close connection between it and what we have been studying throughout the week. Sheep, Calvin told us, by nature need each other. They are truly fed when they are in a flock and with their shepherd. A solitary sheep is a sad creature indeed. This is what we see also in the life of the early church. Comfort does not come to the early Christians individually, as if each one led a private life in secret communication with God. Their comfort comes to them in their fellowship.

The word *koinonia,* here translated as "fellowship," means much more than that. It was the word used also for a business partnership, in which partners jointly owned the assets of the company. Thus, what "fellowship" means is not just the warmth that exists among people who like each other. It is also the commonality of a people who know that they are one and who, in order to be who they are, must truly share with each other, "as any had need." In this early community, the flock fed jointly, not only in spiritual matters, but also in sharing of their material possessions whenever someone was in need.

The Lord who feeds the flock often feeds it through other sheep of the same flock. How do we express this reality today, in our everyday living as Christian communities? Or do we insist on being like cattle, each feeding separately and wandering wherever greener pastures call us?

Prayer: *Show me, Lord, how to feed your flock, and how it may feed me, so that we may be one flock under one Shepherd. Amen.*

133

Sunday, May 2   Read Acts 2:46-47.

We are told in Luke that the risen Lord made himself manifest to the disciples in the breaking of the bread. This strange flock of sheep who are also shepherds of each other gathers in order to be fed and to feed each other.

In this feeding there is both joy and generosity. They did it "with glad and generous hearts." The two go together. There is a sharing that does not begrudge what is given. And, also, there is a receiving that is not humiliating but empowering. The flock in the pasture do not envy each other's grass. Nor are they embittered by depending on each other. They are, rather, empowered.

Throughout the ages, the church has found power and renewal in this simple act of feeding together, as many of us will do or have done today. We often remember that this is a sign of our dependence on God for our very life, both physical and spiritual. We particularly remember that this life has cost the death of our Lord Jesus Christ. But we should also remember that this feeding together symbolically in church is a sign that our entire lives are lived in communion and dependence on each other. Partaking of good "with glad and generous hearts" is a sign of the partaking that makes us a flock; of the partaking through which our Shepherd feeds us. The common table reminds us that we are sheep of the same Shepherd, feeding at the same pasture. It is as sheep of this one flock that we can proclaim again and again, "The Lord is my shepherd, I shall not want."

Prayer: *We thank you, great Shepherd and Guardian of the flock, that you feed us. In communion we remember that you feed us out of your own being and suffering. Do not let us forget that you have other sheep, and that you call us to feed them too. Amen.*

FOLLOWERS OF CHRIST

May 3-9, 1993   **Susan Ruach✝**
Monday, May 3   Read John 14:8-14.

What does it mean when Jesus says that we who believe in Christ will do the works that he did and even greater things?

When I think of what Jesus did, I think of the miracles—walking on water, healing people, turning water into wine. I cannot do those things. Yet, Jesus also calmed peoples' fears, taught them about God and how to relate to others. He told them about God's love, which helped them be freer inside. He encouraged people, helped them see their lives and their world differently. He treated each person with care and dignity. And he critiqued what did not follow God's values.

Don't we do many of these "works" as Christians? Don't we offer words of encouragement and teach about God; calm fears and talk about God's love to others? Don't we try to help people to see their lives differently? Don't we evaluate whether or not things are following God's values?

We as individuals do not have to do everything that Jesus did. The church, the Body of Christ, is the Christian movement. All of us together will do these things that Christ did, and even greater things.

And what a wonderful promise we have in verses 13-14. Whenever we ask for something that Christ would want too ("in my name" means that it would be in the spirit of Christ) and that would glorify God, Christ will do it!

Prayer: *O Christ, we ask to be more like you and, with your help, to be able to know and to do that which is in your spirit and which you have gifted us to do. Amen.*

✝Minister; Associate Council Director, South Indiana Conference of The United Methodist Church.

Tuesday, May 4   Read 1 Peter 2:9-10.

Can you remember sometime in your life when you were not chosen—perhaps to be on a sports team or to be part of particular group? Not being chosen for something we want is a painful experience.

What this passage is saying to us is that in fact we *are* chosen. We who are Christians are very special people to God. Yet we are not special in the sense that we will never have problems or be sorrowful. We are not special in the sense of having an insurance policy that will keep bad things from happening to us.

Our specialness has to do with the fact that we are selected for a task. We are selected to tell other people about this marvelous, awesome God who has called us out of darkness into the light. To be called from darkness into light at its simplest level means to be called from not knowing God into knowing God.

For example, did God, through Moses, lead the Hebrew people out of slavery in Egypt to freedom and the promised land? If so, then we need to proclaim it with our words by telling this story and by proclaiming it with our lives. We need to be moving from those things which enslave us to the freedom offered by God through Christ. To proclaim the mighty acts of God means to live out in our lives these themes, even as we tell the biblical stories.

Suggestion for meditation: *How has God led you from slavery to freedom? Where does that still need to happen in your life? What are the things to which you are still enslaved and the things from which you need to be free?*

Prayer suggestion: *Several times today pause and remind yourself that you are special to God. Ask God to show you how you might proclaim God's mighty acts in the following hour.*

Wednesday, May 5   Read John 14:2-14.

It must have been frustrating to Jesus when his disciples did not understand what he was saying. In this passage, Jesus makes a wonderful promise to his disciples about preparing them a place in God's house and coming for them. Thomas (probably all the rest, too) could not understand. Jesus tried again to explain, and once again the disciples missed the point. This time Philip expressed the question that seemed to indicate his lack of understanding. But Jesus kept on trying, explaining again and again, using different words to help Philip understand.

As we struggle in our faith, as we fail to understand, ask the wrong questions, and miss the point, we can trust that Jesus will handle our questions in the same way that he did the disciples'—with patience. As with the disciples, Jesus continues to coax us to grow a little more, to stretch our minds and hearts to take in this new understanding or that new way of acting.

It is striking that even in the midst of the disciples' misunderstanding of what was occurring, Jesus gave them two incredible promises. The first is that Christ prepares a place for us in God's house and comes to take us there so that we may be with Christ. The second promise is that whatever we ask in Christ's spirit, Christ will do. It is almost as if Christ gave the disciples promises to hold on to, encouraging them even as they struggled to understand.

When we do not understand something such as soneone's death, why certain circumstances exist in our life, the mysteries and paradoxes of faith, we can count on Christ to encourage us as well.

Prayer suggestion: *Ask Christ for both the answers and the promises you need today.*

Thursday, May 6   Read Acts 7:1-3, 51-60.

When our son was young and I would offer some parental advice or information or press a point too hard, he would cover his ears with his hands, saying eloquently if non-verbally, "I don't want to hear any more." Similarly, the people in this scripture from Acts did not want to hear any more of what Stephen was saying. Not only did they cover their ears to drown out his witness to God, they also shouted.

But someone must have been able to hear Stephen because we have his final prayer recorded here, a prayer that partakes of the same spirit of forgiveness as Christ's prayer on the cross. And even the people who covered their ears and shouted to drown out his voice would have seen the way he chose to die, on his knees praying for forgiveness for them.

Are there times when we want to cover our ears to what God is saying to us? Sometimes we may fill our lives with work or activities, leaving no time to listen to the quiet voice of God. Other times we may keep the TV or radio on all the time so that we cannot hear the voices in our own heads, much less God's voice. Or perhaps we tune out God's speaking to us because the words come through someone we do not like. Or we avoid the ways we have heard God before. Do you have other ways that you shut your ears to what God is saying?

Even when the crowd in Acts tried to shut out Stephen's words, they saw his example. Just so, even when we try to shut out God, God continues to speak to us, to use other means to reach us with this wonderful love God has for each of us.

Prayer: *Lord, help us to keep our ears and our hearts open always to you. Amen.*

Friday, May 7   Read Psalm 31:1-5, 15-16.

Focusing on verse 2, we read that God is asked to incline God's ear to the psalmist. It is as if the psalmist were saying, "Lean a little closer, please, God, so you can hear me really well."

I have certainly had those times in my life when I wanted to make sure God heard me clearly—the times when I was in some crisis, had a loved one very ill, or cared deeply about something. I tried to figure out some way to let God know these requests were especially urgent.

Yet as a parent, I want to listen carefully to all the joys, concerns, feelings, and requests of my own children in whatever state they are. Surely God is even more attentive than I as a human parent am able to be (though, of course, God has many more children than I). Perhaps the real issue here is my ability to trust that God hears and responds appropriately. Sometimes what I need is simply a chance to pull out feelings and thoughts and look at them in God's presence.

Sometimes we are asked to be God's listening ear for someone else. We are called to listen with as much of the compassion and love of God as we can manage to have. Perhaps in those moments we will need to pray for help to listen well, to "incline our ears" toward this other person on God's behalf. Sometimes what that person may need is simply a chance to pull out his or her thoughts and feelings and look at them. I have come to believe that when we really listen to one another, we are like God and the spirit of God dwells in us.

Prayer suggestion: *Pray that God may use you as a listener today.*

139

Saturday, May 8   Read John 14:1.

In these two sentences, Jesus gives us the whole approach to life. It is not the cliché "Don't worry; be happy." It is "Don't worry; trust Jesus."

Not worrying is hard for many people, so perhaps it is best to approach this verse from the second sentence that tells us to believe in God and in Jesus. It seems like Christ means more here than just believing that God exists and that Jesus lived, died, and was resurrected. Rather, Jesus is our invitation to know God intimately—to know that God loves each one of us incredibly and wants good for each; that God cannot be separated from us (see Romans 8:38-39); that God is always with us. (It is not that we can always feel God's presence but that God is present with us whether we can feel it or not.) How might our lives be different if we knew in every fiber of our being this belief, this trust about God's love for us?

When we believe in God and in Christ in this way, our moments of worry can become a call to prayer. When we find that we are worrying, we can immediately pray about whatever it is that we are worrying about. We can even use our prayer to ask God if there is anything we can be doing about the situation or cause of our worry besides our praying. Our worrying can also become a call to re-center ourselves in God, to re-orient our ways of thinking, feeling, and acting to God's love and God's purposes.

Our prayers will usually not be "magically" answered, but they will be answered even if the answer is simply some new insight into or clarity about what's going on.

Prayer suggestion: *Memorize John 14:1 and repeat it silently or aloud throughout the day.*

Sunday, May 9   Read 1 Peter 2:4-8.

In these verses the words *living stone* stand out for two reasons. First, we usually do not think of stones as living. But to be a "living stone" means solid or whole, not cracked or broken. The second reason that these words stand out is that Jesus is referred to as a living stone. Later the metaphor is expanded in that Christ as a living stone becomes the cornerstone, the stone of pivotal importance in the building. Then we, too, are invited to become, like Christ, living stones, to become a part of this spiritual house that is being built by God.

If we are living stones in a spiritual house, we obviously must be whole. Yet we are broken people; often we have many cracked places in us. We can only become whole, living stones as we allow ourselves to be transformed by God into Christ's likeness.

A part of this transformation is spiritual sacrifices. Sacrifices were offered originally to renew and strengthen communion with God. Sometimes the communion had been broken by sin or by some perceived uncleanliness. So a sacrifice was offered. Other times the desire in sacrificing to God was simply to strengthen the communion. When I think of spiritual sacrifices, I think of prayer and of anything else which opens us to God.

Since it is God who works the transformation toward wholeness and not ourselves, what we are to do is to open ourselves to God so that God can heal us, strengthen us, and transform us into that which is no longer broken, but whole, living stones. And just like the tiny drops of water which wear away stones, so God will use the tiniest opening we give to work in us.

Prayer: *O Lord, today help me to open myself to your transforming love. Make me more like Christ, the living stone. Amen.*

SEARCHING FOR GOD

May 10-16, 1993   **Harriet E. Crosby**✝
Monday, May 10   Read Acts 17:22-28.

Our week begins with Paul's eloquent sermon to the Athenians in front of the Areopagus. In today's reading, Paul's sermon acknowledges that Athens is a city of seekers. Paul knew all about being a seeker. The former Saul of Tarsus was zealous in his pursuit to keep the law of God, even searching out members of the infant church, imprisoning, and killing them. Then God sought and found Saul on the Road to Damascus, transforming Saul's search for Christians into Paul's search for gentile companions on the Way of Christ.

The Athenians are clearly on a religious quest as evidenced by so many objects of worship in the city. These Greek seekers even had a shrine to "an unknown god" in case they overlooked a god in their pantheon. Paul admired their zeal, but found their search misguided. God, who created the universe, is not contained in shrines made by human beings. God, who is self-sufficient, does not need sacrificial offerings. But God did create human beings to be seekers after God, so that they would search for God and perhaps grope for him and find him—though indeed he is "not far from us." In fact, the unknown god is the Creator for whom the Athenians searched for so long.

This week we join the Athenians to search for God who is "not far from us." When we seek God, we are found by God just as God found Saul, just as God found the Athenians through Paul's ministry.

Prayer: *Lord, sanctify this week. Grant me the wonder of searching for you. Grant me the joy of being found by you. Amen.*

✝Editor and writer; member, The Presbyterian Church (U.S.A.).

142

Tuesday, May 11   Read Acts 17:29-31.

Paul's sermon before the Areopagus climaxed by giving the Athenians a glimpse of God. He told the Athenians they ought not to search for God in objects made of silver, gold, or stone. Instead, Paul exhorted his listeners to first look at themselves, God's offspring. Since the Athenians were not images made of stone, there was no reason to think God is like a work of religious art either.

Then Paul told his listeners their long search for the unknown God was over—that God had found the Athenians. Judgment Day will include Greeks as well as Jews. The instrument of God's judgment is the one whom God raised from the dead. The Athenians' search ends with God offering them the assurance of resurrection on the day of judgment.

Like the Athenians, we too have searched for God in strange places. We look for the assurance or security only God offers in so many other things—success in our work; the love of our families and friends; the accumulation of things that give us pleasure. It is not wrong for us to pursue these things, but it is wrong to believe these good things offer us eternal assurance. The search for this kind of security ends in the knowledge that we have already been found by God in resurrection. We are resurrected because we are God's children, not because of our accomplishments, the quality of our relationships, or the number of our possessions. Our search for God ends in the blessed assurance of the one whom God raised from the dead, the Firstborn of all creation.

Prayer: *Lord, I offer thanks that all of my searching brings me to the Resurrection. Today, let me rest in the knowledge that I am your child. Amen.*

Wednesday, May 12   Read 1 Peter 3:13-22.

Paul's sermon to the Athenians proclaimed that they (and we) are God's children, heirs to resurrection. But being the children of God and living a new, resurrected life in a fallen world is never easy. Today's passage in 1 Peter is addressed to Christians who suffered because they followed the resurrected Lord.

The church to whom 1 Peter was written consisted of people obedient to God, people who were doing what was right and good, yet who were afflicted and persecuted because they followed Christ. This letter reminded them that they not only follow a resurrected Lord, but also a suffering Christ. Suffering is part and parcel of new life in Christ.

Like those early Christians, it is easy during times of great suffering to lose hope even in the midst of new life. To endure suffering we must search for the hope that is in us, sanctifying Christ as Lord. Our search for hope in God during painful times leads us into our hearts. We find in our hearts the crucified, suffering Lord, who is also risen and reigns with God over all angels, authorities, and powers. Our search for hope in God leads us back out into the world. Renewed with the hope that is in us, the crucified and living Lord, we continue to do what is right and good in spite of fear and intimidation. We do not fear what the world fears, but in our hearts sanctify Christ as Lord.

Prayer: *Lord, grant me the courage to search for you in suffering as well as in resurrection. And give me the strength to do what is right. Amen.*

Thursday, May 13   Read Psalm 66:8-10.

Yesterday's reading from 1 Peter showed us that we are able to endure suffering when we hold in our hearts the knowledge and love of the crucified and risen Christ. Our search for God must always be a search for the suffering Jesus, as well as for the resurrected Lord. Psalm 66 also holds in tension the suffering of God's children with their deliverance at the hand of the Lord.

Psalm 66 is a hymn of praise to God for delivering his people out of slavery in Egypt. The psalmist praises God for his awesome deeds in bringing his people safely through the Red Sea (vv. 5-7). But in today's reading the psalmist also praises God for keeping his people among the living in spite of suffering tests and trials. It is the memory of those trials and God's deliverance that drives the psalmist to worship God (vv. 13-20).

We, too, are a people whom God has kept among the living and whose feet God has not let slip. For God has tested us and tried us as silver is tried. Psalm 66 shows us that the search for God's deliverance includes suffering trials and testing. There is no liberation without some painful experiences. Nonetheless, it is God who keeps us among the living when pain dominates our lives. We follow a Lord who feels our suffering and brings us resurrection. It is the resurrection of our crucified Lord that keeps us among the living when trouble surrounds us or when we are overwhelmed by pain. Our search for deliverance ends with the living Lord, who leads us through fire and water to new life.

Prayer: *You brought us into the net; we went through fire and water; yet you have brought us out to a spacious place. Blessed be God, the One who has not rejected my prayer, the One whose steadfast love holds me. Amen.*

Friday, May 14   Read John 14:15-17.

This week our search for God has led us to the crucified and risen Christ. We have found that suffering various trials is often a sign of new life among God's people. With that in mind, we come to one of the most poignant moments in John's Gospel. The next three days we will reflect on John 14:15-21.

The setting is the Passover meal, the evening before Jesus is to suffer death on the cross. During dinner, Jesus has been preparing his disciples for what is about to take place. He now addresses that which their hearts fear most—Jesus is about to leave them alone in a world hostile to the gospel. Jesus tells his followers that he will send to them an Advocate, a Counselor, the Spirit of truth. The word Jesus used to describe this Advocate is *parakletos,* "one who walks alongside." Jesus' disciples will not suffer alone in a hostile world. Instead, they have a constant Companion walking with them through all the adventures and trials yet to come.

We have learned that suffering is often a sign of new life in God's people. Suffering drives us to seek the crucified and risen Lord. God's people have only to search inside themselves for the Holy Spirit, which provides new, resurrection life: You know him, because he abides with you, and he will be in you" (v. 17*b*). The followers of Jesus do not face the trials and tribulations of a hostile world alone. The spirit of God searches for each of us, comes to abide in us, walks beside us, and comforts us.

Prayer: *Spirit of the living God, give me courage today to love and serve you with gladness and singleness of heart. Amen.*

146

Saturday, May 15   Read John 14:18-19.

In today's reading Jesus gets right to the heart of the matter. Time is growing short. The next day he goes to his death. Jesus has spent the evening preparing his disciples for what is about to take place—that Jesus is leaving them in a hostile world, but sending them the Spirit, who is Comforter and Companion. The disciples must have been terrified at the thought of being abandoned by Jesus, in spite of his talk about the Spirit. Jesus was real flesh and blood—the Spirit was still only a promise. The disciples could face anything as long as Jesus was with them. It must have seemed to the disciples that Jesus was leaving them alone to face all the suffering the world would inflict. And then Jesus speaks to the secret fear of abandonment in each disciple's heart:

"*I will not leave you orphaned; I am coming to you. In a little while the world will no longer see me, but you will see me; because I live, you also will live*" (italics added).

Disciples throughout the ages have clung to these words of Jesus. We all experience dark times filled with suffering trials and tribulations. We exorcise despair from our hearts with the knowledge that we are not orphans in this world. We can face anything if we are not alone—and we are never alone. We belong to Jesus, who always comes to us to live in us and through us. Because Jesus lives, we also live.

Prayer: *Lord, live in me today and always. Search out the secret fears of my heart and let me know the comfort of your presence. Let others look into my eyes and find you there. Amen.*

Sunday, May 16   Read John 14:20-21.

On Jesus' last evening with the disciples, he tells them how he will remain with them. Death and resurrection are imminent, seeming to indicate that Jesus intends to abandon his followers. But he tenderly tells them that their relationship with him is about to be more intimate than ever: "On that day you will know that I am in my Father; and you in me, and I in you." Their earthly relationship is about to be replaced with a mystical union, a new relationship that is invisible, mysterious, and powerful.

Yet this new, mystical relationship with Jesus and his Father is not just "pie-in-the-sky" talk. There is a concrete, tangible side to this mystical union—Jesus' followers will keep his commandments because of love. Jesus' disciples will thrive in spite of suffering, trials, and temptations because they are bound together, keeping Christ's commandments out of love for him and one another.

Today we know that we are in the Father, and that Jesus and the Spirit abide in us. Our search for God reveals that we are not alone in the world. In our hearts we find the Trinity at work loving us and encouraging us to love others deeply. We search the faces of those who worship with us today and find the Trinity at work in people like us keeping Christ's commandments, not out of fear, but because each of us has found a love that overcomes death and brings resurrection. We are not orphans but children of God, bound by love in Father, Son, and Holy Spirit, united by that same love to sisters and brothers in Christ.

Prayer: *Lord, I give you thanks and praise for this love that has found me and will not let me go; for your indwelling in me and in all who love Christ; and for the privilege of honoring and keeping your commandments. Amen.*

THE POWER AND THE GLORY OF GOD

May 17-23, 1993   **Charles R. Gipson✣**
Monday, May 17   Read Acts 1:6-8.

To whom does the power and the glory belong? To God, of course. The disciples were aware of their human weakness in contrast to God's power experienced in the Resurrection. It was natural to think that whatever was to happen next, Christ would do it; for God's power and glory was visibly present in the risen Lord. "Lord, has the time come for *you* to restore the kingdom to Israel?" (NJB, italics added)

Jesus corrected their question, saying in effect, "Don't be concerned about *when*. It is *who* bears God's power that you need to understand now. You are seeing God's power in me and not in yourselves. But the same power of the Holy Spirit will come upon *you,* then *you* will be spreading the reign of God over all the earth."

The power and the glory belong to God. Yet Christ has chosen ordinary people like you and me, baptized and confirmed in the strong name of the Trinity, to be bearers of the power that will extend the sovereign reign of God throughout the earth. Whatever you do this day for God's glory has the possibility and the promise of being empowered by God's spirit and of contributing to God's purposes on earth. Too small a contribution, you think? Perhaps it is not for us to know how great or small. It is for us to be faithful in our time and place—today.

Prayer: *God, keep me trusting your power in and through my life. Amen.*

✣United Methodist minister at The Methodist Temple, Evansville, Indiana.

Tuesday, May 18   Read Acts 1:9-14.

"He ascended into heaven." We affirm it regularly in the Apostles' Creed. The luminous cloud of God's glory *(shekinah)* enveloped the risen Christ, and the disciples saw him lifted up and taken out of their sight. It was a remarkable event, eclipsed in meaning and relevance for Christians by the Crucifixion and the Resurrection.

A visit to the small closet-like rock enclosure that marks the traditional site of the ascension of Christ on the Mount of Olives near Jerusalem left me a little shocked by its obvious lack of attention as a holy site. Scraps of paper floated on muddy puddles on the very bare ground of the walled-in area. On Mount Zion, the Rock of Abraham, where the prophet Mohammed is said to have ascended to heaven, is revered and protected by the magnificent Dome of the Rock, a very sacred site of Islam.

The stark contrast caused me to reflect on the relevance of the ascension of Christ for my journey. The outward visible glory of God which enveloped Christ that day was also within him throughout his life. What happened to that glory? It is still here, with the Holy Spirit (within us).

I believe that Christ, having plumbed the depths of human nature, and one who reveals God's dream for humanity, has been ascending in human consciousness ever since.

No glory remains at the earthly site of the Ascension. The glory of God in Christ shines on in the world in the faces of Christians. The light of Christ is in your eyes and my eyes. The mind of Christ is in your mind and my mind.

Prayer: *Jesus Christ, risen from the dead and ascended to heaven, help me to draw upon your glory and live this day in your joy. Amen.*

Wednesday, May 19   Read Psalm 68:1-10, 32-35.

How would you describe the power and the glory of God experienced in your life journey?

In this epic song of the triumph of God in the journey of Israel from Sinai (v. 8) to the sanctuary (v. 35), the psalmist recalls the desert wanderings, the conquest of the promised land, and the bringing of the ark to Zion, and issues a call for all nations to acknowledge the power of God. Dramatic images abound. God is "Rider of the Clouds," "Father of the fatherless" (NIV), "Protector of the widows." God's power is like a fire before which the power of the wicked melts like wax. The earth quakes, and the heavens pour down rain in response to God's presence. God's glory is revealed in saving justice and generosity. God gives the homeless a home, leads prisoners out into prosperity, provides for the needy, and gives strength to the weary.

As I look at my own life journey, I may use different images, but the power and glory belong to the same God. In my epic song, God is Defender of the defenseless, Strong Deliverer, and Restorer of joy. God's power is the power of a love which can perpetually forgive, heal, and renew. God's glory is like a light that leads out of self-imposed darkness and saves us from self-destruction. God's grace unravels knots within, eases pain and tension, and brings freedom and peace at last.

Amazing isn't it? Our times, our world, differ so markedly from those of the psalmist. Yet our experience of God's power and glory calls forth the same affirmation: God gives power and strength to God's people.

Prayer: *God let it be so in my life and in the lives of all your people on earth, today and always. Amen.*

Thursday, May 20   Read 1 Peter 4:12-13.

Peter is writing to Christians who are under persecution because they are Christians. Social and economic sanctions, assault, imprisonment, torture, maiming, or a martyr's death could be the cost of naming Jesus Christ as Savior and Lord. The apostles viewed such persecution as inevitable and nothing new or alien to the life experience of Jews or Christians. Jesus foretold it, and they experienced it as a sharing in the suffering of Christ.

Christians still confront persecution in our time. In Central America, South America, Africa, the Middle East—on any continent at any time—Christians may still be persecuted for following Christ. The words of the scripture are the consolation of God for such suffering and the bestowal of God's spirit of glory awaits the faithful.

Even such a wonderful promise of the bestowal of "the Spirit of glory, which is the spirit of God" (v. 14) upon those who suffer for Christ's sake may need discernment in applying it to our personal lives. Not all suffering is suffering for Christ's sake. More common than persecution is suffering from sickness or injury, mental or emotional suffering, and abuse of various types, all of which need the healing touch of God. For some forms of suffering within ourselves we need to seek help and work for change rather than embrace and rejoice in the situation as a means of sharing in the suffering of Christ. And so we pray for discernment in applying this message to our particular type of suffering.

Prayer: *God, we pray for those around the world who suffer persecution for their Christian faith. Grant them strength to witness to the good news of your love and salvation. Amen.*

Friday, May 21   Read 1 Peter 5:6-9.

"The mighty hand of God" is a phrase used in the Old Testament for the experience of the power and glory of God in *deliverance* (Exod. 13:9; Deut. 9:26). The Hebrews looked back on their deliverance from Egypt and realized they had gained their freedom only by the mighty hand of God. Can we look back on times in our lives when we did not think we could go on, yet we did and were able to say, "Only by the power of God"? That is deliverance!

To be humble before God's mighty hand means to be willing to accept God's saving power offered to us rather than to pridefully insist on our ability to deliver ourselves. That the humble will be exalted is a principle Jesus taught by word and example. Peter—who once pridefully tried to refuse Jesus' act of humble service in his washing of feet—has become a faithful witness to the way of Christ.

"Cast all your anxiety upon him, for he cares for you." Here is a word for all seasons and for this day. It is not easy to do, this "casting." The image is one of *throwing*. It requires letting go, not just placing something in God's hand with our hand still upon it. To release requires deep trust. We may find that we simply cannot let go of all anxiety. Still we can trust the promise. God cares for us.

The exhortation to watchful vigilance against evil may well have come from Peter's own experience on the night Jesus was arrested. The "roaring lion" is an image of evil constantly hungry for power over the soul. But vigilant resistance to evil keeps the soul in God's power and glory and causes the evil one to flee.

Prayer: *Lord, here are the worries of this day in my life.* (Name these to God.) *Dispose of them according to your will as I live this day with my soul trusting deeply in your power and glory. Amen.*

Saturday, May 22   Read 1 Peter 5:10-11.

Even though Peter was writing to Christians who were suffering primarily because of persecution for their faith, this scripture seems applicable to all manner of suffering.

Deep trust, moment by moment, that this is God's promise to the faithful helps the human spirit to triumph in the midst of suffering. We are reminded that God is the "God of all grace" (unconditional and unmerited love) and that our life in Christ is both eternal and glorious. We may face unexplainable suffering in this world, but we are given these inward spiritual resources to enable us to endure as we await God's ultimate intervention and healing.

The words Peter uses to describe the way God will act on behalf of those who are suffering are rich in meaning. They have the sound of stages of healing of human woundedness. God will act to "restore, support, strengthen, and establish." In the Greek, the word translated "restore" is the word used for the setting of a fractured bone. God first puts back together that in our lives which needs mending. *Support* means "to make firm." This is the stage of a healing broken bone when the body forms a strong inner protective covering over the fracture to support the vulnerable area. Likewise, we often speak of the support of the Christian community in times when we are in a healing process. The next stage is to "strengthen." Now the area of vulnerability is becoming an area filled with strength. Then God will "establish" us, which here is a word for the establishment (erecting) of a building on a firm foundation. With God's help and that of the community of faith, we can emerge from suffering stronger than we were before.

Prayer: *Yes, Lord, restore, support, strengthen, and establish me by your healing power and grace. Amen.*

Sunday, May 23   Read John 17:1-11.

This prayer of Jesus for his disciples truly needs to be experienced more than analyzed. To have someone you love pray for you, speak to God on your behalf in your presence, is to receive a gift of love. In such a moment what matters most is receiving the gift with awareness of the presence of God and a sense of oneness and unity in God.

After reading today's scripture, you may wish to use the following as a personal guided meditation. At the end, allow Jesus to pray for you.

Guided meditation: Close your eyes and visualize that upper room in Jerusalem. Using the gift of imagination, put yourself in the scene as one of his followers. Walk up the steps and enter the door. Notice what the room is like, the light that is present, the people who are there, the food and drink that has been prepared, and Jesus, who beckons you to come in. You know that you are not intruding; you are welcome, wanted, and invited by the host.

Take your seat at table as one of those whom the spirit of God has brought to Jesus as follower and friend. See him arise from the place of the host and take up the towel and basin of the servant and begin to kneel before each person to wash their feet. See Jesus kneel before you and wash your feet. Receive as fully as possible this act of love.

Now, aware of love, forgiveness, and peace, we are prepared for the next gift. Jesus wants to pray for us. When you are ready to receive the gift, open your eyes and slowly read the scripture. Hear Jesus pray the words for you. Feel the love that is in the prayer. Know the yearning of Jesus for us to be one with him in intimate relationship with God, and one with each other. Let Jesus do the praying. Just receive the gift of his prayer.

May 24-30, 1993 **Lawrence H. Tyler Wayman**✠
Monday, May 24 Read Psalm 104:1*a*, 24-34, 35*b*.

...Watching

I watched the sea bird dive and splash through the wave and then emerge, peaceful and bobbing on the water's swell.

If the psalmist had been this bird, then it would be at this place where the psalm would have been sung.

In peace one encounters God's greatness. In peace one hears the word and sees the light.

An indispensable requirement for peace is *readiness* for peace. One can work and search and shout and weep and even pray; however, peace requires readiness to see and to hear. Peace really is from God. The psalmist knows of the storms, the darkness, and the silence when one's eyes do not see, when one's ears do not hear. Human activity alone seldom has an effect on bringing peace to a storm or light to darkness.

Only God provides for peace. When one hears the silence, understanding speaks. When one sees the darkness, light comes like the sun. Then God's world bursts upon us like the waves of the sea. Our dive was merely our readiness to begin.

On re-emerging from the watery dive, one must see and listen, so that sight and hearing may adjust to new horizons and sounds. At that moment God appears and speaks. Our peace comes from being ready to see and to hear.

Suggestion for meditation: *Ask: Am I in a state of* readiness *for peace? Listen: to the silence and the sounds surrounding and within you. See: what God is showing you.*

✠Clergy member of the California-Pacific Annual Conference, The United Methodist Church; editor, Pan-Methodist Coalition on Alcohol and Other Drug Concerns.

Tuesday, May 25   Read Acts 2:1-6.

...Gathering

For centuries storytellers have told funny tales of leaders who failed, because no one would follow them. All leaders risk facing the possibility of appearing foolish. People risk appearing foolish if they follow foolish leaders. One must listen carefully to others in order to determine how foolish or reliable their words and ideas may be.

The disciples at Pentecost ran the risk of appearing foolish. People had not come to Jerusalem to hear funny stories. Pentecost was a time for faith stories.

The people were listening, together. Although God speaks personally in the privacy of heart and experience, God's voice is heard, often most clearly, in stories and experiences shared with others. Even in the silence of private daily meditations, one hears the voices of others in prayer.

God spoke in a surprising way to the people who had come to Jerusalem. They did not know the disciples; yet, somehow, they knew the words. Each heard an invitation, individually; however, together they responded to words that excluded no one. Some who heard the words concluded that the disciples were drunk. They walked away in continuing confusion. But others stayed to hear more. The voice that they heard attended to the questions that pressed upon their minds. And they wondered, together.

Suggestion for meditation: *What word could be spoken to you that would catch your attention? cause you to think that it is not foolish? invite you to live in a new way? affirm the value of who you are? alert you to listen for the voice of God in unexpected places?*
Prayer: *Surprising God, startle me with an unexpected word for my faith in you and my life for others. Amen.*

157

Wednesday, May 26   Read Acts 2:7-14.

...Listening

The Pentecost word is a listening word. It is a word that is heard before it is spoken.

The disciples had been silent following Jesus' crucifixion. All the Gospels tell how they would gather and wait, sometimes in darkened rooms; at other times observing normal routines, but later returning to wait. They would talk among themselves about the meaning of what had happened. Some doubted. Some believed. All waited and listened for a word of life.

Can a word be heard before it is spoken? Words of faith seem to have an unspoken quality. They are used when no one knows what to say. When a person is sad, what should a friend say? What words can ease another's pain? Can mere words express great joy? In time, words will be spoken; however, at first, one has to listen.

Some words prepare a listener to hear before they are spoken. A word of love needs an embrace. A word of forgiveness springs from a bent knee. A word of salvation draws its sound from the silences of despair and yearning.

The day of Pentecost was the first of many days when the people's silence became heard into speech. (Imagine a curtain being raised for an audience that has waited a long time for the first act to begin.) The sound is like the breath of God. It pulsates with the beating of each heart:

...yes, you are not alone...Yes, I am with you always....
YES, DEATH HAS NO DOMINION....YES!

Devotional exercise: *In your prayers, place the word "Yes" in a silent place of your imagination, and listen. If no reply comes, wait and watch your daily routine. Gather as often as you can with persons who care for you. If a reply comes, accept it as real; speak it to others; and listen for it to be returned to you.*

Thursday, May 27   Read Acts 2:14-21.

...Speaking

Do you think that some of the disciples may have asked during the days after Jesus' crucifixion and resurrection, "Can we still tell the stories of Jesus, now that Jesus is no longer with us?" Following their experience on the day of Pentecost, they had the answer to their question.

The disciples discovered that the stories of Jesus were the same ones they had heard from the rabbis in the Temple. The difference was that the stories were no longer stories of what had been or of what might be. The stories had become presently real. The disciples discovered also that the stories of Jesus had become their stories. Jesus was still with them.

Peter locates the stories of Jesus in the lives of the disciples. The disciples have become the ones of whom the prophet Joel spoke. They are the sons and daughters who will prophesy, see visions, and dream dreams.

The stories of Jesus include liberating words: "Don't be afraid." "Your sins are forgiven." "Love one another." "I am with you always." These words are spoken and understood in many ways: a touch, a smile, an embrace, a prayer, a meal, a pitcher of water, a tear. The gift of the Spirit is one of knowing what to say and how to say it. Such a gift comes from one's having received the earlier gift of patient listening.

Peter encouraged everyone: Keep speaking. Now is the time to make some commotion because this day that God has made is a new day in Jesus Christ.

The Spirit speaks. We listen.

In a word, Christ comes among us.

Devotional exercise: *Listen for a story of Jesus today. When you hear it, tell it to another, listening to the other's silence for an invitation to speak.*

Friday, May 28   Read 1 Corinthians 12:3*b*–13.

...Connecting

Being a follower of Jesus is different from choosing sides. None of the stories of Jesus have him looking for opponents or enemies. They show him connecting with people rather than cutting them off.

Paul invites those who follow Christ to connect with others in the inclusive attitude of a "good mind." Such an attitude, as developed in the spiritual traditions of Native American people, finds wholeness in all created life and in the human family. In his letter to the Corinthians, Paul identifies the qualities of persons and communities that confess their faith with a good mind in Jesus Christ.

God is the source of all spiritual gifts, services, and activities. They are for everyone. God's good gifts are neither secret, exclusive, nor conditional. In each person's life they work for the common good. An attitude of wholeness is the expression of the good mind of God. Such an attitude is an expression of human spirituality.

With a good mind one refuses to call another "enemy." With a good mind one seeks out sisters and brothers. With a good mind one sees and hears the voice of God in all God's world. Paul identifies the Christian family as "members of one body in one Spirit."

Devotional exercise: *As you read the newspaper or talk with friends today, listen for words that deny the spiritual identity of others.*

Suggestion for meditation and prayer: *In your prayer identify specifically the occasions of denial of another's spiritual worth that you observed during the day. Include those occasions when you denied the value of your own spiritual worth. Pray for a "good mind" in your relationships with others and in your love for yourself.*

Saturday, May 29   Read 1 Corinthians 12:4-11.

...Respecting

How does one ask for respect? Such a question may be impossible to answer. One loses respect in the act of asking. Popular comedians make people laugh when they include in their monologues this longing that many people have. All people want is a little respect!

The members of the Corinthian church wanted a little respect; however, Paul's words hint that the members were not looking in the right places. He reminds them that it has already been given by God. In all that they do for the good of all, they will find God's respect.

Paul does not say that God's respect requires or results in human perfection. His letters are full of his sorrow over his own broken spirituality and humanity. What Paul does say is that respect comes from God who makes all things new.

Saint Francis of Assisi's familiar prayer for permission to be "an instrument of God's peace" may be the only way that one can ask for respect. He prays for help in using God's gift of respect for the good of all people.

Such a prayer for respect underlies the expression "to God be the glory," which is used by many persons in their daily activities. This is the prayer of this writer. Athletes have prayed it during their competitions; artists have expressed it in their painting; carpenters have spoken it with each strike of their hammers. In all activities for good God offers respect as an unconditional gift through the love of Jesus Christ.

Prayer: *Giving God, answer our questions by showing us the way of your peace for the good of all and for your glory. Amen.*

Sunday, May 30 (Pentecost)

Read John 7:37-39.

...Inviting

Jesus invited people to come to the water. By doing so, he laid his life on the line. He was surrounded by the Temple police, sent to arrest him. John describes the scene as one in which Jesus is among his enemies. It is the last place that Jesus should have preached his sermon.

Jesus, however, was always placing that which is last, first. He noticed the need of the people, particularly his opponents, for living water. He invited them to be with him and to be thirsty no more. This was the time and the place to invite people to live.

Jesus was not arrested, this time. Later (v. 46), the police explain their reasons for not arresting him. They had never heard anyone speak as he did. Jesus said that the water of life is for everyone. Jesus did not let the police do their job. He invited them to put aside the label that separated them from others. He included them in his invitation to live.

"Come and drink" is such a simple offer. The only requirement for accepting is to believe that Jesus' words are true. They refocus one's vision of who one is. All that matters is the love of God for all people. Nothing is impossible for the faithful Christian. If a person will only take one step toward the water, Christ will take two.

Devotional exercise: *Do you know someone who hasn't been invited to the water? Have you heard the invitation lately? Listen for it. It's so simple, you may not notice it. Listen for it with a friend. Accept it together in worship this week.*

Prayer: *God of water and life, bathe me in the tides of your time. Strengthen me on the shelter of your shore. Bring me to those to whom I may give your invitation to live. Amen.*

I AM WITH YOU ALL YOUR DAYS

May 31–June 6, 1993
Monday, May 31

Evelyn Laycock✢
Read Genesis 1:1-26*a*, 31.

"In the beginning when God created...." When the Creation was finished, according to Genesis, God saw that creation was very good.

Just as a musical composition tells so much about its composer, so does creation about the Creator. When we look at a rose or a sunrise we see that God enjoys beauty. To see a newborn infant, so tiny and complex yet different from every other child, informs us that God cares for us as individuals, that we each have a special place in God's heart and purpose. To observe the beautiful mosaic of colors, form, and purpose in creation points to God's desire for variety with an inter-connectedness that helps creation remain good.

God's acts of creation continue today. Creation of new life and a better world is taking place as we find cures for diseases that plague humankind; find peaceful purposes for nuclear energy; and remove physical, social, spiritual, and mental barriers that divide humankind. Developing technology, delivery systems, education, and other opportunities that will eliminate hunger, poverty, crime, and other social ills moves the world toward goodness. God, actively involved in this mission, calls us to be co-creators in returning the world to its original condition: "In the beginning...it was very good."

Suggestion for meditation: *In what ways am I a co-creator with God today in helping the world become good?*

✢Hiwassee College Professor Emeritus; Director of the Lay Ministries Center at Lake Junaluska, North Carolina.

Tuesday, June 1   Read Genesis 1:26-31.

Almost beyond comprehension is the realization that humankind is created in the image of God. What a gift, responsibility, and opportunity! Our sin, not being what we are created to be, has tarnished this act of creation. However, thanks be to God in Christ, this does not have to be the final condition of our lives. We may be forgiven and experience the sanctifying process of being shaped back into "the image of God."

To bear the image of God means that:

1. *We have the ability to love and to respond to love*. The deepest and most basic need of all humanity is to give and to receive love. This we learn through experiencing love from others; love does not develop in isolation. The more we are open to God's love, the more we have to share with others.

2. *We have the ability to create beauty and to respond to it*. God is the creator of beauty; therefore, we have the ability to create and respond to beauty. It may be a work of art, a composition of music, a loaf of bread, a computer program, a garden. Within us is the capability of giving and responding to beauty in its many forms.

3. *We have the ability to know justice and to pursue it*. God desires justice and righteousness as the norm for all humanity. God seeks persons to be co-workers for such to become reality.

4. *We have the ability to know God and to have fellowship with God*. Augustine was describing a universal condition when he stated, "My soul was restless until it found rest in Him." God is not playing hide-and-seek with us. God seeks us, and in fellowship together life has meaning, joy, and purpose.

Prayer: *Creator God, I am open for your sanctifying grace to shape me into what I am created to be. Amen.*

Wednesday, June 2   Read Genesis 2:1-4*a*.

God rested on the seventh day "from all the work that he had done." Isn't it interesting that God took a day off? The Sabbath is carved into history as a witness to the God who can relax. What a powerful message this can be for us!

Do we equate our worth by how much we accomplish? Are we important because our calendars are filled—our days and nights busy with meetings, work, and a myriad of other events? Many times Jesus says, "Do not keep worrying...after all these things....your Father knows that you need them" (Luke 12:29-30). These words may enter our minds but not our lifestyle. Consider this: Our salvation comes by grace, not by works. We are children who are loved unconditionally by an extravagant God. We have the promise of life, and that abundantly. What then is the problem?

Can it be we are our own worst enemies? We need to remember the fact that God rested. This is an example for us. From rest that includes celebration of God's goodness toward us comes renewal of body, mind, soul, and relationships.

The Sabbath was God's idea from the beginning. God knows what is in humankind's best interest and lets us know. "Six days you shall labor and do all your work. But the seventh day is a sabbath to the LORD your God" (Exod. 20:8-9*a*).

Prayer: *O merciful Creator, your hand is open wide to satisfy the needs of every living creature: Make us always thankful for your loving providence; and grant that we, remembering the account that we must one day give, may be faithful stewards of your good gifts; through Jesus Christ our Lord..... Amen.*[*]

---

[*]*The Book of Common Prayer*, The Episcopal Church, (1977), p. 259.

Thursday, June 3   Read Psalm 8.

Psalm 8 is a musical echo of Genesis 1–2:4*a*. The psalmist has taken time to really look at the grandeur of nature. In surveying such beauty, the psalmist breaks forth in an outburst of praise, "O LORD, our sovereign, how majestic is your name in all the earth!" An expression of true worship!

At night the psalmist is under the canopy of a star-filled sky, perhaps studying the constellations, thinking of the vastness that lies in space beyond view, or perhaps contemplating the moon with its changing images. In the context of such grandeur, the psalmist asks the Creator a question that is filling his mind. "What are human beings that you are mindful of them, mortals that you care for them?" The response to this question has given men and women through the ages a definition of worth and mission.

To be created human, says the psalmist, is to be made "a little lower than God." This indicates that persons are made different from the rest of nature; our affinity is with the Maker, not with the made. However, there is an inherent danger that should be addressed: Persons are created a "little lower than God"; we are not God. We tend to want to crown the creature instead of the Creator. There is great value in remembering that all we do in the realm of nature is to discover what God has placed there. God was the inventor of penicillin; researchers just discovered it. But the human ability to discover such truths is as awe inspiring. It results from being made "a little lower than God."

Prayer:
O LORD, our Sovereign,
   how majestic is your name in all the earth!
                    Amen.

166

Friday, June 4   Read Psalm 8:5-8.

God made human beings "a little lower than God," says the psalmist, "and crowned them with glory and honor." The psalm continues by saying this is to be accomplished now on earth, for God has given persons dominion over the works of creation, and all things have been put "under their feet." Thus, we are to manage the world in such a way that it will bring glory and honor to God.

For several years I had the opportunity to teach Bible study classes at Oak Ridge, Tennessee, a city that is known for nuclear energ. In those classes sat many renowned scientists who were seeking peaceful uses for nuclear energy. One evening a group of seven scientists told the class about the real possibility of producing a bumper food crop as a result of the research currently going on in their work. This group had recently taken some seeds to India, had helped community leaders plant them, and had given careful instruction about how to tend the plants until the researchers returned. With great feeling, one in the group said, "Maybe this can be one way of helping to eliminate hunger from the world."

Sitting in the class was a man who had been a part of the Manhattan Project—the splitting of the atom. With deep emotion this great scientist responded, "Gentlemen, let me remind you that science is morally neutral; it is who controls it that makes science good or evil. With the same technology you can also starve a community into submission."

Yes, God wants humanity to manage the world so that there is righteousness, justice, and peace for all persons.

Suggestion for meditation: *Does my dominion over God's creation bring glory and honor to God?*

Saturday, June 5   Read Matthew 28:16-20.

The eleven disciples went into Galilee to the mountain where Jesus had told them to go. It was their last meeting with Jesus, and here they were told their mission. The disciples were now entering into the most difficult phase of their ministry. Before, they had had Jesus to lead them, but now they were on their own. Jesus told them three things:

1. *He assured them of his power.* Not just a little power was to be given, but Jesus told his disciples, "All authority in heaven and on earth has been given to me." The disciples were challenged to go out in and with this power to win the world.

2. *He gave them a commission.* A commission grants certain powers and authorizes the performance of certain duties. The disciples were commissioned by Jesus to go and make all the world his disciples. This must have seemed an impossible task, for the world was filled with many religions as well as persons who gave the impression they wanted nothing to do with religion. But the mission was given—they were to go and make disciples of "*all* peoples everywhere" (TEV)—to bring them to a vital relationship with Christ.

3. *He promised them his presence.* It must have been a staggering thing for eleven humble Galileans to be sent forth to the conquest of the world, but Jesus tells them they do not go alone. His presence is what makes such a challenge possible.

In our lives we are called to be daily disciples of the risen Christ. We, too, may feel overwhelmed by the commission, but the promise of Christ's power and presence to accomplish the mission still holds today.

Suggestion for meditation: *The presence and power of Christ are with me every moment. Am I open to receive this gift?*

June 6 (Trinity Sunday)
Read 2 Corinthians 13:11-13.

Today's reading is Paul's response is to those who are trying to discredit him and the gospel he is proclaiming. One charge is, "His letters are weighty and strong, but his bodily presence is weak, and his speech contemptible" (2 Cor. 10:10).

In response, Paul writes this bold letter. His words reflect the deep pain he is experiencing, but he seems to believe his direct, open, and bold response is necessary for the church. As we read, it is as if we are permitted to lift the rooftop off the church and observe events inside. There are divisions within the congregation, power struggles, lies, slander, and sexual immorality.

Paul pleads with them to examine themselves to see if they are living the faith. "Test yourselves," states Paul. "Do you not realize that Jesus Christ is in you?—unless, indeed, you fail to meet the test!" (v. 5) What is the test? How does one take it? For Paul, the question is: Is Christ living in me?

Paul's closing appeal is that the church put things in order, listen to his appeal, agree with one another, and live in peace. Knowing the condition of the Corinthian church, does such a transformation seem possible? Only because the "God of love and peace will be with you." This is the hope for the church; this makes possible such radical change.

The benediction (v. 13) asks that "The grace of the Lord Jesus Christ, the love of God, and the communion of the Holy Spirit" be with the church. Grace, love, and the Holy Spirit are always extended to persons. The question then becomes, "Am I open to receive what God offers to me?"

Prayer: *Help me, God, to see myself as I am. In this realization give me the desire to be what you want me to be. May my life flow out of you, your Son, and your Holy Spirit. Amen.*

SERVING THE LORD

June 7-13, 1993   **Roy I. Wilson**✠
Monday June 7   Read Psalm 116:1-2.

"The LORD...has heard my voice." How beautiful this relationship is which has developed between us and our God! God hears our voice! This is sweet music to our ears in a day when lack of communication has become the number one problem in marriages. So many couples are complaining that their mates do not hear what they are saying. Our relationship with God must be an exceptional one, for God hears us.

This God not only hears us, but according to the prophet Isaiah of old, "Before they call I will answer, while they are yet speaking I will hear" (Isa. 65:24). This God not only hears us but responds to us before we speak.

The beauty of this truth comes home with powerful force when we read: "He chose us in Christ before the foundation of the world" (Eph. 1:4). God, by foreknowledge, knew all of my heart through and through. This God looked down through the catalog of the human race and knew me and heard me millions of years before I became a reality on this earth. God certainly has good ears!

Prayer: *Sacred Mystery, we celebrate your matchless love and grace. Amen.*

✠Retired clergy member of the Pacific Northwest Conference, United Methodist Church; retreat leader; writer. Member of tribal council and traditional spiritual leader, Cowlitz Indian Tribe; Bremerton, Washington.

Tuesday, June 8   Read Genesis 18:1-15.

The reward for faithful service—"Your wife Sarah shall have a son." Is this a kingdom promise?

Three strangers approached Abram. He addressed them as "lord" and declared himself to be their servant. Abram recognized that these travelers must be tired and hungry. As their servant he proceeded to serve them. He washed their feet—how refreshing! He fed them sumptuously—killing for them his own fatted calf.

How does this translate into present day North American culture? How do we treat the stranger we meet each day? Do we favor those who are dressed well, those who appear to be successful? How about the strangers we meet who appear to be tired, dirty, and hungry? Do we avoid them by crossing over to the sidewalk on the other side of the street? Do we do this by simply saying to ourselves that this problem is too big for me; therefore, it is the government's problem?

Some of us may pride ourselves on being good resource persons, knowing how to network the available agencies, and therefore being able to help the tired, the homeless, the hungry. But how many of us are willing to put ourselves out to wash their feet? How many of us are willing to dig into our own resources and give our own fatted calf to feed the hungry?

Those who do will receive their reward—in Abram's case, he would have a son. But Abram's son was more than just another son. Abram became Abraham and was given a kingdom—all of Israel.

Prayer: *Creator God, help me to be more caring by extending myself to others. Amen.*

171

Wednesday, June 9   Read Psalm 116:15-19.

"Precious in the sight of the Lord is the death of his saints." Is death the reward for Christian service?

A human fetus develops inside the mother's womb for a period of approximately nine months. There are eyes but they cannot see. There is a nose, but it cannot smell. There are ears, but they cannot hear. There is a brain, but it cannot think. There are legs, but they cannot walk. They do not seem to fulfill any particular function in this stage of existence.

After approximately nine months we died to that stage of existence, and we were born into this present one. Soon we saw a light and blinked at it. Then we heard a voice that was more familiar than the others and we began to coo. We began to crawl, walk, run, leap, and jump. We learned to reason and to rationalize. All of these capabilities that were seemingly unneeded in our first stage of existence, now came into their full fruition and use.

How many of us would like to return to the darkness of our mother's womb? This life, with all of its problems and struggles, is far superior to that first stage of life. Likewise, our death to this stage of our existence will allow us a birth into another stage that will be of even greater dimension.

John wrote, "It does not yet appear what we shall be" (1 John 3:2, RSV).

Prayer: *God, who is the holy essence of all, we celebrate that the end of this life is the passing to another world. Amen.*

Thursday, June 10   Read Romans 5:10.

The reward for Christian service—"We shall be saved." Shall be saved? Have we not been taught that this is a past tense experience? An experience that took place when we converted to the Christian faith? Are we reading here that this is a future tense experience?

How many Christians think of salvation, regeneration, reconciliation, the words of justification and sanctification, or being born again as all being synonymous? We would only need one of these words if they all said the same thing. They all speak of different experiences, not only in their essence of being but also in their sense of timing.

This is an interesting verse because it contains two of these words and uses them in differing time concepts. Paul says that we were reconciled to God by the death of his Son. Reconciliation is past tense. It took place at Calvary long before I was born. I am not reconciled because of my repentance. Every human being who has ever lived was reconciled to God at Calvary, "While we were yet enemies."

Being saved is revealed here as Christ living his life through us. As we serve the Lord his kingdom is made manifest through us and we go through the process of becoming saved. "Work out your own salvation" (Phil 2:12, RSV).

Western Christianity has become extremely anthropocentric, with the salvation concept being one of saving the soul of the inner person. Salvation is also of the outer world, and not only the inner soul. Salvation is of the entire creation. We need to turn to the needs of the world allowing our faith to be seen in our works—our service unto the Lord. Then the work of salvation *shall* take place.

Prayer: *Creator God, help me to be more sensitive to the entirety of your creation.*

Friday, June 11   Read Matthew 9:35.

What does our service unto the Lord involve? Where can we turn for a good model? How about the Lord himself being our model? This verse reveals a model of his service unto God. There are three aspects of service in this model: teaching, preaching, and healing. Shall we walk in his steps? Would this be considered as walking in the spirit?

What percentage of professing Christians are involved in a teaching ministry? Some adult Christians say, "But I have not been trained to teach," or "I don't know the scriptures that well," or "I don't know how to talk to others very well." All of these are "lame duck" excuses. Jesus said that even a little child shall lead them. Some of the most powerful lessons I have learned have come from the mouths of children. We need to allow the child within us to come alive once again.

We not only need to teach the good news, but also to preach it. No, you do not need to be ordained, nor do you need a pulpit. To be a Christian is to be a minister. If you are not ministering, then you are not living a total Christian life. Why did the primitive first century church spread so quickly across the face of its then known world? Every Christian was teaching and preaching. Most times our preaching is louder through our actions. What better way to preach the gospel than through service to the tired and hungry of this world, to those who are tired and hungry physically and sociologically as well as spiritually? Is this not the ministry of healing?

Prayer: *Great Healer, help me to develop and practice Jesus' model of ministry in my life. Amen.*

Saturday, June 12   Read Matthew 9:36–10:8.

"You received without pay, give without pay" (Matthew 10:8, RSV).

Is this verse addressed to those in the professional ministry, or to the lay ministry? Is the paycheck we pastors receive each month our reward for service unto the Lord? Do we find that which is more rewarding than the pay? What motivates us to serve? In our materialistic American culture we often find ourselves asking the question, "What is in this for me?"

Jesus is here addressing his twelve disciples. They did more to turn the world upside-down than any other group of twelve who ever lived. They would be considered as lay pastors according to the standards of many churches today. They served the Lord without a contract for pay. We cannot class them with today's professionally trained clergy.

Jesus did not direct this statement to the priests (the "professional clergy" of his day), but to the disciples—lay ministers. Do lay members of the church, when they are asked to serve, ask themselves, "What is in this for me?" What motivates them to serve?

I believe that there are probably a few of both the clergy and the laity who, with the powerful politics that exists in the church, serve for what is in it for themselves. But, I would like to believe that most of us serve out of the motivating sense of being called by God to service.

We may not have been called with a sensational Damascus Road experience like Paul, but we may have heard God call us through the great cry of the people for justice, or for greater depth in their spiritual teachings, or through the cry of those in need.

Prayer: *Lord of all life, help me be sensitive to hear your call. Amen.*

175

Sunday, June 13   Read Psalm 116:12-14.

Bounty! Bounty?

Throughout this week we have been considering our service unto the Lord and rewards we receive for that service. Now the question arises, "What shall I render to the Lord for all his bounty to me?"

A Native American may feel a great need to approach the Creator with a request: therefore, he desires to give the greatest gift possible to the Creator. He could give a gift of a hundred horses, but if he owns a thousand horses he hasn't given his greatest gift. He would gladly give all of his possessions to regain his health if he had lost it. There is nothing more sacred to we Native Americans than life itself.

The greatest gift that any person can give is that of one's life. Where does service unto the Lord fall in the list of priorities of my life? Where does it appear in the list of priorities of your life? Do we give our greatest gift? Paul, the Apostle, said that you are not your own. "Do you not know that your body is a temple of the Holy Spirit within you, which you have from God? You are not your own; you were bought with a price. So glorify God in your body" (1 Corinthians 6:19-20, RSV). Paul spoke of himself as a "servant" of Jesus Christ.

"What shall I render to the Lord for all his bounty to me?" What less can I give than my life in service to him?

Prayer: *Great Spirit, Creator God, my bountiful love for you compels me to make the commitment of my life to you. Amen.*

THE OPPRESSION THAT SLAVERY BREEDS

June 14-20, 1993   **Ronald N. Liburd**✛

Monday, June 14   Read Genesis 21:8-14.

Our lection for today deals with the fallout in Abraham's household over a breached contract between Sarah and Abraham on the one hand, and Hagar, their slave, on the other. With the birth of Sarah's own son, the question of estate put her earlier decision to the fundamental test, evoking from her the remark, "The son of this slave woman shall not be heir with my son Isaac" (Gen. 21:10, RSV). Sarah's offer, made from altruistic motives, now looks like a mistake in judgment.

Modern society is plagued with a somewhat similar circumstance. I think of the story of Hagar when I consider some of the well-publicized cases of surrogacy in the United States. Even though the story of Hagar and Ishmael reflects a particular custom of that time, there are, to my mind, some similarities to our present day dilemma regarding surrogate parenting. It seems that when conflict arises, the child suffers in the extended litigation. In our age of scientific and technological advances, we sometimes make life more difficult rather than using these advances to relieve suffering and to help us be more fully the type of persons God intended. The advances we have made in the biomedical field sometimes tempt us to replace *gloria Dei* (glory to God) with our own doxology: *gloria homini* (glory to humankind).

Prayer: *O God, grant us the vision and courage to live out our faith in a manner that testifies to our trust in your ultimate rule, and not in our own. Amen.*

✛Assistant Professor of Religion, Florida A & M University, Tallahassee, Florida.

Tuesday, June 15   Read Genesis 21:15-21.

From the time I received this assignment to the time of writing two events occurred that have helped to bring some perspective to the meditations on the lections for this week. First, a Middle East peace conference, under the sponsorship of the United States, was convened in Spain to find a resolution to a conflict whose origins are traceable in part to the events of Genesis 16-21. Second, CBS featured an hour long program on surrogate mothering. I recall this pointed remark from one observer: "Nobody ever remembers to treat the offspring as a real human being."

That attitude is reflected in today's reading, which reveals the cruelty of the desert to which Hagar and her son were exposed after their expulsion by Sarah and Abraham. This episode both brings to mind the issue and illustrates the cruelty of what I call the evil of the domestication of women. In some cases, the practice of surrogate mothering dehumanizes both birth mother and child.

I note how the electronic medium, in discussing these issues, caters to the entertainment of society's emotional instincts that seek to satisfy an immediate, personal need. The godly medium, however, informs us how to place divine will above the personal, and in the process it shapes our lives for the long haul. By invoking the divine will here, I wish to remind us that it is the voice of God in the desert that sustained Hagar in her moment of great grief as her son gave what she thought was his last cry. Even so does God sustain us in our greatest moments of anguish by offering to us the divine Presence.

Prayer: *Let me hear of your steadfast love in the morning,*
            for in you I put my trust.
        Teach me the way I should go,
            for to you I lift up my soul. Amen.

Wednesday, June 16   Read Psalm 86:1-10; 16-17.

Hebrew tradition attributes this psalm to David, and although we may never be able to determine the circumstances that occasioned its writing, we can identify with the lament of the supplicant. For, it will always remain true that godly people suffer, despite the wisdom tradition which informs us that righteousness begets wealth and averts want. The continual daily cry of the poor and needy for God to deliver the means for their subsistence strikes us as being particularly absurd when those means are delivered, instead, to the very ones who defy God and assail the faithful.

In circumstances like these the question is, ought one to give up trusting in God's power to control human affairs? The answer, we conclude, comes in the psalmist's unshaken confidence and proven experience that in the final analysis wicked rulers and nations will be humbled and God's name will be glorified (Ps. 86:9). This answer appears fanciful to the modern mind, socialized as it is to take the responsibility to correct human-created injustice.

Indeed, the very message of Christianity calls for such action already exemplified in the life of Jesus who declared that he came "to preach good news to the poor,...to proclaim release to the captives and recovering of sight to the blind, to set at liberty those who are oppressed, to proclaim the acceptable year of the Lord" (Lk. 4:18-9, RSV).

But how often one finds that human efforts are overcome by the massive accumulation of global evil! In the face of such overwhelming odds faithful champions of justice can, like the psalmist, beseech God to give us strength to withstand the oppressor.

Prayer: *Pray Psalm 86:10, 16-17.*

179

Thursday, June 17   Read Romans 6:1*b*-5.

The words of our text for today take us into the mind of the apostle Paul as he invokes the sacrament of baptism to describe the problem of sin. We should not ignore the context preceding in 5:18-21 where Paul addresses the human condition of sin caused by one man, Adam, and the removal of that condition by one man, Jesus. No matter how gross the acts of sin Paul declares, God's forgiveness is more abundant. But sensing the need to correct any misreading arising from his emphasis on the abundance of God's grace to cover sin, Paul gives the explanation we find today's meditation: our baptism symbolizes our break with sin and our walk with Jesus.

On the basis of Romans 5:20, the Russian monk, Gregory Rasputin, taught that salvation becomes more effectual when the sinner becomes more indulgent before he or she repents. The idea here is that those who have more to repent for receive more grace and hence a greater sense of joy.

We scoff, rightly, at Rasputin's literalism. But isn't a part of many of our religious communities replete with cases of new converts being used to "display" their former life of sin? In every instance one gets the impression that the spectacle is created to highlight how much more efficacious is their forgiveness than that of those whose only testimony is that God impresses them to surrender their place of comfort and privilege and work for the destitute and homeless.

Would that we learn the truth about sin: that its seriousness lies not in its quantity but rather in the qualitative separation that it creates between us and God.

Prayer: *"O LORD, you have searched me and known me" (Ps. 139:1).*

180

Friday, June 18   Read Romans 6:6-11.

In reading today's text we come across, once again, the slave metaphor that we encountered so often in the readings for the week. Here, the power of sin over the individual Paul describes as a state of enslavement. It appears that he knows of nothing more tyrannical with which to compare sin domination than the institution of slavery.

The imagery here is one of a body of persons held captive, for in the language of verse 7 only death can free the body from the captivity of sin. Paul has in view, of course, the spiritual death which goes into effect at one's baptism, an act that symbolizes death to sin because one has renounced it and resurrection to a new life in God because one has pledged to live godly.

Every act of sin we commit is with our body either against itself or against others; and even when the act is against someone else we do not escape the mental trauma that accompanies guilt. This fact, if no other, should give us reason to pause and reflect on the tyranny we place upon the human body as it cries out daily to be released from the tyrannical reign of sin.

If we show concern for social justice by working for the eradication of oppression, then the slavery metaphor for our bodily captivity to sin should serve to sensitize us to the freedom that our bruised body seeks to enjoy. The advantage in this instance is that we are masters and mistresses of our bodies and as such are uniquely positioned to grant that freedom from sin.

Prayer: *God, give us faith to accept your assurance that our lives would be better under your control, and then strengthen our resolve to live for your cause. Amen.*

Saturday, June 19   Read Matthew 10:24-33.

Those who work for social reform, particularly as it re-
lates to social justice, are bound to encounter opposition
from people who benefit from the status quo. It is this hard fact
that occasions the words of our text for today, in which Jesus
warns his disciples that the call to discipleship involves great
risks: family dislocations, derisive name-calling, persecution,
and even death. But in outlining the consequences, Jesus assures
his disciples that it is not the enemy and persecutor of whom
they need be afraid, but rather God who demands right action.

In the Greco-Roman world where society placed a very high
premium on class status, Jesus' call for his disciples to identify
with his mission was crucial, for only by identifying with Jesus
and his cause would he be able to represent them before God as
deserving a place in the kingdom of God (Matt. 10:32-33).

Christians today who claim to be Jesus' modern disciples
are faced with similar opposing demands from society and
Jesus. On the one hand there is the pressure to gain prestige
in society, which often seems to require a blindness to
suffering and injustice. On the other hand, there is the call to
eradicate injustice in our midst. Those who heed the call of
Jesus identify with him and the Beelzebul epithet. We are
well acquainted with the derisive epithets hurled at those
whites who worked resolutely for the civil rights of blacks;
we recall with shame the murder of young civil rights
workers and assassinations of civil rights leaders. These
modern disciples received contempt from society; but, I
believe, they will receive final approbation as Jesus
remembers them before God.

Prayer: *Lord, grant us holy discernment that we may know those
instances of oppression that need the reform of your justice; and
give us the courage to work toward those ends. Amen.*

Sunday, June 20   Read Matthew 10:34-39.

A profound paradox is that Jesus' message of peace, though not inherently violent, threatens the existing social order in a manner that triggers a violent response from the powerful. As Jesus discerns it, when all the powers of darkness are unleashed everywhere against his disciples of peace, family ties, the most cherished of relationships, will be broken.

It is significant that Matthew arranges this passage immediately after the one describing the master-slave relationship in the Greco-Roman world. Society that values human relationships, be they social or economic, on the classist model is not in harmony with the kingdom of God.

Today's reading lays down the consequences of peaceful attempts to address the evils and injustices of such a society. Family ties will be broken when betrayal becomes commonplace as Christians remain committed to the advancement of God's kingdom on earth. It is a scenario reminiscent of the period and words of the prophet, Micah (7:5-6). As Jesus describes it, violence against the peacemakers will result in the "sword" and the "cross," symbols of execution.

The violence of oppression in today's world is the result of the greedy seizure of the planet's resources and the partitioning of its people to benefit the powerful. Many modern prophets against this injustice (such as Gandhi, Martin Luther King, Jr., Steve Biko, Jean Donovan, and Oscar Romero) have been silenced by the bullet. We are left mourning the loss of such prophets, while seeking to know our place in changing the tide of such oppression.

Prayer: *O God, show us how to be peacemakers, according to your will, in a world rift with violence. Strengthen us with the courage of Christ that we may be your intercessors and peacemakers in today's world. Amen.*

THE TEST OF FAITHFULNESS

June 21-27, 1993   **Jane Allen Middleton**✤
Monday, June 21   Read Genesis 22:1-14.

God's faithfulness

"Take your son, your only son Isaac, whom you love, and go the land of Moriah." What kind of god would make such a requirement? What kind of god would then set Abraham and Isaac free? And what of the obedience of Abraham? The account gives no evidence of resistance or even anguish. Was he foolish? An unloving father? Obedient? Faithful? His obedience was rewarded. "Do not lay your hand on the boy...for now I know that you fear God."

How often does it happen in life that one is "put to the test"? Certainly the blows of living sometimes feel like a test: the death of a loved one; sudden loss of a job or lack of adequate employment to meet daily needs; overwhelming health problems; feeling helpless when friends are burdened; signs of injustice manifested in people dying of starvation, economic hardship, and struggles for freedom.

The story surprises us with its powerful, happy ending. We can almost see Abraham and Isaac in a wondrous embrace of joy. The message is, "This God does not ask for human sacrifice. God will provide the sacrifice."

The broader message to us is: God can be trusted to provide. Can we hear that message? It is a hard one when the resolution does not come immediately or is not one we would choose. Yet, faithfulness is rewarded.

Prayer: *Creator God, help me to trust, even when I cannot see or understand, that you are with me. Amen.*

✤Senior pastor, New Canaan United Methodist Church, New Canaan, Connecticut.

Tuesday, June 22   Read Genesis 22:1-2.

Whom do you love?

As I gazed upon the precious face of my infant daughter, I was in awe of the miracle of her. I realized that life without her would have no meaning whatsoever. She was the center of my life. With a start I thought, "Have I made her my 'God'?" In a sense I had. Neither she nor I could survive the pressure such expectations would put on our relationship. Yet, by simply asking myself that question, I was able to put my love for her in perspective. At the same moment I realized I loved her profoundly, I knew I loved God even more.

God asks of every one of us, "Take your child, whom you love and…offer him.… " To do less is to impose upon that child a life which is out of balance. We are not, of course, talking about offering our children as sacrifices to God—not at all! But we are talking about offering them into God's care, rather than making them—or whoever or whatever is most precious to us—the very center of our lives.

More importantly, God is asking us to offer ourselves, to offer our deepest yearning and allegiance. God requires nothing less than our central loyalty.

God asks us to be very clear about who *is* our God, who *is* finally the center of life. God requires our ultimate allegiance. The redemption in this story is that God does not ask us to sacrifice our children. Rather, God asks us to give ourselves.

Prayer: *Holy God, you and you only you are the center of life. To you I offer myself and all that I have in joyful and willing obedience to your yearning for my wholeness. Amen.*

185

Wednesday, June 23   Read Matthew 10:40-42.

God's generosity

I was one of a group on retreat in Cuernavaca, Mexico. A part of the retreat experience was to spend time with people who were struggling to live faithfully despite difficult circumstances. We walked across a deep ravine to a remote hillside with several scattered makeshift dwellings. It was a hot day, and we had climbed down a steep hill, across a precarious foot bridge, and up the other side. As we made this trek we were keenly aware that everyone who lived in this area had to bring everything—all food, all household goods, even water—by foot, along this same path.

One of those on retreat was overcome by what seemed to be heat exhaustion. Another of our group hurried to a nearby house, hoping to get help. As I looked up, I saw running toward us a little girl with a clean cloth and a basin of very precious water. That day we were recipients of "a cup of cold water." Comforted by a cool, damp cloth on her forehead, our companion revived, and we completed our visit.

The instructions of Jesus in today's scripture reading are similar to those found in Mark 9:41 and remind us of the relationship between Jesus and those who come in the name of Jesus. He challenges us to measure our discipleship by our willingness to give ourselves, not only by word but also by deed. Further, we are to receive others with the same spirit of openness and generosity. Do we receive others with a spirit of suspicion? Jesus is challenging us to receive willingly and to respond by offering all that we can, even a cup of precious water. To do so is in reality to receive Jesus.

Prayer: *Jesus, help me in faithful response to your call to give generously of myself to those in need and to receive your word with a willing, eager heart. Amen.*

Thursday, June 24   Read Matthew 10:40.

God present

"Whoever welcomes you welcomes me, and whoever welcomes me welcomes the one who sent me." With these words, Jesus is inviting all of us to live with a welcoming heart, looking at every moment of life for the presence of Christ.

To live with a welcoming heart requires, first of all, living with a constant awareness of the presence of Christ, to live "practicing the presence of Christ." One way to practice the presence is to live in an attitude of prayer. Paul said, "Pray without ceasing" (1 Thess. 5:17). In our fast-paced secular world such instruction seems impossible to fulfill. Yet a very simple prayer technique can assist in the awareness of Christ. A word or short phrase can become one's companion. The word might be discovered in daily scripture reading or in one's journey. In such a way, one "welcomes" Jesus.

Secondly, to live with a welcoming heart requires inviting Christ into every moment of life. Jesus yearns to participate in the heartache, in the struggle, in the "fray," in the joy, in the midst of the total living of one's life. How often when confronted by a crisis or even a problem, we look to many other coping mechanisms, many decision-making techniques, rather than looking first to Jesus. To truly welcome Jesus is to be open to the guidance offered in the midst of life and to turn to that guidance before any other.

Prayer: *Lord, I am your hands, your feet, your presence. Help me to live in such a way that I am always aware of the power you offer to me. May I respond with faithfulness in all of my life. Amen.*

Friday, June 25   Read Psalm 13.

God sustains

"How long, O LORD?" Four times that phrase rings out from the psalmist. "How long?" Isn't that a question many of us have asked?

A friend describes herself as a recovering workaholic, which is said to be the only socially acceptable addiction. In fact, workaholism is often admired and rewarded in our society. Yet workaholism, like every other addiction, leads finally to isolation. My friend often finds herself crying, "How long...?" What she confesses is that she must begin opening herself to the steadfast love that God is revealing all around her.

God is ever present. Even in the midst of the psalmist's laments, God did not move. To see with the eyes of faith is to become conscious of God's presence in every moment. Living the spiritual life is being attentive to the presence of God. That attentiveness assists us in moving beyond the trials and burdens of life. It draws us into communion with God.

When we take time to be attentive to God's presence, we are less likely to become enmeshed in concern for bearing pain, having sorrow in our heart, or feeling forgotten by God. Then we can become much more aware of God's "steadfast love" and the ways in which God deals bountifully with us.

Suggestion for meditation: *Consider recent weeks in your life. Reflect on a moment when you were particularly aware of God's presence—perhaps a moment of joy, or struggle, or sorrow. Relive that moment, and offer a prayer. As you increase your awareness of these "God moments," you will increase your awareness of God's presence in every moment.*

Saturday, June 26   Read Psalm 13:1, 5-6.

Believing during tough times

The structure of this psalm, which is a lament by an individual, includes the complaint, the appeal, and the expression of confidence in God's help. These could be said to be the stages of struggle. They perfectly match my own experience of life. A crisis happens and I complain to God that such an event has befallen me. I then beg God to hear my prayers and grant me freedom. Finally, I achieve some sense of peace.

In the midst of a crisis, it is sometimes difficult to trust in God's steadfast love and salvation. When I look back at my whole life journey I can say without exception that the Lord "has dealt bountifully with me." But when I am in the midst of crisis, I am more likely to cry out "Will you forget me forever? / How long must I bear pain in my soul?" In the midst of the crisis, God has not yet revealed *how* I will be dealt with bountifully. The pleadings of the psalmist resonate with my own pleadings.

Too often the pain of being in a desperate, desolate place is exacerbated by a feeling of guilt. "If only I had more faith I would not feel such despair." To realize that I am not alone in complaints and pleadings to God is comforting. The psalmist has gone before me, saying, "How long, O LORD?"

The good news is that the place of despair is not the last place, or "the last word." Rather, the last word is the reassurance of God's steadfast love. God is faithful. We are not alone.

Prayer: *Even in my times of despair, O God, help me to trust in your steadfast love. Protect and guide me in your way. I will sing to you because you deal bountifully with me. Amen.*

Sunday, June 27   Read Romans 6:12-23.

God conquers sin

This passage is a strong warning against sin. One clear definition of sin is that which separates one from self, neighbor, and God. Sin is the failure to accept one's acceptability, to acknowledge oneself as loved by God. Sin is any act that creates a barrier between persons, including acts of betrayal, injustice, injury, or derision. Sin is denial of God by thought or deed. The end of this sin truly is death—death to any possibility of new life.

As our world moves closer together, we may have an opportunity for greater reconciliation. Perhaps we can replace the Cold War hostility with a new understanding of the global community. God calls us to unity and to the possibility of using the wondrous resources of the earth for common good. Such is the gift of grace, a grace not cheap.

In *The Cost of Discipleship* Dietrich Bonhoeffer reflected, "Costly grace is the gospel which must be sought again and again, the gift which must be asked for, the door at which [one] must *knock*. Such grace is *costly* because it calls us to follow, and it is *grace* because it calls us to follow Jesus Christ. It is costly because it costs [us] our life, and it is grace because it gives [us] the only true life."[*]

The final, most significant symbol of victory over evil is the death and resurrection of Jesus Christ. Sin cannot prevail. New life is the "free gift of God, eternal life in Christ Jesus."

Prayer: *Help me, O Lord, to accept your love and acceptance of me and to live as a free being, bound only by the possibilities of your grace. Amen.*

---

*(SCM Press, Ltd., 1959), p. 35.

ASSUMPTIONS AND CHOICES

June 28–July 4, 1993   **Alec Gilmore**✢
Monday, June 28   Read Psalm 45:10-17.

This week we will look at ways that people's assumptions affect how they live and make choices, and at how God's interaction with people can challenge and change some of these.

We begin with Psalm 45, which, as most of the psalms, is difficult to date. Whether it goes back to the time of Abraham nobody knows. More than likely the ideas it presents and the assumptions it makes do go back that far.

On the surface it seems a straightforward secular poem, and for that reason there has often been a tendency to spiritualize it. As a psalm used by Israel, it could reflect their strong need to throw off anything "foreign" or alien to their current life. Therefore, Israel (the bride) must throw off everything that belongs to her past and all that is around her and give herself unreservedly to her Lord.

But it could equally be taken as a straight story of a king and his consort, in which case it may be seen as a reflection of the social and cultural assumptions of the day. It is a world in which not just the king but the male is supreme. Not only will his wife-to-be leave her people but she will actually be enjoined to forget them in favor of her husband's family. Her compensation is to be that she will have sons who will rule other lands. Her reward is to be that she will enjoy the loyalty of her new subjects.

Suggestion for meditation: *All cultures have good and bad points. List what you take for granted in your own culture.*
Prayer: *Lord, help me understand the good points in the culture I have inherited, but make me sensitive also to its failings. Amen.*

✢Baptist minister, West Sussex, England, and Baptist chaplain, Sussex University.

Tuesday, June 29 Read Genesis 24:34-38.

Abraham's instruction to the servant are very clear. It is not enough to find a wife for Isaac. She must be found back among Abraham's family. Nothing could be clearer. Nothing could have been more straightforward. But the consequences were far-reaching, and nobody could have foreseen them. They were inherent not so much in what was said or done as in what was assumed. Assumptions are like that.

Abraham assumed that Isaac must marry and that he had the right to choose a wife for his son. Isaac assumed he had to accept what was done on his behalf. Abraham assumed his daughter-in-law must come from his own people, and it was left to the servant to question what at least might happen if the one chosen said no.

Assumptions have their value, and we could not live without them. Imagine what life would be like if we had to stop and consider everything and present reasons for it. This assumption strengthened the family network in which Abraham and his descendants would live. They needed to know their roots and to feel the security that came from them.

And yet they have a down side as well. They could not know how future generations were going to find it both exclusive and troublesome. An elderly and wise Sri Lankan once said to me that 90 percent of the world's problems were due to people making the wrong assumptions.

Suggestion for meditation: *Select one or two of the assumptions on the list you made yesterday and try to assess their consequences to see whether they are good of bad.*

Prayer: *Lord, help me to examine some of the things I take for granted and to work out their consequences for today and for the future. Amen.*

Wednesday, June 30   Read Genesis 24:42-49.

The method the servant uses to choose a wife for Isaac will be interpreted differently by different people. Putting out a fleece (Judges 6:36ff). An answer to prayer. Potluck! An abdication of responsibility. All are possible descriptions and explanations, according to one's viewpoint.

But what is clear is that we have now moved away from a world dominated exclusively by assumption. Assumptions alone are not enough. They cannot find the future wife. The servant must think it through and plan a new strategy. Rationality begins to creep in. Question marks appear alongside assumptions. How to choose? What happens if her family says no?

As the servant reflected on his mission while he traveled, he came to see that loyalty meant finding a wife who was loving and of a generous disposition; in short, someone who was willing not only to observe the basic assumption of her culture by responding to the needs of a stranger but also was prepared to go beyond the assumption (the second mile) by drawing water for the camels as well.

Rebekah had no idea that in simply discharging the normal duties of the day and living as she believed she ought to live she was shaping not only her own destiny but that of succeeding generations also. That is what happens when assumptions become tempered by reason.

Suggestion for meditation: *Choose one assumption from your list and see if you can discover how it may be strengthened by reason.*

Prayer: *Lord, teach me today that it is in the ordinary things and the way I take them for granted that I shape my life and that of others. Help me to see that I must think carefully when I have a choice to make. Amen.*

Thursday, July 1   Read Genesis 24:58-67.

Rebekah has a choice of a different sort. Will she go with this man or not? But how are we to read her response? Was it really as quick, simple, and decisive as it reads; or is this the brevity of a reporter who summarizes in one sentence events that took place over hours, days, or even weeks? Were there no questionings? no heartaches? no soul-searchings? We shall never know. But what comes ringing through loud and clear is that for Rebekah, choice is acceptance, as indeed it was for Mary two thousand years later (Luke 1:38). Rebekah's choice is the choice to obey, to love, to sacrifice, and to take life as it comes, even if that means alienation from her family and personal suffering.

The nature of the sacrifice is different for different people. In Rebekah's case it was a clear recognition that there are times when new life today is possible only if you are prepared to make a conscious break with yesterday. This was what Abraham found difficult to do with all his assumptions. They were like shackles around his feet, rooting him forever and a day to where he was. Rebekah had the capacity to break away, and it was that break which enabled her new life to begin and helped her to be the means of bringing new life to others, as, indeed, it was for Jesus when he began his ministry.

Suggestion for meditation: *What must I let go of from the past so that I may be able to accept the new life that the Lord offers me today? When you have named these, ask the Lord to help you move into the gift of new life through Christ.*

Prayer: *Lord, help me break with the past that keeps me in chains and to grasp the new life you are waiting to give me. Then help me build on that foundation day by day. Amen.*

Friday, July 2 Read Romans 7:15-25*a*.

By now we have moved a long way from the world of Abraham and Isaac. Stories and people have given way to ideas and theology. Many of the old assumptions have been questioned at some time or other, and not least by Jesus. New assumptions and new priorities have also come on the scene. By the time we get to Paul in the Epistle to the Romans, rationality has almost taken over. *Almost*, but not quite!

And that is the problem. What happens when assumption and reason are in conflict? Men no longer assume a responsibility to love and care for their wives. Women no longer meekly accept a destiny in their husbands' houses. Some even speak up in church! The search for reasons is on, and assumption and reason challenge each other. And that is only one example.

Inside Paul there is a much bigger battle raging in a different way. On all rational grounds certain things ought to happen, but they do not. Or if they do, they do not occur in the way we might expect. Paul knows the rules. He intends to keep them. But there is something there beyond the reason that turns even his best endeavors to dross.

What Paul has to discover is a new kind of acceptance. It is the acceptance of himself, just as he is, "warts and all," and the realization that if only he can accept Christ, Christ will accept him and forgive. Then he may be able to accept himself.

Prayer: *Father God, help me accept the things in myself and in others that I cannot change, as you in Christ have accepted me. Amen.*

Saturday, July 3   Read Matthew 11:16-19.

If accepting yourself is one problem, accepting other people can be more of a problem, especially when they do not make the standard responses. If they reject your arguments, you can at least reason with them, but what if they do not even have your basic assumptions?

If music is *your* life and you make music for others, it is reasonable to expect some response. If you offer dance music, it is reasonable to expect people to dance. If they don't dance because they say they are in mourning, then it is reasonable to respond to them by finding someone to comfort them. But if they then say they don't want to be comforted, it is difficult to know what to do next.

This, it seems to me, was the experience first of John the Baptist and later of Jesus with their contemporaries—only it had very little to do with dancing or mourning. It had much more to do with their assumptions. Their contemporaries didn't start in the same place, for all sorts of reasons. They were brought up in a different generation. They were afraid of where the teachings of John and of Jesus might lead, for they had a very different agenda.

When we meet people like that, we are often tempted to get angry or to dismiss them. But sometimes, if we can see behind their behavior to their assumptions, we can experience spiritual growth and a new relationship with that person or persons.

Suggestion for prayer: *Pray for someone whom you find difficult, and ask God to help you better understand that person that you may reach out to them in care and ministry.*

Prayer: *Lord, help me better understand those who do not begin where I do and to be tolerant of those who never seem to understand me. Amen.*

Sunday, July 4   Read Matthew 11:25-30.

Do we detect a note of cynical exasperation with the "learned" and the "wise" when Jesus begins his prayer? It would hardly be surprising! It is not that the learned and the wise are incapable of understanding or of response. Rather, in their cleverness they have so many defenses they can call up to protect themselves. They know how to dig behind any assumptions and to reason them almost out of existence.

It often seems that more straightforward people, by contrast, live out of very different assumptions. They are sometimes described as innocent, sometimes naive. They seem to have a certain vulnerability. Yet such people often have an openness which makes them receptive to others as well as to ideas.

In a way we end this week where we began it, with someone who accepts and trusts, even to the point of sacrifice and suffering, rather than one who questions. Except, now it is not someone accepting and trusting because he or she has *never* questioned the assumptions. It is someone who has raised all the questions and challenged all the assumptions and yet can still, through faith in God and God's plan for humanity, trust and accept others and their ideas.

Maybe Jesus himself was in that category, and it is because of his straightforward acceptance of the cross that he has so much to offer to us all.

Prayer: *Lord, I accept your yoke. May it be easy to wear, and may my burden be light. Amen.*

JACOB: A CHEATER'S INHERITANCE

July 5-11, 1993
Monday, July 5

Betsy Schwarzentraub✞
Read Genesis 25:19-26.

"If it is to be this way, why do I live?"

For twenty long years, Rebekah and Isaac had waited for a child—and was it all for this? In the overwhelming pain of her pregnancy, she prayed in anguish as the children fought within her.

God's response was both a comfort and a warning. Her babies would sire two nations! But the two peoples they would become would war against each other.

Even in birth, the twins fought. As Esau emerged, Jacob grabbed hold of his heel, to make his brother do all the work! While Jacob's name actually means, "May God protect," it was others who needed protection from him. No wonder the storyteller changed a dot or two in the Hebrew to say the name "Jacob" comes from 'ageb, meaning "heel!"

Raising children is hard enough when we expect family unity. But what do we do when those we love prefer to fight and deceive? How do we care for a fragmented family? Can we love both parties when they're in conflict? At times we may join Rebekah in feeling overwhelmed.

God's anguish over us is greater than any human parent's anguish, for often we violate the bonds for which we were created, that is, to live as God's family, true sisters and brothers.

Suggestion for meditation: *How can I help heal divisions in my home? my church? my community?*

✞Church consultant; clergy member of the California-Nevada Conference; Davis, California.

Tuesday, July 6   Read Genesis 25:27-34.

It is not that Jacob was evil. He simply knew how to get others to give what he wanted—and what he really wanted was Esau's inheritance. With a custom by which all family property went to the firstborn son, Jacob knew he would have to trade Esau for his birthright and then deceive his father for the blessing.

One day, a famished Esau burst in upon Jacob's presence just as he was cooking a mouth-watering stew. After a long day of luckless hunting, Esau would give anything for a tasty bowl of it.

Here was Jacob's opportunity. Without warning, he asked his brother, "Will you sell me your birthright for a bowl of this?" (AP)

Now, it is not that Esau thought so little about his birthright, but that just then he was thinking more about his survival. Letting hunger dictate his priorities, he said yes.

"Swear it to me first," retorted Jacob, knowing that oaths were inviolate.

So it was a double deception: not only did Esau lose his claim to being firstborn but neither did he get meat stew! What Jacob had been cooking was nothing more than red bean soup, cooked to look like the real thing.

Eager for a full inheritance, we may find ourselves in a scheming soup of deceptive relationships. Sometimes like Jacob, we want to have it all, both position and possessions. Other times like Esau, we give away what is valuable for a mere illusion of what is good. Yet, God loves us even in the midst of such games. God loves us and offers us a more authentic way to live.

Suggestion for meditation: *When have I been like Jacob? Like Esau? How could I be more truthful in my relationships?*

Wednesday, July 7   Read Genesis 27:18-38.

Despite Esau's increased wariness against his brother after the sellout over soup, Jacob tricked Esau again. This time Jacob took something far more valuable: Esau's full inheritance, given through the blessing of his father.

Isaac knew the time for blessing Esau had come. He told Esau to hunt some game, and then fix him a bowl of stew before receiving the blessing. With that blessing would come the home and everything that Isaac and Rebekah owned, as well as rank over all of Esau's brothers and sisters.

Overhearing this, Jacob went back to the kitchen to fix some more scheming soup. He scented himself with game fat, to smell like his hunter brother. Then he put hairy goatskin over his hand so that Isaac might not feel his smooth skin and know him to be Jacob.

As Jacob entered his father's home, nearly blind Isaac asked, "Who are you, my son?"

"I am Esau," Jacob said.

Because Jacob could not mask his voice, once again his father asked, "Are you really Esau?"

Jacob replied, "I am."

So Jacob received what Isaac had meant for Esau: not a mutual sharing of assets, but an all-or-nothing plan. Jacob got it all, and Esau got nothing. Discovering the deception too late, Esau wept in rage. "Jacob is his real name, all right," he said, "for he has supplanted me in my right to your inheritance, and has deceived me now twice over!"

Suggestion for meditation: *Have I ever misled or deceived those who trusted me? How can I change my focus from what I can get, to what I can give? Is there anything that is worth violating human ties in order to gain?*

Thursday, July 8   Read Genesis 33:1-17.

Dawn finally broke upon an exhausted, limping man. No longer Jacob, now he was named Israel, meaning "the one who wrestles with God."

In his wrestling he had not won out over God's sovereignty. Yet strangely God's victory was his own, for in the darkest hour of night—in confession of his hidden, feared self—had come his true dawn: a personal relationship at last with this fiercely forgiving God.

Israel looked around him in awe. "I shall call this place Peniel," he said, which means "the face of God." "For I have seen God face to face, and my life is preserved."

Now he could face Esau with the truth. His fear as great as before, now he would cling to whatever was left of his brother's love.

This is the irony: It is precisely when we have given up everything, when we know ourselves as hopeless, that God's love sustains us and builds bridges between people.

So Israel at last offers Esau a blessing, or gift, in return: everything he had worked so hard to steal from others. It is all he has, offered, no longer as a bribe, but because in this newfound relationship with God he has everything he wants.

At last Israel sees Esau as his brother. Esau's forgiveness is a sheer gift of grace, which comes only from God. Seeing Esau's weeping eyes filled with love, anger, and forgiveness, Israel knows that Esau's face is the very face of God.

Through God's grace, for us all, even a cheater's inheritance is still the entire inheritance of God.

Prayer: *Dear God, I thank you for your grace! Struggle with me, I pray, until I struggle with You, to find the love which you have offered me all along.*

Friday, July 9   Read Psalm 119:105-112.

In contrast to Jacob and Esau's winner-take-all legacy, Psalm 119 speaks of an inheritance which cannot be diminished in the sharing. "Your decrees are my heritage," the psalmist cries. "They are the joy of my heart!"

Joy can well up from within, as our commitment grows. This is Israel's view of God's Law. The Hebrew term *Torah* does not mean "law" in a modern sense, but instead "instruction," "teaching." It is not merely a moral guide for the community of faith, but the entryway into a relationship of vital communion with our Creator.

In this psalm (as in Psalm 1; 15; 24), God's teaching is linked with creation. Just as every living thing depends upon God's power, faithfulness and grace, so the Torah expresses the very structure of life, and Israel's place within it. Even before it is a human response, the Torah is a gift of grace.

This gift is connected with God's Word. The Greek term for "Word" is *Logos,* meaning "order." Honoring the intricacy of God's creation, the poet followed a careful pattern of an eightfold acrostic poem, each eight-line section beginning with the same Hebrew letter. There is a delight in God's order here which calls us to reproduce it as far as possible in daily life.

At first this extraordinarily crafted psalm seems far removed from the struggles of Jacob. Yet Jacob first had to admit his greedy style in order to receive the inheritance of God's teaching, which this psalmist already claims.

Peace can come, even in the eye of a storm, when we say to God, "Give me life, O LORD, according to your word."

Suggestion for meditation: *What does God want to teach me? How can I claim what God has wanted to give me all along?*

Saturday, July 10   Read Romans 8:1-11.

How in the world could it have come to this? The young church of Paul's day had barely begun and already cultural issues were threatening to destroy it.

The division ran deep. Must a Christian follow all of Judaism's ceremonial laws? Rome had already survived a riot over Jewish-Christian relations, and clarity within the church required serious reflection. Paul's bottom line message was this: our acceptability before God is sheer gift. It cannot be earned in any way. We can accept God's acceptance of us only by trusting God's grace, beyond any laws.

So here Paul refers to the law, not as God's Torah, but as a religion which attempts to earn God's love. He speaks of the contrast between law and grace in terms of flesh and spirit.

Independence and self-sufficiency are what many people seek to achieve. Yet, when we strive for independence from God, our very Source of life and of new life as God's people, we become estranged from the One who is all grace. This is what Paul meant when he spoke of "the flesh."

We can choose, instead, to live "in the Spirit," in harmony with the pattern God created within us. The Spirit is God's activity in creation. This means that all who live "in the Spirit" are literally a part of God's movement in human life. When we choose this option we receive the fullness of life—not only after death, but also before it.

Cultural divisions and the desire to control our lives can threaten us today no less than they did the Roman Christians. Yet, when we focus our living on God's grace, even our smallest efforts fall into the right perspective.

Suggestion for meditation: *Where have I glimpsed the mystery and movement of God? How can I focus upon these things, and contribute to them through my living?*

Sunday, July 11   Read Matthew 13:1-9, 18-23.

Scholar and activist Clarence Jordan called a parable a "literary Trojan horse."[*] Like that great wooden wonder of ancient Greece, he said, we bring the parable into the court-yard, behind our defenses, for the common story that it seems to be. Yet, like the horse's hidden soldiers, once the parable is inside, its truth springs out unexpectedly. So it is with Jesus' parable of the sower.

We can identify with the sowing of seed. All of us de-pend upon the fruitfulness of crops to sustain our lives. We are concerned about having enough food, in a world where much land is poor, weather harsh, and distribution unequal. We are desperate for good seeds of abundant growth.

In this parable Jesus is not concerned with the sower or with the seed. He knows that the seed is life-giving, the seed that is the gospel, the good news of God's love. This seed Christ is spreading over the land, even now. The seed will sprout and grow, becoming enough crops, not merely for our subsistence, but for abundance.

Then comes the Trojan surprise! We are not to worry about seed or sower. Our concern is to be with the nature of the soil of our own lives. Are we receptive to God's word of love? Have we put our energies into growing useless but entertaining weeds? Have we dug deep furrows of confession to prepare for the gospel? As we face these questions, we find lasting answers to sustain one another with love.

Suggestion for meditation: *What do I allow to take root in my life? Where have I resisted the seeds of God's teaching? What needs to be rooted out of our faith community for us to receive God's presence and Word?*

---

[*]From *Cotton Patch Parables of Liberation* by Clarence Jordan and Bill Lane Doulos, A Herald Press Original., 38-42.

GOD IS FAITHFULLY PRESENT

July 12-18, 1993   **Minerva G. Carcaño✛**
Monday, July 12   Read Genesis 28:10-19*a*.

Jacob was aware of God's presence in his life, but what he experienced at Bethel surprised him. God entered his quiet time of sleep and dreams saying that God's presence wanted to be with him. God's promise of divine presence would impact Jacob's life and the lives of generations to come. Jacob could be sure of God's promise because of God's track record: as God had been with Abraham and Isaac, God would be present with Jacob.

And what a presence God promised! An alien to the land where he lives and a single man on his way to find a bride would—through God's presence in his life—become owner of the land and parent to a family that would extend to the four corners of the earth. And to think that all this became known to Jacob in the wilderness while he had nothing more than a rock for a pillow and the reaching of a neighboring province as his goal!

Even as Bethel was a place of divine surprise for Jacob, wherever we are in our own life journeys can become a sacred place for the revealing of God's presence.

Prayer: *Come, Divine Presence, and journey with us. Interrupt our steps and surprise us. Amen.*

✛Pastor, South Valley Cooperative Ministries, Albuquerque, New Mexico; clergy member of Río Grande Annual Conference of The United Methodist Church.

Tuesday, July 13   Read Psalm 139:1-6.

David must have been a man with many thoughts to preserve for just his knowing. His reputation pointed to actions that were best left forgotten. Even in those moments of splendor when he triumphed in wisdom and courage, he must have often longed for the comfort and rest of solitude.

Yet, there is one who penetrates David's every thought, his every movement, even his forthcoming emotions and responses: "O LORD, you have searched me and known me." David is conscious of the fact that he is totally and always surrounded by the presence of God. He could have rebelled at such an intrusion into his being. Instead, he rejoices, for while knowing God's presence as one of exhortation and judgment, of authority over his life, and as one who daily calls him to accountability, David has also experienced God's love. It is because God loves him that God chooses to be with him from the simplest to the most important hours of his living. And though God knows David in all his imperfection, God embraces him with love. God's choosing to be present with David is a wonderful blessing beyond David's comprehension.

Like David, we fall short of becoming the persons God wants us to be because of imperfections, weaknesses, and sin. And like David, God is present with us also. Though we shall always come out short in God's examination of our lives, God will not abandon us. Such is God's wonderfully incomprehensible love.

Suggestion for meditation: *Take a moment to be still. In the tradition of the psalmist, invite God to search you and know you. Take comfort in God's love that surrounds your every thought and movement.*

Wednesday, July 14   Read Psalm 139:7-12.

God's presence is not to be experienced only through the human heart and spirit. Indeed, all of creation gives witness to God's infinite and eternal dwelling in our midst. The psalmist recognizes that even a conscious effort to separate self from the Holy would be to no avail; for the heaven, the morning, the uttermost parts of the sea, darkness and light alike—even the remote abyss of Sheol—would declare that God is all around. And how is the psalmist encountered by God? The psalmist's own testimony is that God's extended hand leads him and God's right hand holds him.

What a blessing it is to know that the discerning of God's presence is not left simply to our own ability to find God. I am painfully aware of moments in my own life when I felt that God was absent and nowhere to be found. But always there has been a fellow or sister creature of God's handiwork who has helped me in my times of disbelief, bringing God close to me. I recall a rainstorm upon a cotton field that assured my tired body and weary spirit that God had not forgotten us sons and daughters, a bright sunlit morning that broke through the shadows of death with God's love, and a cool dusk that helped me to know God's presence in the turmoil of a failed marriage. Sisters and brothers, sometimes unbeknownst to them have also at important moments provided just the right word or expression of care to affirm God's presence in my life. Yes! In all things, in all places and spaces under God's creation, God is present!

Suggestion for meditation: *Consider God's creation all around you. What is creation saying to you about God's presence at this very moment in your life?*

Thursday, July 15   Read Psalm 139:23-24.

It is one thing to reach out to God in times of struggle or in an hour of thanksgiving. It is quite a different matter to invite God in to examine our hearts and thoughts and to uncover what is wicked and evil within us. The psalmist was truly a brave person to bare himself in such a way before God, thus running the risk of being condemned for any wickedness within his being. But the psalmist also knew God's compassion that faithfully and with constancy leads in the way everlasting.

The psalmist's brave stand is possible because as he stands trusting in God's compassionate and forgiving ways, his deepest desire is to be made perfect through God's intervention in his life. The psalmist's earnest hope is to be of clean heart and pure thought. The psalmist recognizes that only God can perfect him thus and enable him to walk in perfect communion with the Creator.

As human beings we have been given the capacities for thought and action. Persons can grow in their understanding of right and wrong and direct their thoughts and actions in ways that lead to righteousness. In this growth process I have at times caught myself thinking that through my own wisdom, sensitivity, and desire to do what is right, I can perfect my being and living. The psalmist's words cast loving judgment upon my life.

Only God can fully see our weaknesses and wrongs and make clear for us the way everlasting. While there is much each of us can do to achieve right living, God's participation with us is absolutely necessary. Are we ready to invite God in to reveal to us our failings and to help us to perfection?

Prayer: *"Search me, O God, and know my heart; test me and know my thoughts."* Amen.

208

Friday, July 16   Read Romans 8:12-17.

While God's presence in our lives is constant, experiencing its fullest blessings requires that we be willing to be shaped and led by the divine Spirit.

In no greater way does God's presence manifest itself than in the cross of Jesus Christ. Christ himself is the measure of God's love and mercy for us. Through Christ's death and resurrection God's intent for humanity—life—is made evident. The fullness of life and life eternal, however, are left to human choice. Only through Jesus can we experience such a gift, but it is a gift that we must be open to receiving. We can receive the gift and live according to God's spirit and have life; or, we can reject the gift and live according to our own sinful desires and face death.

Living for life, living by the Spirit as scripture says, is a willingness to be shaped by the Christian disciplines of love, mercy, justice, and peace. It is a disposition toward being led by what Christ would do were he in our place. This living God assures us of support beyond ourselves.

While we are yet pulled by human sinfulness that tends to enslave us, God frees us from the slavery of sin and unrighteousness by making us God's own. With Christ we are made children and thus heirs of God. The power that lifted Jesus from death is also ours when we live as Jesus lived.

May the spirit of God that was with Jesus and is with us be our guide and our strength.

Suggestion for mediation: *Give thought to what is happening in your life and ministry. What would Jesus do were he in your place? Remember that as you turn to Jesus for guidance he offers you his power.*

Saturday, July 17   Read Romans 8:18-25.

After having recently given birth to a daughter, the imagery of creation groaning in labor pains is painfully yet joyfully real for me. The broader picture of humanity joining the rest of creation and together anticipating a birth of redemption excites me and fills me with hope.

The apostle Paul paints a vision as only he can. The fulfillment of God's promise of glory and freedom from bondage and decay for those who are faithful is coming. It is like giving birth though. We and all of creation feel growth in the womb of our spirit, but the child is yet to arrive. In the meantime we struggle with change and the pain that it causes. Like a pregnant woman who observes her changing body and feels the burden of her seed, what keeps us trusting and hoping is that there is no denying that something meaningful is occurring. We have experienced the first fruits of God's presence through the Holy Spirit who promises us glory.

In the travail and pain of giving birth a woman has a hard time seeing glory, but the hope of holding her child in her arms keeps her struggling. If we can just keep struggling in hope despite the sufferings that we may encounter, glory will be born and bless our lives, and it will be known that we are daughters and sons of God.

Prayer: _Lord, stay be our side and give us the patience to wait for the birth of glory. Allow your spirit to bear fruit in our spirit that hope may abound. Amen._

Sunday, July 18   Read Matthew 13:24-30, (36-43).

Though God may be present in our world, it is tough sometimes to stand in goodness because evil seems to grow and prosper all around us. The condition of the world we live in pushes us to want to declare to God with the servants of the parable, "...did you not sow good seed in your field? Where, then, did these weeds come from?" The underlying question is, "God, where are you?"

God's response, according to the parable, is that God is present and aware of what is happening but also has a sense of God's own time. When God determines that it is harvest time, the good and the bad will be dealt with appropriately. God is with us and is taking account of how we live. The question then becomes, "So, where are we?"

Are we able to stand firm as Christians even though sin prevails? Can we remain standing in the face of oppression, hate, violence, and destruction? If God be with us, can we wait for the harvest?

I confess that I too often focus on where God is while forgetting to check on where I am in relationship to God. It is precisely at these moments that I lose perspective and become overwhelmed by the evil that grows around me. As I reconsider my faith experience, I am reminded of the fact that God has been faithfully present in my life. It is God's merciful presence that makes life's weeds tolerable. By seeking to be in close relationship with God we will be among those to see a harvest of goodness.

Prayer: *Loving God, we thank you for your presence with us. We confess that we do not always give you of our presence. Forgive us and strengthen us with your abiding spirit, that we may someday reap with you the fruits of your blessings. Amen.*

211

FOUND IN GOD'S GRACE

July 19-25, 1993
Monday, July 19

Kil Sang Yoon✞
Read Genesis 29:15-28.

Ambition frustrated

Jacob is an ambitious person. When his ambition gets its way, he is willing to walk over his own father and brother. In his ardent desire to win his beloved, he is determined to work seven long years! He acts as if he could get whatever he desires on his own terms. But he is caught at a vulnerable time and is cheated. He is awakened to the realization that there are other peoples who live by different mores and customs.

Laban may have been wrestling with the predicament of the younger daughter about to be married before her elder sister. Laban may have tried, unsuccessfully, to persuade his nephew, "It's not the way we do here in our country."

A blind ambition can drive us to be extremely individualistic. Being controlled by one's desire to achieve a certain end, one tends not to care for others in a communal life. Jacob has pushed to get his own way to the point of bringing animosity to a filial relationship. Now he experiences the thwarting of his single-minded desires. He is found within the web of family traditions, customs of a community, and the desires of others. He has come to a new realization: he is not and cannot be the center of the world. A new horizon opens to him, and he has to find his place in God's community.

Prayer: *Gracious God, help me find my own place within the communal life with others and with you. Amen.*

✞Clergy member, East Ohio Conference, The United Methodist Church; on staff of United Methodist Board of Higher Education and Ministry, Division of Ordained Ministry, Nashville, Tennessee.

Tuesday, July 20   Read Genesis 29:15-18.

Not deceived but graced

When one is blinded with one's ambition, she/he is usually not ready to listen to others. As many concerned parents try to convey to their children what they think may be best for them, so, too, Laban may have tried to persuade his nephew to marry Leah first and then Rachel. But Jacob, knowing his own capability to deceive others for his gains, may not be able to accept the surface value of what Laban has tried to tell him. He insists on marrying Rachel, the younger.

Now Laban pulls his trick. When the wedding party runs into the late night, the concerned father uses his authority to send the older daughter in the place of the younger one to the groom's bosom. (Many of us shudder at this kind of custom practiced in the patriarchal society.) This father even tells the angered groom that he is ready to give his second daughter in a week, at the end of the wedding celebration.

When an unchecked ambition dulls the individual and collective conscience, an awakened spirit can help us find the interest of self, community, and country within the interrelated nature of life with God, others, and the natural world. If the Jacob in us tries to seek one's own interests at the expense of others, the Laban in our integrity reminds us of others' interests as well. Jacob is blinded by an individualistic attitude. Laban helps Jacob see that he is not isolated from the rest of the community. Jacob is found in the realm of grace generated by Laban's gracious giving and invitation to come back to the web of a communal life.

Prayer: *Grant us the wisdom, Lord, to understand that we do not live isolated lives, but that we are all part of a community. Amen.*

Wednesday, July 21   Read Romans 8:18-30.

Setting the groaning world free

Humans are caretakers of God's creation. We are entrusted with the responsibility for taking care of the natural world, including ourselves. But when we fail to be and do what God intends us to be and to do, the created nature suffers as "the victim of frustration" (NEB).

We are part of God's creation. Our life is only possible within a right relation with this created world. Both humans and the natural world are interconnected, interdependent, and interrelated. When we abuse nature, the whole creation, including ourselves, is endangered and God's intention in creation is thwarted. We are witnessing that all creation is under the assault of abuse and exploitation. We and the whole world are plagued and deprived; we suffer disconnectedness and brokenness. This fractured state needs to be mended, healed. The wholeness of creation must be restored.

For this ministry and mission, God has come to the world in Jesus to claim the whole nature as God's creation. God in Jesus, the Anointed, heals the brokenness between ourselves and others, between ourselves and nature, between ourselves and God, the Source of our life. In Christ we can be put right with each other, with the natural world, and with the Creator of all. God wants to set the groaning world free.

God invites us to participate as God's partners in this ministry of healing and restoring. As we respond to the call, we need to be convinced by God's call, empowered by God's spirit, and trained with wisdom and new skills. It is not always easy to be part of God's mission. It requires of us our complete submission to God's leading.

Suggestion for meditation: *Why has God chosen us? To what are we called?*

Thursday, July 22   Read Romans 8:31-39.

Strength for persevering

Being chosen is a privilege accompanied by responsibility. Those who are pulled into a covenant relationship with God are called to participate in the work of mending what is broken, healing the wounded, liberating the captives, and fighting injustice in the hope of restoring God's order to the fractured world.

This task often runs into conflict with the established order of the disconnected world. The vested interests of the legions resist the work to connect the broken pieces. The might of the resisting forces has tried to silence the voice of the prophets with seduction, bribery, and persecution. What can be the source of wisdom and strength for the chosen ones to stand tall in the face of various demonic powers?

Paul has experienced the transforming power of God in Jesus Christ. That is the source of Paul's strength to be a champion of God's cause. Trusting the God "who did not withhold his own Son, but gave him up for all of us," Paul has endured trials, hunger, insult, physical beatings, imprisonment, and threat of life. Paul's life is firmly rooted in the One who is the Maker and Ground of all being, the Lord of world history, known in Jesus's life, teachings, sufferings, death and resurrection and present with people as the sustaining, empowering Spirit. Paul utters boldly, "If God is for us, who is against us?'" And nothing, he says, "will be able to separate us from the love of God in Christ Jesus our Lord."

Suggestion for meditation: *Am I convinced by this faith? What is the degree of my conviction? Is it consistent, strong, and resilient to keep participating in God's redeeming work in the face of threatening forces?*

Friday, July 23   Read Matthew 13:24-43.

Are we not the salt and yeast?

When we are moved by the nudging spirit of God, we respond to God's leading. We are part in what God intends to achieve for the world. The more strongly we sense the call, the more eager we are to participate in God's mission as we perceive it. However, as we are enthused to do God's work, we may fall into the danger of identifying our positions with God's.

How often do we see that some groups of people use and abuse what they define as "God's will" to legitimize their own self-imposed role as "messiah"? Are we also guilty of this at times? When an individual, a group, or a nation in self-righteous enthusiasm thinks and acts as if they were the only chosen ones, the rest of the human families suffer as the objects to be "conquered," "corrected," and "civilized."

There are various situations where God's chosen ones must learn not to make hasty judgments of others' opinions, beliefs, behaviors, and cultural life as "pagan" simply because they are different from "our familiar ways of life." God, who calls and justifies, is the Creator and Redeemer of all the created world. We must not usurp God's being and doing.

What we each as Christians need to learn is how to become the salt and yeast for the world (see Matt. 5:13 and today's reading). We need to be like the smallest seed which is sown to grow as a large tree to offer shade and branches to others for the renewal of life.

Suggestion for meditation: *At what places are we blinded by our own self-interest to appropriate and abuse God's will? How can we become faithful agents of God's redeeming work?*

Saturday, July 24   Read Matthew 13:44-52.

Seeking the treasure and the pearl

How attractive are the values and norms of our culture! They direct our precious energy. They promise to fill our hunger and thirst. Such factors may be the major stumbling block to an intimate relationship between ourselves and the One who is the Ground and Source of our life. We need to be reconnected to this Source.

As we become immersed in the life-giving Source, we come to realize we have deeper yearnings which the perks of an affluent culture cannot fulfill. In this awakening we are challenged to sell or give away our valued goods and to buy the field where the real treasure is hidden. The "treasure" and "pearl" represent the kind of life which we can taste in our living relationship with God in God's reign. How aware are we that our yearnings can only be met by God?

In a secularly oriented society people of faith face many values different from their own, many seemingly "delightful" things that compete for attention, time, and energy. Surrounded by the things we have made, so often we feel dis-eased, fragmented, and regimented. We sense that we have lost wholeness within us and oneness with each other and nature. How can we restore this oneness with self, with others, and with the natural environment? Don't we need first to restore our oneness with the Ground of all?

We do need to set aside a certain amount of time daily to be in touch with self and God. There the old and new treasures are waiting for us, for the nurture of our souls.

Suggestion for meditation: *How does my life-style interfere with my relationship with God? How have I let the values of my culture affect my relationship with others? with the environment? What is one small step I can take as a first step toward wholeness?*

217

Sunday, July 25   Read Psalm 105:1-11, 45*b*.

"Let the hearts of those who seek the LORD rejoice!"

A myriad of events and things competes for our energy! As we attend to numerous aspects of our contemporary living, we experience dissipation of energy and famine and a dryness of soul. We often feel as if we are drifting aimlessly.

Sunday is the day of re-creation, of resurrection, of a new beginning. Once again we are called to be aware of God's presence with us as the Source of energy and wisdom. Psalm 105 reminds us of God's faithfulness to the chosen through the generations. The worship in Christian community brings us together to reiterate and to remember God's saving acts through the ages. Christian worship is an event where God's marvelous deeds of creation, covenant making, guidance, and liberation are reenacted as a new reality. In corporate worship, as we remember who God is and what God does, we experience that we are re-membered, renewed, revitalized. We are awakened by the fact of who and what we are, where and when we are, and *whose* we are after all.

In this rediscovery of our lot in God's household, we are compelled to respond in thanksgiving and praise, glorifying and proclaiming who God is and what God has been doing.

Do we try to attend to too many things in our daily living? Have we been completely inundated by the trivial, leaving the essential unattended? Let us respond to God's gracious invitation to come to the feast of grace!

Suggestion for meditation: *Take an uninterrupted time alone with God in recollecting and remembering what God means to you. Jot down a list of what God has been doing for you, your family, and the larger world community in recent years. Find some meaningful ways to praise and glorify God's deeds and offer thanksgivings to God.*

OUR STRUGGLES, GOD'S SURPRISES

July 26–August 1, 1993   **Richard L. Morgan**✢
Monday, July 26   Read Genesis 32:22-31.

In a small group participants shared their faith journeys. I asked them to think of their lives as a book and to give that book a title. One said, "I would call my book *Struggles and Surprises,* since my whole life has revolved around repeated crises. But God has surprised me with redemptive endings."

Jacob must have reflected on his life journey in those long hours between midnight and dawn at Peniel. From all appearances, his struggles seemed to end in success. He had gained the birthright and blessing, had outwitted Esau, and had finally won the hand of his beloved. It reminds me of the promise of our own decade just past: "You can have it all."

But Esau still awaited his revenge. The next dawn might be Jacob's last. In the long struggle of the night, Jacob was surprised by the strength of his unknown assailant, whom he later recognized as God. Tenaciously holding on, he cried out, "I will not let you go, unless you bless me." His surprise was that *God* would not let *him* go until he was blessed.

The blessing was a gift, not an achievement. As Frederick Buechner wrote, "Power, success, happiness, as the world knows them, are his who will fight for them hard enough; but peace, love, joy are only from God."[*] In our struggles we, too, may find ourselves blessed with such gifts.

Prayer: *God, our refuge and strength, in all our struggles may we be surprised by joy and peace. Amen.*

---

[*]*The Magnificent Defeat* (New York: The Seabury Press, 1979), p. 18.
✢Interim minister to churches in the Presbytery of Western North Carolina, The Presbyterian Church (U.S.A.); consultant on aging; Lenoir, North Carolina.

219

Tuesday, July 27   Read Genesis 32:31.

I watched him limp on crutches to the pulpit to give his witness. Surgery for a massive brain tumor had left his speech slurred, his vision and hearing partly gone. His courage and contagious humor deeply moved us. "I have learned two lessons from this experience," he said. "Pain is inevitable but misery is optional, and I chose not to despair; and God can use any ordeal as a blessing."

Jacob left that midnight struggle at Peniel with a decided limp. Jacob seemed to be winning the battle through the dark hours of the night, but then suddenly the Stranger touched the hollow of Jacob's thigh, and Jacob was helpless. It was almost as if the Stranger held back until the last, allowing him to use every ounce of his strength, so that Jacob would know the defeat was final.

Only later did Jacob realize that his adversary was God. Was God's presence, then, best known in pain and difficulty? The new person who crossed the Jabbok at dawn was no longer Jacob, the wheeler-dealer, but Israel, the wounded healer. He was broken, yet reborn; crippled, yet crowned.

Our brokenness can be a place of new beginnings. The hurt places in our lives tell our stories—of broken relationships, shattered dreams, physical handicaps. We limp into the future, but like Jacob, we can become new persons. Perhaps it is in just such moments God initiates new beginnings.

The greatest surprise of history occurred when Jesus stumbled out of the tomb into the light of the Resurrection morning. Later Christ showed the disciples the wounds of death that were the beginning of eternal life.

Suggestion for meditation: *What are the experiences of your life which have been most difficult? In the light of God's redeeming power, how have those experiences blessed you? blessed others?*

Wednesday, July 28   Read Psalm 17:1-5.

She told me that her life had been shattered when her husband of thirty years walked out on her. "For a few hours last night I couldn't sleep, replaying the old scenario of our broken marriage," she lamented. "I felt betrayed and angry."

Walter Brueggeman says that the driving power of the psalms are experiences of disorientation and reorientation which characterize human life. Psalm 17 is a lament of a person whose life has fallen apart, devastated by some over-powering enemies. This person cries for vindication and justice. "May my vindication come from you; may your eyes see what is right" (NIV).

As the psalm unfolds, the painful disorder becomes less intense, and in its place, a quiet change. The psalmist discovers the incredible security found in God. "Keep me as the apple of your eye; hide me in the shadow of your wings" (v. 8). No satisfaction for the complaint ever happens. But the "wonder of [God's] great love" (NIV) is enough.

Our stories are full of dislocations and disturbances. It may be some obvious issue like marital separation, a distressing medical diagnosis, loss of needed work, or anxiety about a loved one. Our desperation leads to despair, and we cry for help.

Whether it is our own pain or grief, or the hurt and terror others have, life does not always bring the wholeness we long for. Our surprise is that God's presence is security.

Prayer: *O God, some people claim you help those who help themselves; but there are times when I cannot help myself. I cling to you as a distraught child holds on to a parent. Be my strength and refuge, I pray. Amen.*

Thursday, July 29   Read Psalm 17:6-9, 15.

"It just isn't fair," this quiet man cried as he pounded the hospital wall. He had always been in control, but now life had tumbled in. The surgeon told him that his wife had inoperable cancer. His shock soon turned to despair. "Why her? It just doesn't make any sense. She has been such a compassionate person, caring for others, neglecting herself." I stood with him, my friend, in the deafening silence.

The psalmist poured out his complaint to God. By all standards of justice he had been treated unfairly, and God seemed terribly distant. He protested his innocence. "My steps have held to your paths; my feet have not slipped" (NIV; see vv. 3, 5,). These words described the life of my friend's wife.

Claus Westermann finds three complaints in all the laments: a *You-complaint,* directed toward God; an *I-complaint,* centered on the person praying; and a *They-complaint,* focused on other people. All are present in this psalm, but the major complaint is with God.

In the end, however, complaint turns to trust and even praise. "Seeing God's likeness" is enough. There is no definitive response to his anguished complaint, but a strong presence makes the complaint seem less important. The pain persists; but now comes a deeper peace, not known before.

In the long twilight struggle after my friend's wife died, I often prayed this psalm on his behalf. I had never experienced such a life-shattering loss, but as I thought of him, the psalm called me to be a calming presence for my friend, reminding him that we are held in God's unceasing love.

Suggestion for meditation: *In a quiet moment, think of someone who is having a hard struggle. Feel their pain. Enter their situation. How can you pray for them? be with them?*

Friday, July 30   Read Matthew 14:13-19.

She was a widow, living alone with the memories of her lifelong partner. In her frail hand she held a framed picture of a boat at sea. The caption read, "O Lord, the sea is so great....and my boat is so small." She sighed and whispered, "It was his favorite saying. Doesn't it remind you of him?" So it did. Once he told me, "I never made much out of my life; too many windmills and impossible dreams. But I always reached out to the unfortunate."

When Jesus told the disciples to feed the restless, irritable crowd that day in Galilee, they were horrified and felt so powerless. " 'We have here only five loaves of bread and two fish,' they answered" (NIV).

Jesus made the crowd sit down (which meant they expected to be fed). He took what was available, gave thanks, and multiplied it to feed a crowd. As the miracle unfolded before their eyes, the disciples were dumbstruck. Later they realized the greater truth: Jesus can satisfy our deepest hunger to feel adequate and loved.

Like the disciples, we know our inadequacies all too well. There are times when we feel unable to meet life's demands. But remember God's surprising power. God can "do infinitely more than we can ask or imagine" (Eph. 3:20, JB).

I assured my friend that her husband's life among us reminded us that God gives grace to the humble and resists the proud. She smiled. "Yes, when I remember him, I rejoice how the good Lord used even his idiosyncrasies to help the poor."

Suggestion for meditation: *Think of someone you know who appears to be a "failure." Can you see ways in which God worked through him or her? At what times of failure or disappointments have you felt God's presence in your life? toward others?*

Saturday, July 31   Read Matthew 14:20-21.

An older woman, her body crippled by arthritis, stood before our Sunday school assembly and spoke on the story of Jesus' feeding of the multitudes. Instead of the usual comments, she read Jesus' words, "Pick up the pieces left over, so that nothing is wasted" (John 6:12, JB). She pleaded with us not to discard older people in the church but to use their talents for the Kingdom.

She spoke for many in our work-oriented society: for the elderly, who often feel themselves forgotten by the church; for others who are "outsiders" because of gender, race, or socioeconomic status. The church sometimes does forget its calling to be a house of prayer for all people.

Jesus did not forget the leftover pieces that day. In fact, the pieces must have fallen from his hand as he broke the bread. "Gather the fragments left over, so that nothing may be lost." Jesus was always intentional in including the "smoldering wick" and the "bruised reed" (Matt. 12:20). He never discounted anyone.

I had gone to worship at a low time in my life. Retirement for me had not been the "promised land" some had indicated, but a never-ending wilderness. By my own choice I had left the limelight for the shadows. But it was an adjustment to be alone so much. I knew what it felt like to be unwanted. As the congregation sang "A Mighty Fortress Is Our God," I sensed that God had special plans for my remaining years. The leftover pieces of my life were still usable. Surprise!

Prayer: *God of all peoples, fix our attention now on those whom we often forget. Let us remember those depressed by neglect, infirmities, or unemployment. Help us to offer them hope in your name and through your love. Amen.*

224

Sunday, August 1   Read Romans 9:1-5.

He was a street person, forsaken by his family, the church, and the community. Day after day, he loitered on the town square. There came a time when even his street friends abandoned him.

I visited him shortly before he died. From his dingy bed in a musty room, he glanced toward a faded picture of Christ on the wall and said, "That's the only friend I ever had."

At his funeral, many came to hear what the preacher would say about the town disgrace. I read the parable of the publican and the Pharisee, and Jesus' words, "Truly I tell you, the tax collectors and prostitutes are into the kingdom of God ahead of you" (Matt. 21:31).

Paul experienced unending grief over the plight of his kinsmen, the Jews. His joy that the Gentiles were entering the Kingdom was diminished by the pain he felt over his own people's rejection of the gospel.

God surprised him. As he pondered his problem, he realized that what we see now is what has taken place thus far. But God had not rejected the Jews. His final intention is to save all Israel (Rom. 11:26). Paul's struggle ends in an outburst of praise for God's surprising mercy. "O the depth of the riches and wisdom and knowledge of God" (11:33*a*). For that forsaken street person—for everyone—God's mercy is available.

In South Philadelphia a Wesleyan church has one stained glass window and the words, "Come to the Mercy Seat." Lit from the outside, the words glow like neon for the worshipers to see. But the light from inside the church helps people in the darkness outside read the words, too. For everyone, inside the church and outside on the streets, God is mercy.

Suggestion for prayer and meditation: *Remember people who seem to have rejected God's love. Pray for them by name.*

SENT BY GOD

August 2-8, 1993   **Kit Kuperstock**✣
Monday, August 2   Read Matthew 14:22-23.

Ever since John the Baptist's disciples brought the devastating news that Herod had beheaded John, Jesus had needed prayer as a starving person needs food.

Since Jesus walked this earth, we have struggled to answer: how could he be truly human while also "true God from true God"? If Jesus had all power and knowledge, and knew that at the time, was his human experience—even a brutal death—only a role-play? The church early called that belief heresy.

Hungrily seeking solitude, Jesus seems especially human. Though my little boys have grown into men, I still remember putting grief or crisis on hold until I got them all fed and bathed, read them a story, and finally tucked them in bed. (With a quick prayer that, this once, they would stay there!)

Jesus went by himself in a boat to a deserted area, but multitudes quickly found him. Jesus responded to their needs: healed their sick, fed 5,000 of them with five loaves and two fish (Matt. 14:12-21).

Then he sent them away. No cup can continually run over for others without being refilled. Jesus finally got time alone to pray: to deal with grief—grief for a prophet, his cousin, one crying in the wilderness—and to add this to his abiding knowledge of what it is to be human.

Prayer: *O Love that wilt not let me go,*
I rest my weary soul in thee.*

✣Writer; active in prison ministry; Oak Ridge, Tennessee.
*From the hymn "O Love That Wilt Not Let Met Go" by George Matheson.

Tuesday, August 3   Read Genesis 37:1-4.

As a young man, Jacob fled to keep his twin brother, Esau, from killing him. Jacob had conned Esau out of their father's blessing and Esau's birthright as firstborn. (See Genesis 25:29-34 and Genesis 27.) Years and distance healed the rift between them. Eventually, Jacob and Esau together peaceably buried their father, Isaac.

But hate erupted among Jacob's sons. Like his father, Jacob played favorites. When Joseph, Jacob's favorite son, was 17 he gave his father a bad report on some older brothers. That hardly made his brothers love him.

But that was soon overshadowed by the long-sleeved robe Jacob gave Joseph—especially luxurious beside the short sleeveless tunics his older brothers probably wore.

When Joseph showed off his new robe, some of his brothers clenched their fists and muttered threats. But I can imagine that Joseph was too pleased with his robe—and himself—to notice.

We all make mistakes as teenagers—but few, perhaps, as many as Joseph did. Why would God send this self-centered troublemaker to do anything important? Because beyond our limitations, God sees our possibilities.

When God hands us a task several sizes too large
And we try to explain there's some kind of mistake,
There's a hint of God's smile—
And like water, loaves, fish,
We find ourselves changing.*

Prayer suggestion: *What task have you been afraid to tackle? If you begin it, might you find yourself changing? How would you feel about that change?*

*From the poem "In the Beginning" by Kit Kuperstock.

227

Wednesday, August 4　　　　Read Genesis 37:12-21.

Whatever possibilities God saw in him, Joseph continued to infuriate his brothers. Even Jacob rebuked Joseph for sharing dreams in which the rest of the family bowed down to him (Genesis 37:5-11).

Jacob sent Joseph to check on his brothers and the flocks they were tending. "See how they are doing and bring word back to me," Jacob told him. He had no idea how much most of his older sons hated Joseph.

It was not a very exciting errand, but Joseph set out. Perhaps as he searched for his brothers, he was thinking how dull his life was, would probably always be. With no sense of danger, no excitement about possibilities, Joseph walked into his future.

Can you remember when some casual beginning made an enormous difference in your life? How and where did you meet the person you married? How did you get interested in the field you work in? I know a physicist who said his initial fascination with research dated back to a magnet his grandmother gave him when he was four. He tested every small object in the house to see if his magnet would pick it up.

When I decided to take a few classes at Tennessee State University, I did not know that some of my fellow students would be prisoners. I certainly did not know that I would spend years working with prisoners and their families, studying crime and prisons, and writing books about ways we can prevent crime and work toward *shalom* in our communities.

Prayer: *Our God, we have no way to see the end of the trail, but we know from beginning to end, it belongs to you. Please let us walk with you into our futures. Amen.*

Thursday, August 5   Read Genesis 37:22-24.

When my older children were young, two of them, Eric and Steve, visited with my parents in Nashville one summer. Mother and Dad were driving the boys home after their visit. The other children helped me prepare for their homecoming. We slicked up the house and fixed an extra good lunch.

Then the phone rang. It was Dad. "We had a wreck," he said.

Their car had gone off a 70-foot bluff. Mother had a serious skull fracture and 32 other broken bones. Dad and the boys, though much less seriously hurt, all had broken bones.

Nothing had happened as we had expected. Instead, a friend quickly drove us the many miles to the hospital while a trusted sitter stayed with the children in Oak Ridge.

Nothing happened as Joseph had expected. He thought his brothers were coming to welcome him. Instead several grabbed him and yanked off the long-sleeved robe. Reading the story I imagine the scene to be like this:

"Careful!" Joseph pleaded. "Our father gave the robe to me."

That was the wrong thing to say. One brother thrust his knife toward Joseph's face. Joseph was terrified. Never had he dreamed that his brothers would hurt him. He was relieved to see Reuben whom he trusted more than the others.

"Put the knife away," Reuben said quietly. "We agreed to put him in the pit, not to spill his blood."

Two of his brothers swung Joseph by his arms and lowered him into the pit. Reuben allowed it. Joseph felt like his entire world had turned upside down. Nothing was like he had thought it would be. He was scared and astonished.

Prayer: *When other helpers fail and comforts flee,*
*Help of the helpless, O, thou who changeth not, abide with me.**

---

*From the hymn "Abide with Me" by Henry F. Lyte.

Friday, August 6
Read Genesis 37:25-28
Psalm 105:16-18.

As I read further into the story of Joseph, I picture the events in my mind like this:

While the brothers ate, Reuben tossed Joseph some bread and mutton. Joseph hoped they would not leave him in the pit overnight. At night, wild animals prowled. Then Joseph heard men shouting in a foreign tongue at their camels. They had stopped so the animals could graze.

After awhile, three of his brothers hauled Joseph up out of the pit. He thought the frightening game was finally over. But he had another unpleasant surprise. While his brothers held him, a stranger fettered Joseph's feet, and put a tight iron collar around Joseph's neck. It hurt.

That stranger was an Ishmaelite with goods to sell in Egypt. Other Ishmaelites waited for him with the camels. Joseph had to shuffle along behind the Ishmaelite.

The long-sleeved robe had told Joseph who he was. Not the pain or fright but an iron collar and fetters told him something very different. Not only did they prevent his running away, they also helped turn him into a slave.

In our particular geographic locale, slavery no longer exists. But in my work with prisoners, I have thought there are some similar feelings to the lack of power felt by slaves. When someone is arrested, he is handcuffed with hands behind his back. When prisoners are transported, their feet are manacled together. These are to prevent the prisoners from grabbing a weapon or running away. But I think these are also to remind the prisoners that they are powerless.

Suggestion for meditation: *What experiences in your life have made you feel powerless? At those times was there someone you could rely on? Did you feel the presence of God as your helper?*

230

Saturday, August 7   Read Psalm 105:1-6, 18-22.

We left the 17-year-old Joseph being taken to Egypt to be sold as a slave. Psalm 105 is a poetic overview of God's mighty acts for Israel from Abraham through Moses. It left me wanting to zero in more on specifics.

Though I thought I knew Joseph's story well from Bible story books as a child, it repaid re-reading as an adult. You'll find it in Genesis chapters 37 and 39–50.

Certainly God's confidence in Joseph was well-placed— God saw that it was well-placed. The competent 30-year-old administrator over all Egypt is hard to recognize as the spoiled teenager we first met.

The serious question raised for us is familiar: does God really will that people do evil so that good can result? In Genesis 45:8, Joseph comforts his brothers who sold him into slavery by telling them, "It was not you who sent me here, but God."

Does marvelous cosmic salvage remove the brothers' responsibility for their own actions?

I got into these questions in a very hot crucible. For example, I spent an hour once discussing Paul's "objects of wrath that are made for destruction" with a prisoner. (Romans 9:22*b*). If you were an "object of wrath made for destruction," you would have no responsibility at all for your own actions, would you? Nor any hope. I find it tough to conceive of the God I love and that kind of creation.

Prayer: *I ask no dream, no prophet ecstasies,*
no sudden rending of the veil of clay,
no angel visitant, no opening skies;
*but take the dimness of my soul away. Amen**

---

*From the hymn "Spirit of God, Descend Upon My Heart" by George Croly.

Sunday, August 8   Read Romans 10:5-15.

The Torah, God's law in the first five books of the Bible, is full of wisdom to handle an astonishing number of human problems. God's people were to live by the Torah—yet, as the years went by, the interpretation of its commandments became increasingly intricate and complicated.

The most orthodox Jews, the Pharisees, spent much time and energy measuring legal distances to walk on the Sabbath, and weighing the intent of tiny provisions of the law. As Paul wrote to the Christians in Rome (Rom. 3:2*b*), "the Jews were entrusted with the oracles of God"—a responsibility to take seriously indeed.

But however hard they tried, they could not obey the law in every detail. Paul, a Pharisee for most of his life, saw that "both Jews and Greeks are under the power of sin...None is righteous, no not one" (Rom. 3:9*b*, 10*b*).

God had not given the law to be impossible to keep. In Deuteronomy 30:11, God said: "This commandment...is not too hard for you, nor is it too far away....It is in your mouth and in your heart for you to observe" (Deut. 30:11, 14*b*).

Now Paul reminded the Romans that God in Christ had assumed the consequences of sin—and ended the power of sin. The writer of Hebrews quotes God's covenant as: "I will put my laws in their hearts, And I will write them on their minds" (Heb. 10:16*b*). That is *implanting* God's word—establishing it decisively in the mind or consciousness.

Paul further reminds us: "There is no distinction between Jew and Greek; the same Lord is Lord of all and generous to all who call on him" (Rom. 10:12). All that is needed now is for us to share that good news about our generous Lord.

Prayer suggestion: *Who needs good news and needs to hear it from you? Pray for that person.*

GOD'S BOUNDLESS MERCY

August 9-15, 1993   **William E. Smith**✞
Monday, August 9   Read Genesis 45:1-3;
                                     Psalm 130.

They could not believe their ears! He said, "I am Joseph; Is my father still alive?" Jealous of their youngest brother, their father's favorite son, Joseph's brothers had sold him as a slave to a caravan of traders headed for Egypt. That had been 20 years ago, when Joseph was 17 (Gen. 37:2). Now this Egyptian official, second in power only to Pharaoh, said he was Joseph. They were so shocked they could not even speak. Suddenly the sins of the past rose up to haunt them—the jealousy, the dastardly scheme to get rid of Joseph, the deceitful lie that he had been killed by a wild beast, causing their father's heart to break. What would happen to them now?

Typically, they were thinking not about Joseph or about their father, but of their own skins. Little wonder they were "dismayed...at his presence." In a deeply introspective prayer the psalmist asks, "If you, O LORD, should mark iniquities, LORD, who could stand?"

But something wonderful is about to happen to these scheming brothers: they are to be reconciled to Joseph and to God, encountering, as never before, God's boundless mercy.

> O Israel, hope in the LORD!
> For with the LORD there is...
> ... great power to redeem.

Prayer: *God, we thank you for your great love and mercy toward us..May we show mercy and compassion toward others. Amen.*

✞United Methodist pastor, Professor of the Practice of Christian Ministry, The Divinity School, Duke University, Durham, North Carolina.

233

Tuesday, August 10   Read Genesis 45:4-15.

Joseph's brothers are scared speechless when they learn that the Egyptian official is none other than Joseph himself. They are relieved that he does not intend to punish them. Rather, he assures them that they have been caught up in a divine drama: "God sent me before you to preserve life."

This affirmation may tax both their credulity and ours, but this is nonetheless the central theme in the story. Three times in an earlier chapter the narrator states, "The LORD was *with Joseph*" (39:2, 21, 23*b,* italics added). Now, as he looks at the past, Joseph sees the hand of God at work: "God sent me before you to preserve for you a remnant on earth, and to keep alive for you many survivors."

The motif of rescue is central to the entire composition of Genesis.[*] Noah and his family survive the flood; Abraham, faced with the prospect of no heirs, is promised descendants and land; Lot and his family (except his wife) are delivered from the destruction of Sodom. So here, "God sent me before you."

The focus is not on the devious schemes of humans but on the ultimate purpose of God. We must neither trivialize nor sentimentalize this concept. We do not say to a person dying of cancer, "It's going to be all right," or "It must be God's will." We do affirm that God is gracious and that although we may make a mess of our lives, or may become victims of seemingly hopeless tragedy, God's ultimate will for us, and all God's children, is good. Only those who trust God can really know that for sure.

Prayer: *Lord, help us to believe that your mercy is greater than our sin and that nothing can separate us from your love. Amen.*

---

[*]See Gerhard von Rad, *Genesis: A Commentary*, Rev.ised edition (Philadelphia: Westminster Press, 1972), p. 398.

Wednesday, August 11   Read Psalm 133.

This brief wisdom psalm celebrates the rich fellowship of worshipers gathered in the Temple on a festive occasion. It is from a collection of psalms chanted by pilgrims on their way to worship. The spirit that unites them is compared in a picturesque way to "precious oil" and the "dew of Hermon." These similes would have vivid meaning to devout Jews.

Precious oil is the fragrant ointment used to consecrate the high priest (see Ex. 29:7), descendant of Aaron, who also bears his name. Imagine the sacred oil being poured upon his head, trickling down his luxurious and thick beard (it was never to be cut) and the collar of his robes. Oil is the symbol of God's blessings, and it flows in profusion.

Syria's snow-capped Mount Hermon can be seen from northern Israel. It is a majestic sight. The "dew of Hermon" is simply heavy dew, once again symbolizing God's bountiful blessings. The unity of those who worship together is like the life-giving dews of Mount Hermon; they bring God's blessings in abundance evermore.

Contrast these delightful images with the disunity which separates Christian communions. How can we claim "one Lord, one faith, one baptism, one God and Father of all" (Eph. 4:5-6) while still insisting that our way alone is valid? The unity the psalmist extols is not exclusive; it unites believers everywhere who long to worship God.

As we seek God's forgiveness and grace we will discover the life-giving, restoring spirit of unity that is truly a gift of God.

Prayer: *Deliver us, O Lord, from the spirit of divisiveness that separates us from each other and from you. Remind us that all your children are united by your mercy and love, and help us to rejoice in the gift of unity that is already ours through Jesus Christ our Lord. Amen.*

Thursday, August 12   Read Romans 11:1-2*a*

The question Paul asked—"Has God rejected his people?"—is both deeply personal and highly theological. Why had the Jews not acknowledged Jesus as Messiah? Paul was himself an Israelite, and it pained him deeply that the Gentiles accepted salvation by faith in Christ (Rom. 10:19-21), but the Jews did not believe. Is it possible there was more at stake here than the freedom of the human will to say no instead of yes, and that even the rejection of the Jews is a part of God's larger plan? These issues are foremost in Paul's mind in Romans 9–11.

What in the world is God doing? The question haunts us in times of natural catastrophe, in times of rampant evil such as the Holocaust, and in times of personal tragedy. Our family prayed, apparently in vain, for the healing of our thirteen-year-old son from bone cancer. When the devastating disease claimed yet another victim, we were reassured by the magnificent claim of Paul: "We know that in all things God works for good with those who love him...nothing...will ever be able to separate us from the love of God which is ours through Christ Jesus our Lord" (Romans 8:23, 38, TEV). For Paul, God's boundless mercy is demonstrated supremely by Christ:

> Christ Jesus is—the Lord....for it was in him that God elected us in love, and it is with him that we shall enter into God's glory beyond history. In Christ Jesus, God is *for us;* and it is in Christ Jesus that we know him and trust him.[*]

Prayer: *"Christ has died; Christ is risen; Christ will come again."* Amen.

---

[*]C.K. Barrett, *The Epistle to the Romans,* Harper's New Testament Commentaries (New York: Harper and Row, 1957), p. 174.

Friday, August 13   Read Romans 11:29-32.

Paul is thinking long thoughts. He is still troubled by the seeming arbitrariness of God. The Jews by their own free will rejected Christ, while the Gentiles accepted him. Does that mean that God's promise to Israel no longer holds? On the contrary, "God does not change his mind about whom he chooses and blesses." (TEV). Even the disobedience of humanity can serve God's greater purposes. As the Gentiles disobeyed God and yet were saved, so the Jews, in rejecting Christ will, in God's plan of salvation, eventually receive him. So God will be "merciful to them all" (TEV).

Note the universality of sin, a familiar Pauline theme: "since all have sinned and fall short of the glory of God" (Rom. 3:23). The fact is that we, not God, are responsible for our sins: our tendency to love ourselves more than God; to avoid, rather than seek, God's will; to look with indifference on the poor, the homeless, the oppressed. This is what it means to be "imprisoned...in disobedience."

Note as well, however, the universality of salvation: "While we still were sinners Christ died for us" (Rom. 5:8). It is God's undeserved grace that is at the heart of the gospel, and no one affirms this central truth more forcefully than Paul. Four times in this brief passage he mentions God's mercy, a reflection, no doubt, of his own personal experience.

Here is much-needed assurance for our lives: God is ultimately in control of history. God's purposes cannot be thwarted. God's mercy, revealed supremely in Christ, is not for a chosen few, but for all humankind.

Suggestion for meditation: *Read Romans 11:33-36 as an affirmation of faith. Let Paul's words voice your own thanksgiving to God: "To God be the glory forever. Amen."*

Saturday, August 14　　　　Read Matthew 15:10-20.

Jesus is at the height of his popularity. People throng to hear him and witness his miracles. His disciples, awed by his wisdom and power, have proclaimed him "the Son of God" (Matt. 14:33). The Pharisees and scribes, keepers of traditional faith, are uneasy. For them religion has become a matter of faithfully practicing those rituals that separate the pure from the impure.

When they inquire why Jesus and his disciples do not conform to their outward displays of piety, Jesus reminds them it is they who are breaking God's law. The words from Isaiah are reenacted again in them: "These people...honor me with their lips, while their hearts are far from me" (Isa. 29:13).

Then to the people, and later to his disciples, Jesus explains that it is not what goes into the mouth but what comes out that defiles. For what is spoken comes from the heart, and very center of one's being where the religious life is formed. If one's heart is defiled, evil will result, and no amount of hand-washing will make it clean.

It is not enough to be outwardly strong or even respectable. The test is whether our hearts are pure: Do I neglect my spiritual life? Do I tend to look down on others in order to boost my own ego? Am I envious of others? If my fantasies were projected on a screen, would I be ashamed?

If we are honest with ourselves and God, we can only join the tax collector praying in the Temple, "God be merciful to me, a sinner!" (Luke 18:13)

Prayer: *"Lord, I want to be like Jesus in my heart."*[*] *Amen.*

---

[*]From "Lord, I Want to Be a Christian," Afro-American spiritual.

Sunday, August 15   Read Matthew 15:21-28.

The woman would not take no for an answer. Jesus' disciples regarded her as a nuisance: "Send her away! She is following us and making all this noise!" (TEV). It was unusual to find someone in Phoenicia, home of the Canaanites, long-time enemies of Israel, who believed.

Jesus had not brought his disciples here to do public ministry; in fact, they were on retreat. Besides, he understood his mission as being centered on "the lost sheep...of Israel" and said as much to the woman. She came and knelt at his feet; "Help me, sir," she pleaded. Testing her faith, he replied, "It isn't right to take the children's food and throw it to the dogs" (a term frequently used by the Jews then to refer to Gentiles). With rare wit and keen insight she responded: "But even the dogs eat the leftovers that fall from their masters' table." "You are a woman of great faith," Jesus declared. 'What you want will be done for you.' "(TEV).

The key to the woman's persistence was her great faith. Somewhere, somehow, she had heard of Jesus, and although she was not a Jew, she called him "Son of David." She believed that he could heal her desperately sick daughter.

In this encounter we also see Jesus redefining his mission. While he was sent to his own people primarily, compassion forces him to extend the scope of his ministry. So here, in this most Jewish of the Gospels, we see glimpses of things to come, such as when Paul, a Jew, writes to gentile Christians, "There are no more distinctions between Jew and Greek, slave and free, male and female, but you are all one in Christ Jesus." (Gal. 3:28, JB). There are no limits to God's mercy!

Prayer: *Lord, we thank you for the faith of the Canaanite woman and for Jesus' compassionate response. Help us to know that all things are possible to those who believe. Amen.*

GOD'S STORY AND OURS

August 16-22, 1993 **Carmen Utzurrum Pak✝**
Monday, August 16 Read Exodus 1:8-14.

A ninety-three-year old member of the congregation I serve loves to tell stories. When I began working in this parish, his stories helped me discover, in part, what being a pastor in La Verne meant and what I was expected to do.

Anthropologists have known for years that when they want to find out about a society, they listen to the stories that the community tells. Our stories tell who we are.

As Christians we are heirs to a treasury of stories that hold our faith convictions. In understanding these stories, we discover who we are and what we are called to do.

Today's passage is clearly part of a continuing story, one that began in Genesis with the Creation and the call of Abraham and Sarah and continues here with the oppression of the Israelites. It is the story of God calling these people into a community to live in covenant with God.

Our identity as this faith community calls us to a certain way of life, to do things differently from the way we would if we were just living for ourselves. We do not always take care of each other, but our stories make it clear that we have to try. God's story continues in us each time we respond to the word and Spirit of God moving through these stories.

Prayer: *Eternal Word of Love, help us as we read your story and ours, to discover who we are and what we are to do. Amen.*

✝Pastor, United Methodist Church at La Verne, California.

Tuesday, August 17   Read Exodus 1:15–2:20.

In today's reading, the lives of the covenant people were made bitter with hard service with mortar and brick. While we see the grandeur of fortified cities and of the pyramids, God saw the oppression of the people. And God did something about it. Nothing spectacular, no lightning bolts or crashing thunder. Our text reveals God's love, not as a supernatural rescue but as a divine sharing in human suffering.

Shiphrah and Puah, midwives; a mother; a sister;—all ordinary women. But these women outsmarted the Pharaoh and his men. How this story must have been told again and again with hilarity; how the great Pharaoh was thwarted by the cunning of ordinary women! Indeed, the future challenger to Pharaoh's power was raised to manhood under Pharaoh's nose. We discover how God often confronts the powers of the earth with the power of love in forms of lowliness, weakness, and servitude.

The more the Israelites were oppressed, the more they multiplied; and "God dealt well with the midwives." The Pharaoh's plans were thwarted. We see how the word of hope for the poor is a word of challenge to the powerful; justice for the oppressed means judgment of the oppressor.

When the poor were being trampled the prophets pronounced God's judgment (Amos 5:11; Jer. 5:28-29). Mary praised God who put down the mighty from their thrones and exalted those of low degree; filled the hungry with good things and sent the rich away empty (Luke 1:52-53). This is our story as well. In Jesus' dying and rising, God creates a new human community. We are called to tell God's story today.

Suggestion for meditation: *Where is God confronting the powers of the earth with love in the forms of weakness and servitude? Could God be using you? your church?*

Wednesday, August 18   Read Psalm 124.

The psalmist celebrates Israel's deliverance and gives all credit to God. Happily, the psalmist does not suggest that God is on the side of Israel because its cause is just; nor does the poet exult over the achievement of Israel's armies.

Many in our nation celebrated what was seen as the undisputed superiority of United States technology and sophisticated weapons during the Persian Gulf War. They affirmed a belief that "by the grace of God" the Allied Forces won the war because their cause was just.

Those who vaunted the allied victory are a stark contrast to the psalmist who makes no claims for a just and righteous cause, nor even that Israel deserved to be preserved. The psalmist simply acknowledges that the deliverance was God's doing: "If it had not been the LORD...."

How restrained and sober is the psalmist's expression of thanks for the deliverance! While our commanders exulted over the rout of Iraqi soldiers, the psalmist expresses no satisfaction over the enemy's defeat. The poet simply states: "Blessed be the LORD who has not given us up as prey to their teeth....We have escaped...Our help is in the name of the LORD who made heaven and earth."

Recognition of our creatureliness leads to acknowledgment of the continuous providence of God. The world and all that it holds belongs to God; we merely have the privilege of using it. Such a sacred trust must reflect the care and love the God has for *all* of creation.

Prayer: *Gracious Sovereign, we are the work of your hand. You alone are our security. Amen.*

Thursday, August 19 Read Matthew 16:13-17.

"Who do you say that I am?" The big question is not who this itinerant teacher is but where Jesus fits in God's story. Jesus asks the disciples the question that many in the community are asking. They answer, "John, Elijah, even Jeremiah, or one of the prophets." When Jesus asks them the critical question: "But who do *you* say that I am?" the disciples nudge Peter to step up and answer Jesus' question. Peter then makes the amazing declaration: "You are the Messiah, the Son of the Living God!" In that great statement of faith, Peter answers the question of where Jesus fits in God's story: Jesus is the one in whom we see God!

Simon comes to see who Jesus is through a revelation from God; that is, Simon has received insight into a deeper world, a world not of "flesh and blood." For Peter, Jesus is now the one in whom the invisible world becomes visible: God is seen in Jesus.

Can we begin to see our story not as something bound by time, but open for such an explosive insight? Imagine what would happen if we found ourselves in the presence of a living God, not bound by our tribalisms and our timidities.

"Blessed are you, Simon, son of Jonah." This blessing marks Peter as the one in whom and through whom God's story will be told. Jesus is saying here that God can and does choose the most unlikely persons to be entrusted with God's work.

The mandate to Peter was not a purely personal one. Jesus was speaking to the church struggling to be church, a church rooted in the question, "Who do *you* say that I am?" This is the greatest question of life.

Suggestion for meditation: *Who do you say that Jesus is? Are we open to such an experience of insight as Peter had and to the indwelling in our lives by the living God?*

Friday, August 20   Read Matthew 16:18-20.

Jesus meets Peter and calls him the Rock. It is a call to all Peter is, which is much more than Peter knows himself to be. Jesus is entrusting Peter with the leadership of the community—Peter who proved untrustworthy and even denied Jesus. Jesus is saying here that God can and does choose the most unlikely people to tell God's story.

Jesus empowers Peter when calling him the Rock. Could it be that this story is nudging us about our own ability to see our possibilities? We are so unsure about our own worth. Some of us feel that we are too far gone to be repaired. Peter had every reason to regard himself this way, knowing his denial and his fear. Yet, Peter was used in a great way by God. God sees what we do not. God comes to us as if we are the people God wants us to be. We are never far from the transforming power of God.

God's power does not make us perfect and blemish free, but it does release our potential. This is what God does in Jesus Christ. We cannot remain the same after being with Christ. Being with Jesus changed Peter. All this is God's doing. It does not depend on our goodness.

This story suggests that God loves us and knows us, including those parts of our lives we ourselves refuse to acknowledge. And, knowing us completely, God accepts us and empowers us. Such an experience disarms us—this acceptance of ourselves, warts and all—then frees us from the need to prove ourselves worthy. We are freed to be *for* the other, to accept the other as we have been accepted. We are empowered to tell God's story in our lives.

Prayer: *Thank you, Eternal Love, for knowing us completely and loving us. Help us to accept others the way you accept us, and free us to be all we can be—like Jesus, our Savior. Amen.*

Saturday, August 21   Read Romans 12:1-3.

When we have been the recipients of gracious hospitality or of generous sharing, or when we have been forgiven, our response is, "What can we do to show our appreciation for such a blessing?" That's how it is with the Christian. Our experience of the "mercies of God" moves us to respond in some way.

Paul suggests that this response is not simply one of gratitude; it involves a new way of seeing ourselves in relation to God and to God's creation. Our response must mirror God's action, God's mercies; it is *imitation* of God's love. This renewal of our mind makes us new persons—*transformed!* Who are these transformed persons through whom God is present to the world? Our faith stories are about widows—a foreigner from Zarephath and a worshipper in the Temple who gave all she had; a tax collector; a humble girl engaged to a carpenter; a Samaritan, another outsider. *It is those who risk everything on God.*

Transformed by the renewing of our minds, we learn that discipleship means giving up false securities and discovering that God wants nothing less than our very selves! Then every aspect of our living is joined with Christ's offering and presented as a living sacrifice, proving what is good. And what is this good? "To do justice, to love kindness, and to walk humbly with your God" (Micah 6:8).

There it is: we are to renounce our striving for money, our desire for prestige and power, our hoarding of goods, our competing for success. Instead, we are to form a new human community wholly dependent upon God, embodying God's justice and mercy.

Suggestion for meditation: *Sit quietly, simply being present to God with your whole being. Then offer all that you are and all that you have to God. What changes in your life are needed to do this?*

Sunday, August 22   Read Romans 12:4-8.

Paul reminds us that we, with our differing gifts, are one body in Christ. All of us are to use our gifts, moved by the presence of the Spirit, to prove what is the will of God. *Every one* has received a gift of ministry from the Spirit: writing letters, teaching, listening, sitting quietly with a patient, cooking a meal. Is this something I can do? *Every* gift can be shared for the good of the community. The life of discipleship comes not in isolation, but in the process of doing for others.

The life in community to which we are called does not just happen. The grace of God makes it happen whenever we respond actively in doing for others. Then our life together becomes a sacrament of God's presence. In the sacraments, ordinary stuff become the sign of God's presence. The sacramental life is lived through relationships that involve caring, helping, giving, doing acts of mercy.

In a largely greedy and unbelieving world, it often seems that what we do makes little or no difference. But we can often make a difference in ourselves (transformed, renewed), and find some joy in doing it. And, together with others moved by the Spirit, one Body in Christ, we can have an impact for good and for God larger than we ever imagined. What a power could be released if the whole church could realize that!

Prayer: *Great Spirit, all that we have, all that we are is a gift from you. Enable us, with our gifts, to be Christ's Body in the world. Guide us that we may truly be in unity with Christ and with each other, and united in our ministry to the world. Amen.*

August 23-29, 1993 · **Raymond Fenn**✢

Monday, August 23 · Read Exodus 3:1-6.

Revelation through nature

Moses was a fugitive. His fellow Hebrews remained in slavery, even though the pharaoh whose authority he had challenged had died. Moses had married and was working as a shepherd. Suddenly, while caring for his flock, he was aware of a strange sight: a bush on fire but not turning to ashes.

Perhaps most of us do not live close enough to nature to appreciate how Moses felt. So many people live in cities where the fast pace of life and the potent influence of technology have blunted the edge of our response to the divine. Rushing by in car, bus, or train, we catch but a glimpse of the beauty of nature. The unexpected may attract our attention, but do we have the time to stop? Or do we even appreciate fully what we have seen?

The emphasis on ecology has convinced some of us of the value of the natural world. But what do we have to do so that, beyond the beauty, we catch a glimpse of God? Moses responded to God: "Here I am" (REB). He was tuned in; he heard God speak directly to him. He did not stand hesitantly, only partly attentive, chewing gum and waiting for another divine word. No, he took off his shoes—a symbol of reverence and respect. When we concentrate our total attention on God, that is most often when the Holy One is revealed to us.

Prayer: *I would hear, I would understand, I would obey. Amen.*

✢Associate priest, St. George's Anglican Church, Westbank, British Columbia, Canada.

Tuesday, August 24   Read Exodus 3:7-15.

Revelation through obedience

Perhaps Moses wishes he had only looked casually at the burning but non-consumed bush. But he has come too near. Perhaps Moses had tried to forget the slave-like conditions in which his people lived in Egypt. Now, he is here in God's inescapable presence. His is not simply natural curiosity, nor is it an ordinary worshipful act: God speaks to him.

Moses cannot disagree with the Lord's analysis: "I have witnessed the misery of my people in Egypt....I know what they are suffering" (REB). What could he say in rebuttal? Then, the Lord says: "I...have come down to rescue them." For a moment Moses is unsuspecting, but soon he cannot believe what he is hearing: "Come, I shall send you to Pharaoh." *Me?* And the excuses pour out. God will not accept them. It is not important, I believe, whether it was an inner voice or an audible one. Nor is it important how we assess our own ability: God chooses; we are asked to obey.

The One whose nature is unique in every way—"I am that I am" (REB)—will be with Moses in every aspect of the rescue operation. Revelation is a very intimate, personal matter. Merely listening to God's command will tell us only a little about God. When we hear God saying, "Pray on my behalf; speak for me; touch for me; heal through me; love for me," these will only be words until we obey and thus do that which God has commanded. Then it is as though the darkness is illumined, as if flowers suddenly burst into bloom. We are sustained in spite of weakness and, sometimes, in spite of strength, as we faithfully obey.

Prayer: *Unstop my ears, Lord. Put your word in me and let me reveal you. Amen.*

Wednesday, August 25   Read Psalm 105:1-6.

Revelation through gratitude

There can be no dispute as to which came first: revelation or gratitude. I experience something of God's nature through the physical world or another person, and I respond with gratefulness. It is as if a door had opened from the darkness of a closed room into the brilliance of clear morning light. I cannot see everything there is to see, but I do, in part, grasp another aspect of the divine.

These verses are partly praise and partly gratitude. The only way we can react to God's blessings is to give both thanks and praise. The psalmist is reminding the worshippers of the dramatic rescue from Egyptian slavery. "Remember the wonderful works God has done."

Life is full of uncertainties, and believing in God does not always seem to help. This could be because we are searching for a revelation when we should be seeking the security of already given certainties. The psalmist gives some guidelines. "Make known his deeds among the peoples" (REB). That is, do not be afraid to share with others how you have been blessed. "Be joyful in heart." Or, do not witness somberly. "Look to the LORD and be strong," or be willing to recognize that it is not our ability that is important but the Lord's gift of strength.

There are elements that are essential to our Christian faith: from the Incarnation to the gift of the Holy Spirit. Following a pattern of scripture readings for the church year can make us familiar with the pattern of our faith. Sometimes it is as if we deal with a certain aspect and then wrap it up and put it away until next year. But everything is part of God's continuing revelation. We respond in gratitude, taking note of all the reminders.

Prayer: *Help me, Lord, find the foundation of my faith. Amen.*

Thursday, August 26   Read Psalm 105:23-26, 45*b*

Revelation through history

The psalmist is reminding us of what God did and what God does for us: rescues us from difficulties and constraints. I tend to think of history as events, revolutions, wars, famines, all of which took place in the past. Yet all of these happenings have some bearing on what is occurring now. From newspapers and magazines which analyze the news to television coverage of what is taking place now, everything is mostly dealt with on its merits for the current moment.

In contrast, the Israelites were constantly looking back to the ground of their contemporary position. And the Exodus, the rescue operation which had changed the course of their history, got more attention than anything else. God is viewed as the One who continued to reveal the Divine Self and as the Source of every historical event.

God's self-revelation occurs all the time, not just through selected people and happenings. Thus, as the Hebrew people look back, they see God working for their salvation. They feel themselves to be God's special people. Revelation is constantly taking place but it can also be traced back into the files of history. We, too, through our Judeo-Christian heritage belong to the same historical pattern. Thus, our history, although there may be no event-connection with the biblical story, reveals that we, too, are part of the divine plan. There is a continuing spiritual link, and the only proper response is the closing words of this psalm: "Praise the Lord."

Prayer: *Lord, help me to see my personal history in relation to your revealing of yourself in Jesus Christ. Amen.*

Friday, August 27　　　　　Read Romans 12:9-21.

Revelation through community

In this reading Paul underscores the potency of Christian love. It is the foundation of all secure relationships. It is the corrective for all dysfunctional behavior.

But the community in Paul's day, as in ours, included both Christians and non-Christians. The act of loving one's fellow believer should be easier than exercising charitable feelings towards those in the general community. Yet sometimes it is more difficult. This can be because we apply a higher standard to our fellow believers but are more lenient in dealing with our secular neighbor. Or is it that we are apt to be more judgmental with another Christian since, after all, the Christian has heard and accepted God's word?

There is another difficulty in dealing with fellow believers. Much of our conversation, because we meet only once a week at worship, is on a superficial level. In the short time after the service is over we ask about health, surface feelings, children's progress at school, visitors from other communities—keeping our comments on a safe level. Unless we belong to a small, intimate group that meets regularly, becoming through this process at one with each other, we seldom discover the deep problems or deep joys others experience. When this does take place we can pray more powerfully and share at a deeper level.

There are two aspects of relationships we need to address: First, to love our neighbor because Christ died for all. It is in living love that we exemplify the gospel in its depth and breadth. Second, through this love, we experience the strong desire to share that which has changed us.

Prayer: *Fill me with your love, Lord, so that I may overflow with the desire to share it with another. Amen.*

Saturday, August 28   Read Matthew 16:21-23.

Revelation through suffering

The capital city, Jerusalem, is the focal point for the climax of Jesus' ministry. It is here that he comes in conflict with the religious and secular authorities. In the verses previous to our reading (vv. 13-20) Peter has blurted out what he believes is the true identity of Jesus: "You are the Messiah, the Son of the living God" (v. 16, REB). But messiahship is not a pleasure cruise, either for Jesus or for the disciples who will follow his lead. It involves much more than bearing a title.

Peter, after his amazing insight, completely misinterprets the statement Jesus makes about his suffering, death, and consequent resurrection. It is as if he did not hear Jesus say: "And to be raised again on the third day" (REB). Peter reacted like this because he thought of the Messiah as having power of a kind superior to that of the Romans. Then, at this point he could not conceive of the Messiah undergoing any kind of suffering. The response of Jesus reminds us of his wilderness temptations.

Some Christians equate suffering with any bodily discomfort or mental anguish. But the test is whether the pain is the direct result of witnessing for Christ's sake. When we put our faith on the line, recklessly risking any possible consequences, then we know that the final outcome will be resurrection.

Many also think that the Christian way is about love to the exclusion of suffering, reasoning that if we love Christ enough then we are somehow protected from suffering. However, this attitude is unrealistic. There may even be times in our lives when we must be willing to seek out our "Jerusalem" for the sake of the gospel.

Prayer: *Teach me, Lord, what it means to follow Jesus. Amen.*

Sunday, August 29   Read Matthew 16:24-28.

Revelation through challenge

We, in common with the first followers of Jesus, are faced with a challenge. It is a strange challenge: "Whoever wants to save his life will lose it, but whoever loses his life for my sake will find it" (REB). The normal reaction is that "winning the whole world" is not only legitimate but sensible. This challenge is probably more of a problem for us than for those who lived in gospel times. Our consumer-oriented society is dominated by the manufacture and buying of things. This is what regulates our standard of living, so that income is measured in proportion to its spending power.

Our attitude to life has a lot to do with whether we accumulate things or use them to be more effective as Christian witnesses. Restraint is not a popular topic because of the claim many make that we should have the freedom to do what is right for us. It is not an easy proposition to take Jesus at his word. Thus the questions are: How do I witness? For whom do I witness? The answers must be our own. Nobody else can reply for us. We look at our desires, our plans for daily living, then we make an active comparison with the way of life to which we believe Jesus calls us, and we make necessary adjustments.

At the end of the scripture passage there is a reference to those who will be alive when the Son of Man comes again. Some scholars connect this with the Transfiguration, others to the church, the outward expression of the renewal of Israel. Many believe it is still in the future. But whatever interpretation is put on it, Jesus is the authority who is the head of the church.

Prayer: *Grant, Lord, that I may accept the challenge that comes to me as I accept Jesus as the Lord of my life. Amen.*

August 30–September 5, 1993   **Ruth Heaney**✢
Monday, August 30   Read Psalm 149.

Though short, Psalm 149 runs the gamut of human emotions. At one end of the scale, it is classified as one of six imprecatory psalms (psalms that call for God's judgment on enemies; see Psalms 58; 59; 69; 109; 137). At the other, it is one of the hallelujah hymns (psalms that begin and end with "Hallelujah," or "Praise the Lord"; others are 106; 111–113; and 146–150) that carry the Book of Psalms to a jubilant conclusion.

The "assembly of the faithful" that gathers to sing Psalm 149 is far greater in number than when it entered Egypt as a clan consisting of Jacob and seventy descendants (see Exodos 1:1-5). Still, it is a small nation, totally dependent upon God's divine purpose for its survival. The new song expresses thanksgiving to God for what God has done for the Israelites in the past and a trust that God will continue to help them.

Thanksgiving and trust, however, were tenuous throughout Israel's history. In guiding God's people toward their destiny, the Holy One of Israel has required innovations other than new songs. Sometimes Israel murmured in protest as it experienced the birth pangs of new beginnings.

Prayer: *Lord, how easy it is to identify with a people whose mood swings from victorious to vindictive! Help me to remember that the victories belong to you and that you are the only one who can keep my world in true perspective. Amen.*

✢Christian writer; Wenonah, New Jersey.

Tuesday, August 31   Read Exodus 12:1-2.

God has spoken. This fatal night—the Passover—requires a new calendar for Israel. The month of Abib (see Exod. 13:4) becomes the first month of the Jewish year.

Why a new calendar? Those who claim to have the mind of God in this or any matter deceive themselves. We have already been told that God's thoughts are not our thoughts, God's ways not our ways (Isa. 55:8). We can only conjecture from a human standpoint and from what we know of the human mind.

Psychologists tell us that the mind has a tendency to retain the details of beginnings and endings with sharper clarity than what transpires between the two. By placing Passover in the first month, is the Creator of that mind helping Israel to recall in the future the events leading up to this climactic moment?

The events, as well, lend themselves to being remembered. The fact that people are more likely to remember positive things that have happened to them and block out the negative ones is well documented. It is sometimes referred to as "the good old days" syndrome, because most people remember their past as more pleasant than it actually was.

The events of the Exodus have certainly been positive from Israel's viewpoint. Miraculously untouched by plague, hail, darkness, and death, the children of Israel watched from Goshen as God's incredible demonstration of power was unleashed against the Egyptians (see Exodus 7–11).

The inexplicable, from a human standpoint, will occur even before the Israelites cross the Red Sea. Their courage will crumble as their faith in God's love for them falters.

For now, though, Israel is ready to flee to a new beginning.

Prayer: *Lord, I, too, know fear. Give me courage to face the Red Seas in my life, confident that you will provide paths through them. Amen.*

Wednesday, September 1   Read Exodus 12:3-10.

Although Passover was to be an observance involving the entire Hebrew community, God broke it down into family units. It remained thus until the Passover celebration was discontinued when Israel fell into spiritual decline during the period of the judges (2 Kings 23:21-22).

King Josiah revived the Passover hundreds of years later during a sweeping reform of Judah (2 Chron. 35:1-19). Through Josiah, God added a new requirement for Passover: it was to be observed in Jerusalem. Why did God want the entire nation of Israel to congregate in one location for Passover? Did the pilgrims dare to speculate as they traveled to Jerusalem?

While God's plans for Israel continued to take shape, God's original specifications for the family festival remained. The new addition simply made it incumbent upon each family to plan its festivities in Jerusalem (2 Kings 23:23). Eventually every Hebrew male would be required to make the Passover pilgrimage to Jerusalem with his family.

Such was the case when twelve-year-old Jesus accompanied his parents to Jerusalem for the feast of the Passover (Luke 2:41-42). While in the Temple, he referred to God as his Father (Luke 2:49). This familial address was inconsistent with the Hebrew perception of God as a deity so awe-full, so holy that one dared not look upon God's face (Exod. 3:1-6). It would grate on the pharisaic mindset in the years ahead.

Since the child Jesus was already aware of his relationship to God, what else did he know? Did he realize what his role would be during his final Passover journey to Jerusalem?

Prayer: *Lord, you called the Almighty, Everlasting God your Father and taught us to call him "our Father" as well, that we might know God's nearness to us and love for us. Thank you. Amen.*

Thursday, September 2   Read Exodus 12:11-14.

The Passover lamb was to be eaten in haste by families huddled under God's protective blood covering. With sandals on feet and staff in hand, the Israelites waited to follow Moses out of Egypt. With them they would carry the Lord's command to observe the Passover "for ever" (vv. 24-27, RSV).

Despite lapses into idolatry, these were a grateful people who would recount the mercies of God to succeeding generations. And when, on occasion, they did turn their backs on God, they quickly learned that they were too few in number and too poor in material resources to preserve themselves. Without God they were as vulnerable as a Passover lamb.

Yet even through periods of Israel's unfaithfulness to the covenant, God remembered the Israelites and remained active in their affairs—affairs that continued to carry them toward a new covenant.

A Passover meal was the occasion at which Jesus initiated what would became known as the Lord's Supper, and those gathered in the upper room had a kingdom conferred on them (Luke 22:28-30). No one but Jesus realized yet that the blood of the Passover lamb, even though it once warded off Israel's physical death, would no longer suffice. In order for his followers to take their thrones, Jesus had to shed his blood. A stumbling block for many, Jesus' atoning blood would issue a new relationship between God and Israel.

"I am the way, and the truth, and the life" (John 14:6).

Prayer: *Lord, the depth of your compassion and mercy overwhelms me. How tenderly you guided your chosen people along the portion of their spiritual journey that began at the first Passover and ended at the Lord's Supper! What awes me even more is that you do the same for me as I grope my way along this part of my spiritual path. I humbly thank you. Amen.*

Friday, September 3   Read Matthew 18:15-17.

Jesus ascended to heaven, leaving behind a new church with no clear-cut local leadership. The scattered congregations would have to feel their way through many first-time situations. On certain issues, however, Jesus had left specific advice. One was about the matter of church discipline.

Surely, the implication here is that Jesus wanted church members to shun the unrepentant sinner in much the same way as their contemporaries avoided Gentiles and tax collectors. Oddly enough, such conduct was inconsistent with the way Jesus treated these groups during his earthly ministry.

Still, there may be a logical explanation for this apparent dichotomy. Many Gentiles and tax collectors were included among those who did listen to Jesus and whose lives had changed as a result. The self-righteous unrepentant did not.

On them, Jesus vented his anger and called them such stinging names as "hypocrites," "blind fools," "serpents," "blind guides" and "whitewashed tombs" (Matt. 23:13-36).

The spiritual corrosion that results when an unrepentant sinner is allowed to remain in Christ's church is important enough to warrant his advice. The new congregations heeded it. Do we?

Or do we remain strangely silent because of something else Jesus said? "Let anyone among you who is without sin be the first to throw a stone at her" (see John 8:7). If so, we overlook Jesus' final—and disciplinary—statement to the adulteress. "Go,… and do not sin again" (v. 11).

Sinners not only belong to, they *are* the church of Jesus Christ. Only by refusing to repent can they rob themselves of their usefulness to their Savior and to their local church.

Prayer: *Lord, guide us as we in the church seek to follow your way. Amen.*

Saturday, September 4   Read Matthew 18:18-20.

The promise Jesus has already given to Peter (Matthew 16:18-19) is now extended to all his disciples. It is a familiar concept placed in a new context. The disciples know only that in rabbinical law whatever one binds is forbidden and whatever one looses is permitted.

What is it they are supposed to forbid or permit on earth? Can it mean that they are supposed to decide what is or is not the Lord's will when he is no longer with them? And, further, can it be possible that their decisions will be approved automatically in heaven? What if they err?

It is an overwhelming responsibility, but they will not be expected to shoulder it alone. Jesus assures them that he will be with them whenever they gather in his name—even if there are only two or three of them. To disciples finally beginning to understand their enigmatic teacher, this assurance implies that his tremendous power will also be there. They soon come to learn that they are right.

Unfortunately, the church of Christ today seems to have lost sight of this fact. We tend to reflect society's attitude that strength lies in numbers. How often we hear churches with large congregations referred to as "successful" and those with small congregations as "struggling." Yet we need only to look back at the military victories of tiny Israel to realize that God is not dependent upon size for divine miracles.

God's power can be unleashed whenever two or three are gathered in the name of Jesus.

Prayer: *Lord, help me to feel your presence when I gather with others in your name. Remind me that your very name has far greater power than all my strengths and talents combined, and help me to know your will. Amen.*

Sunday, September 5   Read Romans 13:8-14.

Individual believers, as well as new church bodies, need advice. Here Paul makes two points to help them with their new Christian life-styles.

The first covers what he feels should be their attitude toward debt: If you owe it, pay it and clear the books. He notes an exception, however. The debt of love should remain outstanding and, at the same time, be paid every day.

Paul's claim, that by doing so one will keep all of God's laws, is based on Jesus' second great commandment (Matt. 22:35-40). Love is the umbrella that covers all the commandments. If we *truly* love God and others, the activities that appeal to us will be ones that do not cause us to sin against either.

His second point, the need for a moral life-style, has a sense of urgency about it. Paul believes that Jesus' return is imminent. The fact that we still wait does not lessen the value of his advice. Each day brings us a step closer to either the Lord's coming in glory or our going home to him in death. Does it matter which? We need to be ready.

We have looked this week at some of the new beginnings God's chosen people faced as they journeyed from bondage in Egypt to freedom in Christ. In Romans and elsewhere, Paul highlights the key requisite on which his spiritual journey, and all others, rests. He says that all commandments are summed up in the directive to: "Love your neighbor as yourself," which echoes Jesus' words, "Just as I have loved you, you also should love one another" (John 13:34-35).

Suggestion for meditation: *How do I accept the new beginnings God introduces into my life? Do I step eagerly into the unknown with the sure confidence that God's word will be "a lamp to my feet and a light to my path" (Psalm 119:105)? And do I go with a love that has been generated by my gratitude to God?*

FACING CONFLICT CREATIVELY

September 6-12, 1993   **Robert Corin Morris** ✢
Monday, September 6   Read Exodus 14:19-31.

Right conflict

Facing conflict is inevitable. While we may not be able to avoid conflict, we can choose *how* we fight.

The way of Jesus involves models for "right conflict" rooted in the scriptural pictures of God's loving combat for human good. As in Moses' case, the first step is to present just complaints and seek a reasonable compromise. After Pharaoh's rejection of justice and his display of contempt for the sacred Heart of the slaves' culture, God, through Moses, sends a carefully escalated set of disruptions. But, even now, after the death of his firstborn son, Pharaoh is still locked into the delusion of his own omnipotence, and so he breaks his promise and pursues the fleeing Israelites.

God keeps the two groups apart, as if giving the Egyptians one last chance. Only when all else has failed does the ancient tale picture God unleashing an unrestrained torrent of destructive power against the Egyptian leaders. In all prophetic warning and social conflict, God is pictured restraining wrath, pursuing mercy, offering alternatives, and using catastrophe only when we finally bring it upon our own heads. Personal conflicts, from parenting to partnership and social struggles, from the pastorate to the presidency, can benefit from this model of restraint.

Prayer: *O God, help me remember mercy even when I am angry and restraint when I am fighting. Amen.*

✢Episcopal priest and spiritual guide; Director, Interweave, Inc., an interfaith adult education center in Summit, New Jersey.

Tuesday, September 7   Read Exodus 15:1*b*-11.

A warrior God?

The God praised in this *Song of Moses* comes among us as a Warrior! This image, prized by many warlike generations, may well disturb us who live in an age when shooting war is less and less a realistic option for dealing with human disputes. But in the scriptural saga, God cannot avoid conflict any more than we can and is seen as energizing the people for battle. David praises the Thunderstorm Power that fills his warriors (Psalm 18), while Deborah as judge or tribal leader prays for that Power to defeat the Midianites (Judg. 5), and Jesus overturns the tables in the Temple (Matt. 21:12-17).

Verses from Moses' song are part of Jewish daily prayer, and the Sabbath service's *Hymn of Glory* pictures God as a strong young man in battle, his tanned face a radiant gold. Thrusting and turning in his blood-red garments, his black locks swirling about him in flowing curls and tightly woven plaiting, star-studded by the night dewdrops reflecting the morning sun in them. This shining power is praised as a manly facet of the Divine Glory, even as the Sabbath Bride is welcomed as a womanly aspect. Only one image of the way God works, it is nonetheless biblical.

Since we know God's final goal for us is to "study war no more," ought the Warrior imagery be ripped out of the musculature of the body of biblical images? Or does the warrior impulse in us all, like the sexual flame and even the caring heart, need training and consecrating to grow up into the Christ, who alone knows the art of right conflict?

Prayer: *O God, help me pick my battles wisely and face my opponents in the spirit of the strong and tender Christ. Amen.*

Wednesday, September 8   Read Exodus 15:20-21.

Victory dance

The women dance their own victory dance. Miriam, a prophet like her brother Moses, leads the rejoicing. The repetition of the opening lines of Moses' Song may suggest that the men and women sang the Victory Cry back and forth to each other "with tambourine and dance" (Ps. 150:4). Thus, the Song of Moses is also the Song of Miriam, and some speculate that she may have written the original.

In any case, it is a sign that the sisters are as invested in a successful outcome to conflict as their brothers. Depending on the culture, males and females may have very different styles of battle, but universally, all of us face the challenge of fighting sooner or later.

But does *God* take sides in our conflicts? This idea can be used to justify monstrous behavior and "holy" war. Yet the God known in the biblical story does have a strong taste for justice and a terrible fondness for those oppressed by sin's power or social evil, and this leads to confrontation. We know this much: if God takes sides with one group against another, it is only for strategic purposes, so that, in the end, the whole world will be better for both groups. Pharaoh is defeated for Egypt's sake, and Jesus advocates active love for his crucifiers and our every opponent. Christ's attitude is rooted in the same spirit as the old rabbinical legend which pictures God stopping the angels from joining this hymn of praise with the sad query: "Why do you rejoice when my children the Egyptians lie dead upon the shore?" Presumably the sound of the tambourines and drums was too loud for the humans to hear God's question.

Prayer: *Just and merciful One, keep me from gloating over the downfall of anyone, even those who oppose me. Amen.*

Thursday, September 9   Read Romans 14:1-12.

Christian differences

The "whole group of those who believed" may indeed have been "of one heart and soul" (Acts 4:32) right after the first Christian Pentecost, but the disciples have seldom been of one mind since then. Unfortunately, at times differences about even minor things have led to vicious behavior.

Paul wants the early Christians to be generous in their treatment of some differing ways of devotion and discipleship, bending over backwards to accommodate each other. The disputes may involve Jewish-Christian practices obscure to us. Eating vegetables might be a kind of Messianic vegetarianism, celebrating the restoration of the diet of Paradise in Christ. Or it might be a Jewish-Christian way of eating with Gentile-Christians without eating non-kosher meat. "Judg[ing] one day to be better than another" probably involves minor Jewish holy days, such as full and new moon, or even the Zodiacal beliefs of some Jewish mysticism. Paul, who himself teaches that such practices are "weakness," wants us to look beyond the practice to the heart of the practitioner, who does it "in honor of the Lord."

We are seldom of one mind in the churches, but we can be of one heart and soul if we learn to accept the confession "Jesus is *kyrios*" (Lord, Shepherd-Leader) as the all-inclusive, simple test of family membership, especially over differing devotional and discipleship styles. This spirit is also crucial in facing the more substantial issues of morals and politics and authority that are once again dividing Christians.

Prayer: *Generous Christ, let me see the heart of love for you behind the words and deeds of those who do not follow you in what I think is the "right way." Amen.*

Friday, September 10   Read Matthew 18:21-27.

Living as family

From its beginning the church has been called "family" and its members "brothers" and "sisters." But all of us know that families are likely to cause some of our deepest wounds as well as some of our fondest memories. Forgiving family members is not a remote ideal but a survival tactic!

The radical, revolutionary Judaism in Jesus' day spawned many "brotherhood" groups like the Dead Sea Scroll Community, with strict "Manuals of Discipline." Such a manual may lie behind Peter's question: "Master, this Sect demands that their members forgive an offending colleague as many as seven times. Can people be allowed to go on messing up? What about good discipline?" (AP)

Jesus' answer, in Matthew's own "Manual of Church Discipline" section must have surprised Peter: "Seven times is hardly a beginning! Seventy-seven times is more like it! There can't be a limit to your willingness to stick with a family member to the end" (AP). Good order in functioning groups—families at home, teams at work, churches in mission—comes out of good relationships, and forgiveness is the door to working through problems.

When injury is done, the most important thing is real reconciliation. This does not mean putting up with destructive behavior endlessly. It does mean being willing to give up the grudges we inevitably accumulate, lay our cards on the table, settle accounts with each other, and go on together, learning from our mistakes. Otherwise, the debt load of withheld resentment gets too crushing, contaminating every encounter. Families cannot function well that way.

Prayer: *Discipline me with your own skill in forgiveness, O God, for I am not very good at it. Amen.*

Saturday, September 11   Read Matthew 18:27-35.

Terminal righteousness

Conflict can breed self-righteousness, a terminal disease of the human spirit. Being in the right becomes more important than being in right relation, proving others wrong more important than the struggle for common truth.

The master who forgives millions of dollars is not financially impractical but deeply wise about long-term investment in people. Rather than standing on his "rightness," he seeks the good of all. What monetary good will it do him to put the bankrupt servant in prison or sell him into slavery? The loan needs to be renegotiated or forgiven outright, and everyone will benefit.

Jesus' parable is rooted in the economic ethic of the Torah, which demands the remission of debts every fiftieth year, the year of Jubliee (Lev. 25:8-55). This was designed to avoid a common disaster of ancient societies— accumulation of debt over many generations, leading to the servitude of whole families. Jesus insisted on economic obedience to this law (see Luke 4:19) and used it as a symbol of the emotional economics of personal relationships.

But the forgiven man hasn't learned the lesson. He cares more for his own rightness than for productive relations with his debtors. He goes after his short-term gain rather than investing in *our* common future.

Such refusal to forgive is a short-term, bitter pleasure masquerading as real right-eousness. It has its own lonely reward: being right. We are most likely to fall prey to this pseudo-righteousness when we know society will side with us as the aggrieved party.

Prayer: *Lord, help me note the times today I hold others crossly to standards I break myself. Amen.*

Sunday, September 12   Read Matthew 18:34-35.

Divine torture?

The God of just love described in this week's lessons may take sides for a while with one group against another, but always for the long-term good of all humanity. Sometimes God takes sides against *us!*

From Genesis to Revelation, God is pictured as acting both in both forgiving love and forceful judgment. Some of the most bloodcurdling images of judgment are reported as part of Jesus' own teaching, like this warning about torture.

This is disciplinary action, however, not vindictive revenge. We suffer the consequences of our sins until we realize we must change. The oppressor state must suffer the plagues caused by its own injustice, churches must suffer the consequences of their own self-righteous partisan battles, the disciples must be tortured by their own internal anger and outward wrangling until they change.

Until we learn to cooperate with the inclusive nature of God's just love, which seeks the good of all, God's love must, in part, will be experienced as a threat and a judgment.

Jesus is trying to warn his followers that having a heart ready to forgive is the only way to work through conflicts successfully. Unforgiving hearts face inner torture and escalating outer conflict. We begin to dwell in darkness.

There is a better way. It involves never forgetting that even your worst enemy is still a member of the family and that, sooner or later, you will eat together again.

Prayer: *Try me, O God, and seek the ground of my heart. Look well if there be any way of wickedness in me. Amen.*[*]

---

[*]Psalm 139:2*a, 24*b; from "The Psalter," *The Book of Common Prayer*, The Protestant Episcopal Church in the U.S.A., 1929.

THE FAITHFULNESS OF GOD

September 13-19, 1993   Helen R. Neinast✣
Monday, September 13   Read Exodus 16:2-15.

The scene is the prototype for the Israelites' life in the wilderness. God leads them away from danger, delivers them from oppression. They respond by singing God's praises (Exod. 15). But when the next step goes less smoothly, their rejoicing turns to bitter complaint. One moment, they proclaim God is their Savior and Lord; the next, that God is guilty of neglect and of mistreatment.

In today's passage, the faith of the Israelites is "eroding like the sand dunes."* The people have been led out of Egypt, but now there is a food crisis. Their murmuring grows louder. They complain bitterly. Their complaints turn to accusations—against Moses and Aaron and God.

God's reaction is a curious one. Instead of getting angry with the people for their lack of faith, God responds by blessing them with "bread from heaven" that rains down by day, and with flocks of quail that cover the camp by night. In response to Israel's lack of faith, God is faithful. The manna continues daily to feed the Israelites for forty years.

That is the message of Exodus 16. God's graciousness, God's faithfulness, prevails for the Israelites. The same is true for us. Over the years, through all our life's circumstances, in spite of our complaining, God is faithful.

Suggestion for meditation: *Sit quietly and reflect on the ways God has been faithful to you in the last days and weeks.*

---

*Terence Fretheim, *Exodus,* volume from Interpretation, A Bible Commentary (John Knox Press, copyright 1991), p. 181.
✣United Methodist minister in the New Mexico Conference; writer and consultant in higher education; Tampa, Florida.

Tuesday, September 14   Read Philippians 1:18-26.

Torn between hope and despair. Not knowing whether to go on living or to wish for death. Whether it is a crisis of physical health, of emotional stability, or of grief, loss, or indecision, each of us has known the terrible struggle of which Paul writes in Philippians.

The very difficulty of the passage Paul has written—his awkward wording, his confused sentences—reflects Paul's disturbed frame of mind. He even quotes Job—the quintessential sufferer (v. 9).

It is an odd passage, written while Paul is in prison. The suffering, the torment, the physical drain of his imprisonment are evident. He wonders whether it is better to live or to die. *What is to be gained by living?* he asks. The chance to witness once again to the gospel of Christ. *Yet, on the other hand, what is to be gained by dying?* he wonders. Release from trouble and pain, the chance to know Christ fully, at last.

Paul says that he is torn between the two. In one sense, he knows that this—living or dying—is not his decision to make. But in another sense, he can take initiative: he can decide what his attitude will be in his present circumstance.

Oddly enough, in the midst of Paul's confusion and despair, one belief frames his agony: that God is faithful and will always remain so. No matter what, God will deliver him. It is upon this bedrock that his faith rests.

God's faithfulness—it is on this same bedrock that our own faith, however strong or troubled, rests. The promise is sure . . . God's graciousness prevails.

Prayer: *In times of confusion, doubt and despair, stay near to us, God. Hold fast to us in your faithfulness. Amen.*

Wednesday, September 15   Read Philippians 1:27–2:16.

Although the Philippians reading for this week actually ends at verse 30, it is important to read further in order to gain a fuller sense of what Paul is trying to say to the church in this passage.

Philippians 1:27 begins a new direction in Paul's thought. In the passage before, Paul has been speaking only implicitly to the people at Philippi about how they are to respond in faith. In this next passage, he begins to preach *explicitly* to them about their actions and their faith.

In verses 27-30, Paul exhorts the people to live a life worthy of the gospel of Christ. They are to do this in Philippi, the city in which they live, a city aligned with and loyal to Caesar, a city that could and did make it difficult for followers of Christ to profess and live their faith. The suffering they will go through because of their faith is, according to Paul, a way of sharing in Christ's own suffering.

The rest of the passage (through 2:16) is rich with images on which to model the Christian life—soldiers, citizens, athletes, gladiators. But it is the image of servant that is, according to Paul, the best image for the Christian life. Christ as servant—humble, obedient, faithful—is the best model for the Philippians in their struggle to be faithful.

God's faithfulness—in the form of Jesus the servant— once again prevails. Through many challenges and trials, God is faithful. Because of God's faithfulness, Paul says, we are strengthened in the faith. God's faithfulness prevails in calling us to a strong life of faith.

Suggestion for meditation: *Reflect on the ways God's faithfulness has impacted your own struggle to be faithful. What difference does it make to know that any struggles you face because of your faith are linked to Jesus' struggles to be faithful to his calling?*

Thursday, September 16   Read Matthew 20:1-7.

In biblical times, the working day started with the rising of the sun and ended at sunset, when the stars appeared. The first group of workers went out to the vineyard at sunrise, the next at 9:00 a.m., the next at noon, then another group at 3:00 p.m. The last group would have arrived about 5:00 in the afternoon.

The striking part of this parable is often overlooked. While it is noteworthy that some went to work at sunrise and some did not begin their labor until ten or eleven hours later, these facts do not figure until later in the story.

The poignancy of this story, then, is not in the lateness of the hour that the last group went to work, but in the urgency of the need of these last-recruited workers. These people needed the work and the money, or they would not have waited all day in the marketplace to be hired. The image that comes to mind is not unlike that of the long lines of unemployed people of our time, desperate to provide for their families.

And so a compassionate householder (or else one who had underestimated his labor needs for the day!) gives these needy people the chance to work, even near the end of the day.

Imagine the relief these last-minute hires must have felt. Instead of going home penniless at the end of the day, they would have *something* with which to buy food. However late they were called to work, they were grateful to be called at all.

God's approach to us is not unlike the householder's approach to his last-minute workers. When we feel we have no resources to meet our families' needs, when we worry that we will have nothing but emptiness at the end of the day, God steps in. Even at the last minute, God responds to our need and we, like the workers in the vineyard, are grateful.

Prayer: *Ever-faithful God, you see our needs and in compassion you respond to us daily. Thank you for your faithfulness. Amen.*

Friday, September 17   Read Matthew 20:8-16.

Now for the intriguing and troublesome part of this parable. Workers have been toiling in the vineyard—some since sunrise, some since noon, some only an hour or two. It has been hot and exhausting work: the Palestinian sun, along with the scorching heat of the sirocco off the desert, has made this day seem long, even for those who had spent only the last few hours working.

At the end of the day, all the workers have gathered to be paid. For some reason, the latecomers are paid first. They were given a denarius—a generous wage for the entire day, much less for a few hours' work! But to their astonishment and anger, all the other workers received exactly the same amount as the latecomers.

The householder's—and God's—reply is swift: "Am I not allowed to do what I choose with what belongs to me?"

This is not the reply of a capricious and arbitrary God. It is the response of a God who is faithful, who keeps promises made. The householder had promised one denarius to the first group of workers, and he fulfilled his promise. The fact that he chose to be generous to those who had come later was a sign not of unfairness but of graciousness.

God's faithfulness, the Bible reminds us, is gracious and compassionate. God's faithfulness to us is not based on merit but on grace. For that, the parable says, we must not grumble but rejoice.

This is the true measure of God's faithfulness: "For by grace you have been saved through faith, and this is not your own doing; it is the gift of God" (Eph. 2:8-9).

Prayer: *Focus our hearts on rejoicing in the majesty of your faithfulness, gracious God. Help us to know that we are, indeed, latecomers to the vineyard of your grace. Amen.*

Saturday, September 18   Read Psalm 105:1-36.

Today's reading was written for use by a congregation at worship, and it is a hymn of praise. It might have been used at daily worship services, during festivals, or by an individual in private worship. It was sung as a hymn for renewal of commitment to the covenant between God and Israel.

In Psalm 105, the psalmist launches into a long recital of God's wondrous faithfulness to the covenant made with Israel. This is God's history with God's people. This is a song about God's power, God's faithfulness, remembered by a grateful congregation. The psalmist knew the value of time spent in reflection, remembering, looking back.

By singing this psalm, the congregation began to develop the discipline of remembering, or reflection. There is much encouragement to be gained from looking back and tracing God's involvement in the life of the community. The psalmist knew this, and encouraged it in this hymn.

As Christians, we have ritualized ways of remembering, or reflecting on the history of our faith. Advent, Christmas, Lent, Easter, Pentecost—these seasons build our faith by reminding us of God's involvement in our lives.

What would it be like for us as Christian communities—as local churches and congregations with long histories of God's care and concern for us—what would it be like if we sat down to write our own psalm of praise to God? What events would we include in our "salvation history" to mark with joy and wonder God's power and love for us?

Prayer: *O steadfast and sure God, we give you thanks for the amazing gifts you have bestowed on us, on our parents, and on their parents before them. Our remembrance is filled with joy for all the wondrous things you have done. Amen.*

273

Sunday, September 19   Read Psalm 105:37-45.

In the last verses of this psalm, we are led full circle by the lectionary, back to the story in Exodus 16 of God's provision of manna and quail to the people in the wilderness.

Once again, the psalm reminds us, God remembers the promise made to Abraham and Sarah, and God is faithful. Not only did God provide meat and bread, God also made water gush from the rocks, and at last led the people with joy and gladness into the promised land.

The psalm is a powerful song that lifts the eyes and ears of the worshipper from her or his own crises and problems to the graciousness and steadfastness of God.

But why has God done such great things for the people? Is it because the people have done something to deserve such treatment? Hardly. Recall the Israelites' many stumbling efforts and false starts on the way to Canaan, remember the workers who came late to the vineyard, and see how that mirrors our own meandering paths toward belief.

No, the reason God has done such great things for God's people is single-fold: God has been faithful to encourage us to be faithful. The purpose of God's historic acts—in the lives of the Israelites, in the lives of the early Christians, and in our own lives—is to create an obedient, faithful people.

God's will for us is the same as the gift God extends to us—faithfulness at all times and in all circumstances. The promise is sure: God is faithful. And the message for us is also plain: God, who is strong enough to make such a promise, will be constant enough to keep it. We are called to do the same.

Suggestion for meditation: *Think of the promise God made to you. How does God's faithfulness to that promise affect the way you follow through on your commitments to God? to yourself? to others?*

1994

is just around the corner!
Now is the time to order your copy of
THE UPPER ROOM DISCIPLINES 1994

Year after year, *The Upper Room Disciplines* continues to appeal to more and more Christians who, like yourself, desire a more disciplined spiritual life. Be sure to order your copy today, while the 1994 edition is still available.

SEEING MIRACLES, HEARING THE MESSAGE

September 20-26, 1993   **Glen J. Stewart**✝
Monday, September 20   Read Exodus 17:1-7.

A woman is seated hunched over the unconscious body of her husband, praying without words. Praying that he might be healed of the illness he and she are fighting. They have spent many days in the hospital, and she has prayed like this many times. A surgeon worked on her husband's body today that he might be made healthy again.

The next morning when she comes to the hospital the surgeon tells them both the surgery was successful, the illness not as bad as they originally thought, that all will be well soon.

They experienced a miracle. Such miracles change lives. They lift lives. Just telling and hearing the telling of the miracle lifts lives. Such miracles happen every day, yet many of us are too busy to see or realize the miracles that happen around us. The Israelites could not deny this miracle. The water pouring from the rock hit them in the face. It cooled their hot, burnt brows. But in our hurried world we miss a lot of miracles, miracles that would lift our lives, bringing renewal and confidence that God lives and is active in the world.

Keep your eyes and ears wide open to the miracles that will happen around you today. Light will shine on any life that witnesses a miracle.

Prayer: *Take me to a miracle today, O God. Open my eyes and ears that I might witness a miracle that renews my life. Amen.*

✝Associate Regional Minister of the Christian Church (Disciples of Christ) of Greater Kansas City, Mission, Kansas.

Tuesday, September 21   Read Psalm 78:1-4.

From mouth to mouth the great deeds of God are told. The deeds of God are life-giving and renewing, but even just the telling and the hearing of those deeds are life-giving too.

Stories about grandparents and great-grandparents in my family are numerous. The stories are about humorous events in their lives. I laugh each time I hear the stories. I laugh as I tell the stories as well. While I never knew these people, they seem to come to life in the telling of the stories.

The mysterious wonders of God were first explained and told by word of mouth from person to person, from elder to child, from believer to searcher. The greatness of God is revealed and appreciated each time the story is told and retold. The promise of verse 3 is meaningful: the greatness of God will not be hidden from coming generations but will be told and retold. In Sunday school classes, in living rooms, at kitchen tables, in sanctuaries, around camp fires, the greatness of God is told again and again. And with each telling, faith grows in both the hearer and the teller.

There will be times when stories will be told but meaning not understood. It could be years before the meanings of some stories are understood. Nonetheless, the stories need to be told.

We believers need not only to hear the stories of the greatness of God but also to tell them to others. For as we tell them our own faith grows, our lives are lifted, and we become witnesses to the greatness of God.

Prayer: *May I hear the story of your greatness told today, O God. May I have just the right place and time to tell the story. Amen.*

Wednesday, September 22   Read Psalms 78:12-16.

Today's scripture recounts some of the great events in the history of the Israelites. God performed miracles right in front of people. The psalmist sees all of God's creation as a miracle. And the miracles never cease to happen. God's creation of the earth and sea, God's gift of the sun and the stars—everything around us is seen as the hand of God working miracles in our midst.

How will God work miracles in your life today? For some, life is too busy and full of appointments and work to notice the beauty of a fall day. For others, the cool fall breeze, the changing colors of the leaves, the rain after a hot, dry summer are all gifts to be experienced, enjoyed, and appreciated. There is nothing great enough that it should keep us from enjoying God's continuing creation among us.

We easily get involved in our own work, our own success or misery, our own lives, so that what isl around us becomes invisible unless we can use it to our own purposes. So now we live with the results of dumping garbage on the land, in the streams, and in the air. We pollute our own lives as well by forgetting the importance and the beauty of the environment around us.

In addition to the list offered in the psalm, I would also offer our spouses and our children, our parents and grandparents, our brothers and sisters, our nieces and nephews, indeed, our whole families and all of our friends as gifts that have been especially given to us to love and appreciate and know as God's miracles in our lives.

How will you experience God's saving miracles today?

Prayer: *Thank you, God, for the gifts you will give me today. May my eyes and ears be open to seeing and hearing them and may I be ready to appreciate your gifts even more. Amen.*

Thursday, September 23   Read Philippians 2:1-11.

"I woke up this mornin' with my mind stayed on Jesus."*

This is the first line of a song that for me has been a powerful one. I first learned it at church camp but have sung it many times since. The song tells of the importance of keeping one's mind, heart, soul, and all we have focused on Jesus. Life would be a lot easier if one kept one's life "stayed on Jesus."

This idea is not a new one. It is Paul's theme in today's scripture reading: "Let the same mind be in you that was in Christ Jesus." Be of the same mind, be like Jesus, or, as many of us have sung, keep your mind "stayed on Jesus." Brother Lawrence, the seventeenth century monk who called his constant mind of prayer "practising the presence of God," encouraged others to be in a mind of prayer. Being of a mind like Jesus would be a prayer also.

Verses 6–11 are the words of a hymn sung in the first-century church. As the Christians of Philippi read this letter, they may have sung these lines; some may have hummed a favorite tune for the hymn. And as we do with the great camp songs, members of the Philippi congregation probably went home singing or humming this song. Paul used the words of this song to get across his point; by doing so he gave his readers a way to remember his point: "Let the same mind be in you that was in Christ Jesus."

Prayer: *O God, you have given us so much to set our minds and hearts upon. Today I ask your help to set my mind on Jesus. Help me to keep him on my mind and in my heart this day. Amen.*

*From an Afro-American spiritual.

Friday, September 24   Read Philippians 2:12-13.

"Work out your own salvation." What a task to be assigned on a Friday! Like the Christians at Philippi, we know that is not possible. Paul makes the assignment though to let folks know they need to contribute to this effort, too.

"Work like it all depends on you, pray like it all depends on God" is a phrase I have heard many times. Paul might have written that phrase here if he had heard it. Even more, Paul encouraged the readers to work out their own salvation with fear and trembling. By doing so, Paul is encouraging strength through weakness, greatness through humility, and salvation through weakness and trembling.

I have felt closest to God when I was most vulnerable. When I was weakest, I felt God's support in my life. When we are strong, when we feel our salvation is worked out, when all is going well, we often act as if God isn't needed. God's strength and support aren't felt. Through fear and trembling work on your salvation.

We often fail to realize how God is acting in and through our lives. We must admit our own weaknesses if we are to even begin to appreciate God's strength and support in our lives. I believe God is ever seeking new ways to work in and through our lives. If our own will and ego will only step aside, God will be present and work in our lives so much more.

Prayer: *Like plants that grow in the spring, we are in need of your light and presence in our lives. Speak to me today, O God, that I might recognize your voice in the midst of all the noise of my life. Amen.*

Saturday, September 25   Read Matthew 21:23-27.

Just after Jesus performs a miracle and tells the disciples that whatever they ask in prayer will be received, Jesus is thrust into another conflict with the religious authorities. The chief priests and elders always seemed to want to get Jesus into trouble by trying to trip him up, to get him to say something controversial, or to encourage him to say something against the law. I doubt if the questioners really wanted to know anything about Jesus' authority. They were more interested in protecting their own positions. They did not realize that by attacking him and eventually crucifying him they would kill the Messiah for whom they had waited for so long.

During the first century the Roman emperors wanted to get rid of Christians. They persecuted them, threw them to the lions, and tortured them. All Christians would have had to do to save their lives was to renounce Christ, but few did. And instead of killing of the faith and the faithful, the empire's actions brought others to Christianity because they were so impressed at the courage, the strength, the love, and the faith of the Christians who were put to the test. Christianity might never have caught hold in Europe without the persecution.

Tests draw the best of life from us. We might never know the best we can offer and give in life without being tested, questioned, troubled. Thanks, chief priests, you helped make it possible. Thanks, troubles, I didn't know I could do it. Thanks, God!

Prayer: *May I remember today, O God, that the challenges that come to me will draw the best from me and prepare me for even greater things you have in store for me. Amen.*

Sunday, September 26   Read Matthew 21:28-32.

Miracles are always renewing, uplifting experiences, but hearing Jesus' message is sometimes difficult. We sometimes don't like to hear some messages because we are afraid they might put us in a negative light. Today's parable hits all of us between the eyes. We have all procrastinated, and we have all done deeds we never thought we would ever find ourselves doing. Jesus uses such human ways to shine a light on how he and John the Baptist were accepted. I am sure the chief priests and elders were more concerned about tripping up Jesus than finding their place in God's kingdom, for they believed their place was secure. But for the rest of us who hear Jesus' words many decades later, the message can be sobering.

Like the chief priests and elders, there are times that we, too, feel upstanding, self-righteous about our faith. But the fact is, we have a lot to hear, learn, and realize to establish a place in the kingdom for us. Those of us who read the words of Jesus today feel more convicted by them than the elders did years ago. We should. We, too, are set in our ways, often using scripture to support our bad habits and sins. I doubt if life would be any better for us if we lived a life without Jesus, only to come to him late in life. We would be like the son who finally did as his father wanted him to do.

We are called to repentance and self-examination every day that we live. We need to compare our lives and our way of life to what Christ models for us in light of this parable. Jesus would be tough on most of us, for much is required of those who have much.

Prayer: *Help me to examine my life today O God. Don't let me hide my life in the scriptures, but allow the light of Christ to expose the darkest corners. Amen.*

GOD'S GRACE IN LIFE'S DISORDER

September 27–October 3, 1993   Thomas E. Frank✠
Monday, September 27   Read Exodus 20:18-21.

Imagine the Israelites at Sinai. They had fled from Pharaoh, rushed headlong through a miraculously parted sea, and then traveled on into a barren desert wilderness. Suddenly, it dawned on them that they were in the middle of nowhere, following an eighty-year-old man who had promised a land of milk and honey for them. But first they must stop at this mountain, Moses had said, and hear what the Lord had to say.

When Moses had gotten his charge from the Lord to go to Pharaoh and say, "Let my people go," he had been at the foot of this mountain, also called Horeb (see Exodus 3). Horeb means "wasteland," and that was an understatement! "We would rather go back to Egypt," cried the people, hungry, thirsty, and exhausted (Exod. 16:3).

The Lord sent manna with the dew, but the people whined, "What is it?" (16:15) The Lord made water flow from a rock, but the people were soon thirsty again (17:1-7). Now the Lord called the people to the mountain, shrouded in darkness, thunder and smoke, to hear a word.

But the people trembled, for they could not see the wasteland for what it was: a place of grace, where in their neediness they could learn to rely on God. In the fear and despair of their lives, could the Lord have a word for them?

Suggestion for meditation: *Read Psalm 114. How has God spoken in my wilderness?*

✠Assistant Professor of Congregational Life, Candler School of Theology, Emory University, Atlanta, Georgia.

Tuesday, September 28   Read Exodus 20:1-17.

The people Israel stood skeptically before a rock at Meribah, waiting for Moses to produce some water in the wilderness. "What did you bring us out here for, to kill us with thirst?" they cried. But Moses struck the rock with his staff, and water flowed to quench the people's thirst (17:1-7).

Similarly, I stand before the rock of the Ten Commandments. Where is the water here? Is there life for me in these formidable "thou shalt nots"?

These are only ten of the hundreds of commandments and laws in the Torah, (the first five books of the Bible). Christians do not pay attention to the others, though, such as what to do with an ox that gores someone. What is it that is so compelling about these ten?

Jesus repeated them to the rich young ruler as the basis on which the man could be saved (Matt. 19:16-22). But Jesus went on to say that they were not enough, that the young man should sell all his possessions and give the money to the poor—then he would be perfected in God.

And perhaps that is the water from the rock. The Decalogue comprises ten words (deca—logos) of life, intended to keep my life centered, focused and balanced in God. They remind me of what God has done for me ("I brought you out of Egypt"). They relieve me of the young man's burden of constant work, achievement, and accumulation of possessions by letting me rest in the wondrous grace of God, the Creator of heaven and earth ("Remember the Sabbath").

Jesus said, "Follow me"; and the poor fishermen dropped their nets to come along. But hearing the same call, the rich young ruler turned away. Which one am I?

Suggestion for meditation: *Read Psalm 1. Where do I find the waters of life?*

Wednesday, September 29   Read Psalm 19.

Nowhere in scripture is the unity and order of creation in God more eloquently displayed than in Psalm 19. Nature and humanity are in perfect harmony. For humanity's part, the law of the Lord provides a trustworthy order of life that is righteous, sure, clear, pure, true (vv. 7-10). Such a life even tastes good, sweeter than honey.

As if to mirror that perfection of human order, nature itself proclaims the glory of God in the wonders of the heavens (vv. 1-6). The daily course of the sun across the sky is a sign of God's faithfulness. Indeed, these are joyous rounds, the sun acting like a newlywed emerging from the wedding tent, an athlete exhilarated with the race.

Then what a sour note is struck by the jarring language of warning, error, fault and insolence (vv. 11-13). Where did that come from? What is evil doing in this perfect universe?

I am thrown again into the continual human struggle for a life of integrity and justice. "LORD, why do you hide yourself in times of trouble?" wonders the psalmist (10:1) "The voice of the LORD shakes the wilderness...and strips the forest bare" (29:8-9). And so I call out for God's help in a world quaking with chaos.

I cannot always expect to look at the heavens with Psalm 19 eyes. Shaken by the death of a parent, upset by the divorce of good friends, distressed by the faces of hunger and poverty, I cannot glibly mouth such words of orderliness and glory. My tongue is tied, and the Spirit must give me the words to speak. And what does the Spirit whisper me to say? "O LORD, my rock and my redeemer."

Suggestion for meditation: *In "the meditations of my heart," how am I learning to trust God, Creator of beauty, Redeemer of a troubled world?*

Thursday, September 30   Read Philippians 3:4*b*-9.

Paul was extremely righteous under the Law, observing all the commandments. He was so outraged by the people claiming Messiah had come, he led in their persecution.

But then something happened that turned all these achievements to rubbish. The Sabbath "attendance pins" and the proscribed daily prayer routine came to seem outdated, useless.

It's risky, this throwing out everything from one's past life. Every time I clean out my closet, I stall over the sweater Grandma gave me or my favorite old jeans.

What's wrong with keeping these things another year? I ask. There wasn't really anything wrong with Paul's life; the world could stand more righteous people. Why did he turn away from his old life? Did he find it empty, unfulfilling?

No. That is just my attempt to explain Paul's actions out of my own needs. Paul saw nothing wrong with his life. He just met Jesus, that's all. And after he met Jesus, nothing was ever the same again. "The value of knowing Christ Jesus"—his voice soaring now—"surpasses everything."

Paul was not among the Twelve. He saw none of Jesus' miracles, heard none of his parables. He did not parade with him into Jerusalem, and he was not at the cross. He never sought Jesus at all. But Jesus found him.

I go to church, sing the hymns, give my offering, volunteer to teach. I know how to be a pretty good church member. but what I really want is for Jesus to find me, too.

Prayer: *Lord, hear my longing for Jesus to find me. Amen.*

Friday, October 1   Read Philippians 3:10-14.

I often wonder if Paul's contemporaries doubted his sanity; or, at the least, wondered that he made up what he said had happened to him.

"You say you met this Jesus on the road that runs up to Damascus?" some may have said.

Others may have mocked him, "What did he look like? He was executed years ago."

But Paul was nothing if not tenacious. He was not going to let his experience or his vocation slip away. The resurrected Lord had spoken his name, that he knew for sure. And even if his skeptics doubted the experience, they could not long question the fruit of Paul's calling.

Because of his call, Paul was willing to suffer just as Jesus had. He was fearless, not out of naïveté, but out of courage. He was going to witness to Christ's power to change lives, even if it cost him his safety, his home, or his life.

Once he heard the call, Paul could even forget the past, his guilt, his obsession with saving himself by practicing the law. Now he saw the prize, an all-surpassing life in Christ. And through his witness, people down through the centuries have been drawn to listen.

So Paul's life itself became a sign of what people who did not know Christ for themselves could hope for. Is my life, and my congregation's life, such a sign?

Suggestion for meditation: *How is my life a witness to my calling in Jesus Christ?*

Saturday, October 2   Read Matthew 21:33-41.

Jesus' journey had at last brought him to Jerusalem. Daily, he taught in the Temple courtyard, where disciples would gather around their various rabbis to hear the word of God interpreted, listen to stories, and debate. It soon became apparent that Jesus' stories had an edge to them. People gathered around him, some hoping just for the heated debate, some to hang him up in something heretical.

"Once upon a time,..." Jesus began, and a story unfolded that, like a bad TV show, was laced with murder and mayhem, the tenants so obviously crooks, the landlord so obviously innocent that when Jesus asked his listeners what the owner should do, they were unanimous: throw the bums out.

"Once upon a time," the prophet Nathan had said, "a rich man stole, slaughtered, and ate a poor man's favorite pet lamb." "Oh," cried David, "that's awful! He should pay dearly for that." Nathan looked at the king—who had just taken Uriah's wife as his own and arranged for Uriah to die in battle—and said, "You are the man." (See 2 Sam. 12.)

But when Jesus told his story, he was more direct. "You," he was saying to the scribes and Pharisees, "have forgotten who owns the vineyard."

I wonder sometimes if I am not a Pharisee myself. I find it hard not to think of my faith as a possession. I find myself thinking of *my* church, *my* sanctuary, *my* pew, *my* beliefs.

What a relief to know that nobody owns God's good creation or our faith in God's purposes. It all belongs to God alone and comes to us by God's grace. And that means I am free to follow Jesus, even to Jerusalem, even to a cross.

Suggestion for meditation: *If I am only a tenant, a sojourner in God's creation, then how should I treat the earth and my fellow sojourners?*

Sunday, October 3   Read Matthew 21:42-43.

I suppose everybody has a favorite house. My childhood memories still gather in the spacious, rambling rooms of my aunt's home. My eye roams from the vastness of the wrap-around porch, to the living room's high ceiling with its wooden beams, up a stately staircase to the chain of bed-rooms linked around a huge central bath, to the mysterious stairs leading to a toy-filled attic, back down the stairs to the sunlit kitchen.

It is not only the spaces, of course. It is that I have always felt at home in this house, where there is always room for me.

Jesus is the cornerstone, he tells his listeners, upon which a great house will be built. According to Peter, as we are filled with gifts and graces by the Spirit, we become living stones. Aligned with the cornerstone, Christ, we are built up into a spiritual house where God lives (1 Peter 2:4-5). We receive our calling to be stewards of the household.

Stewardship is not ownership; rather, it is finding the particular grace or gift God has given me, and using it for the good of the household (1 Peter 4:10). When I have found how my gift fits in, I am truly at home in the house (Eph. 4:11-16).

At table with his disciples for a last supper, Jesus washed their feet, blessed and broke bread, and served them a cup of wine. Then he spoke to them of God's house and its many rooms. You will have a place there, he said (John 14:2).

As I grow in discipleship of Christ, I am gradually finding my place in the household. I am learning how God wants me to use my gift. But the best part is that there is room for me here because Jesus is the host.

Suggestion for meditation: *Read Psalm 84.*
Prayer: *"How lovely is your dwelling place, O God." Amen.*

TO BE GOD'S PEOPLE

October 4-10, 1993   **David Randell Boone**✠

Monday, October 4   Read Deuteronomy 14:1-8.

In a few weeks, on November 1, we will celebrate All Saints Day. Celebrating All Saints Day affirms the mystical fellowship in Christ that all God's covenant people enjoy. And the special point of the festival is that this fellowship includes all our spiritual forbears in Israel and all those of the church who have passed on into eternity. On this occasion we often sing William W. How's great lines:

> O blest communion, fellowship divine!
> We feebly struggle, they in glory shine;
> Yet all are one in thee, for all are thine.
> Alleluia, Alleluia!*

In the Bible, to be a saint means to be holy, consecrated, and set apart for God. Christians are part of a people God has chosen to be special or *peculiar* (see 1 Peter 2:9, KJV). Christian life reflects values and practices that are visibly distinctive.

Even Israel's grieving and dietary customs were distinctive, so that God's covenant community could be distinguished from non-covenanted neighbors. Not eating pork reminds Hebrews of the blessings of Jewishness. What practices in our lives remind *us* that we are saints of God?

Prayer: *God of Abraham and Sarah, I am grateful for the joys and responsibilities of being called apart for you. Amen.*

✠Interim Pastor, Blue Ash Presbyterian Church, Cincinnati, Ohio.
*From the hymn "For All the Saints" by William W. How (based on Hebrews 12:1).

Tuesday, October 5   Read Psalm 135:1-4.

Like other psalms, Psalm 135 was used in the worship of the Jerusalem Temple. It was to be sung by "you that stand in the house of the LORD." When any translation (version) of the Bible prints LORD in all capitals, we are to understand that the Hebrew text has God's distinctive, proper name: Yahweh. Actually, Yahweh is only an educated guess about how the name would have been pronounced, since 1) ancient Hebrew had no written vowels, and 2) it was taboo for anyone, even a priest or scribe, to speak this proper name of the God of Israel. Hebrew faith took its responsibility to hallow God's name very seriously indeed.

Not only is Yahweh's name special. For our psalm contrasts Yahweh's power and goodness with the impotent, lifeless gods of neighboring nations. And the later verses (15-18) confirm the impression of the author as a proud national poet thumbing his nose at foreigners with the taunt, "Our God is better than your god" (AP). The writer believed this, not because Yahweh was some sort of mascot for Israel but because of his people's experience of God's saving actions in nature and in human history.

Hebrew faith rather turned the mascot image on its head: Israel belonged to God. God chose Abraham's and Sarah's descendants to be God's own special possession. This notion was heady stuff, and therefore it was sometimes hard for Hebrews to stay humble. It took the prophets to remind their fellow Jews that being God's chosen people was not an inexhaustible bowl of cherries (see Amos 3:1-2).

Prayer: *Mysterious One, whether we are yours by birth or adoption, we can never deserve such steadfast love. Keep us humble and ready to extend the love we have learned from you to every person we meet today. Amen.*

Wednesday, October 6   Read Psalm 135:5-7.

This section of Psalm 135 celebrates Yahweh's lordship over nature. Note in verse 5 of the Revised Standard Version text the two forms LORD and Lord, reflecting God's proper name and, in the second instance, the Hebrew word for one who has mastery and control and therefore deserves respect.

The psalmist reminds us that God does what he pleases meteorologically. I once heard a Protestant theologian say that by asking one simple question he could learn a lot about one's personal theology. The question was: "Do you pray for changes in the weather?"

I asked this of a farmer in my congregation. His answer: Absolutely not. "Even when you are needing rain badly?" I pressed. "No, not even then," he responded, "because what is good weather for one person's pleasure or prosperity can be disaster for someone else. Best to leave it with God." Together we agreed that the petition for "seasonal weather" from the Book of Common Prayer is a good compromise!

Whether the weather is seasonal or extreme, the psalmist's faith is that God is immanently involved in it in a casual way. Our modern passive constructions—"clouds are forming" or "it is raining"—are foreign to Hebrew thought on the weather, which boldly claims that "God makes the clouds rise," and "God makes lightnings for the rain."

The Creator of the natural world is still involved in it. When we witness a variety of climates and seasons, the rich hues and teeming fertility of land, water, forest, mountain, and sky, the lyric beauty of a sunrise, or the awesome power of a volcano, we are moved to adore and respect this God!

Prayer: *Author of all life, open my senses to feel you moving within nature. Amen.*

291

Thursday, October 7   Read Psalm 135:8-14.

We move now from considering the greatness of Yahweh, Lord of nature, to Yahweh, Lord of history. Reflection on God's purposeful directing of human history begins with the exodus experience, conceived here as *the* redeeming event whereby God chose Israel. Yahweh heard the cries of an oppressed slave people and brought them out of slavery to freedom. A compassionate God, Yahweh reached out to help human beings in pain. That God is gracious and compassionate has always been the fundamental belief for Jews and Christians to confess when asked to articulate their faith.

This liberating God still "vindicate(s) his people." We perceive God's work of deliverance today in places where people live in exceptional bondage. In South Africa and in other places humans cry out to God for help in becoming free. And faith discerns God's spirit creatively stirring upon the face of the chaotic waters of political oppression.

What about violence? The repeated verbs *smote* and *slew* provoke the sad thought that liberation movements, whether of the past or the present, are seldom without physical conflict. God smote the firstborn of Egypt, both human and animal. U.S. citizens recall that we have taken up arms in the cause of freedom many times. Yet the terrible reality of bloodshed, now made unavoidable by television news, leads us to hope, along with Martin Luther King, Jr., that freedom for oppressed people may be achieved through nonviolent means.

Prayer: *God, our champion, in choosing us to be your people, you made us free. Show us how we can cooperate with your purpose of freedom for all people. Amen.*

Friday, October 8   Read Philippians 4:1-3.

When Paul pleaded with Euodia and Syntyche to agree in the Lord, he probably did not think they were going to achieve an identical understanding on whatever it was that had caused their argument. What he meant was: "For God's sake, put your differences in perspective and stop allowing them to disrupt the church's corporate life. Don't let your conflicting pride destroy the community of God's people you have both worked so hard to plant."

All congregations have a Euodia and Syntyche problem from time to time. It is a human problem, and many Christians get caught up in it. What is important is how we handle disagreements.

City dwellers often choose simply to leave one congregation for another, seeking to avoid unpleasantness or seeking a group where our will can dominate more easily. Sometimes that works. More often, we find that we are faced with new conflicts in the new situation. Chronic church-hoppers seem to have little capacity for real community life.

Euodia and Syntyche were without such options. For it is almost certain that they belonged to the only Christian group in Philippi. Unless they wanted to drop out of the church altogether, they had to stay. Enter Paul's one word of conflict management advice: *forbearance*. Some of us like to call this being subject to brothers and sisters in the Lord, meaning: (1) you are free to argue your view, but (2) you are also expected to defer to the collective wisdom of the community, and (3) the health of the whole church is more important than one person getting his or her own way.

Suggestion for prayer: *Picture someone in the church who is a thorn in your side. Pray for that person. For yourself, pray for the grace of forbearance.*

Saturday, October 9　　　　Read Philippians 4:4-9.

A friend once remarked to me that he found it difficult to trust anyone who smiled all the time. He was reacting against a version of proper Christian demeanor that demands constant cheerfulness and backslapping jollity. Now this behavior may be the genuine expression of a personality. But it may also be compulsive. Anyone who has ever been exhorted from funeral pulpit or graveside not to cry or be sad about a tragic death will recognize what I describe.

The joy Paul recommends, on the other hand, is not rooted in the variations of human personality or disposition, but in Christ. It is a gift that transcends our glandular differences. It is the joy of Christian freedom. Those who trust Christ are put right with God apart from the demands of the law, any kind of law. Earlier in this letter, Paul depicts Christian life as free. That is, God has called us for a life of knowing Christ and the power of his resurrection—and of suffering for the gospel in the hope of our own bodily resurrection with Christ (see Philippians 3:8-11). We can forget keeping the rules as a way of being good enough for inclusion in the chosen people. We are already in. We are free. And that is a cause for joy.

This being true, I am free to practice a joyful *piety*—a good old word meaning an intentional and conscientious walk with God—without worrying about whether or not I am appearing to be conventionally *pious*. God does not require me to wear a stained-glass persona! And when I am secure in this freedom, I need not be threatened when disagreement within the church arises.

Prayer: *Lord, when life becomes grey and depressing and doleful, keep me aware that you are for me no matter what happens. Amen.*

Sunday, October 10   Read Matthew 22:1-14.

Matthew has reworked a parable of Jesus (see Luke 14:16-24) into an allegory of God's way with the covenant people. The characters in the allegory have direct historical counterparts that Matthew's audience of Jewish Christians would have immediately recognized. The king is God; the marriage feast, the Messianic age; the servants who are sent out, prophets such as John the Baptist; the invited guests who will not come, the Jews; the king's army, the Roman army; the inviting of street people to the banquet, the Christian mission to the Gentiles; and the close review of the guests by the king, the final judgment.

The daunting phrase is this: "Many are called, but few are chosen." How are we to interpret it? The use of common sense may be best. Many hear the message of the kingdom of God, but only a few accept it. This affirms one's personal responsibility to accept or reject the gospel.

And yet, the forcible removal from the feast of the man in the allegory who offended because he was not wearing a wedding garment disturbs us. We want more information to assure us of the fairness of the king's action. Was the fellow thrown out because he *could* have dressed appropriately but did not care enough to do so? Or did he find himself embarrassed before the king because he did not own a wedding garment? More information is not available. So if we feel uneasy about the harshness of this last part, we can read Luke's version; or else we can consider that *uneasy* is exactly how Matthew intends us to feel.

Prayer: *Lavish God, we thank you that by calling us into your kingdom you have invited us to a banquet. Clothe us with your righteousness, that we may not be found wanting when crises come upon us. Amen.*

FROM IDOLATRY TO THE HOLY ONE

October 11-17, 1993   C. Gordon Peerman, III✣
Monday, October 11   Read Exodus 33:12-17.

Following the fashioning of the golden calf, Yahweh alternately threatens to destroy and then to abandon the people of Israel. In the face of divine wrath, Moses argues that despite their transgressions, these are still Yahweh's people whom Yahweh delivered from Egypt. Moses pleads with Yahweh not to abandon him and to accompany his people to the land promised to them. Yahweh relents, assuring Moses, "My presence will go with you, and I will give you rest."

Thomas Keating reminds us that "the word 'rest' has a precise tradition in Christian spirituality. The early contemplative monks of the Egyptian deserts understood this term to mean something more than sitting under a heavenly palm tree. Rather, they were thinking of the 'rest' that comes from wanting what God wants and not being compulsively forced to do their own will, because their own will, along with everything else in their own ego, had been sacrificed to God."[*]

Centered on the devices and desires of my own ego, I will fashion an idol that I imagine will give me security. Yet, paradoxically, it is the idol that gives me no rest, and it is the great "I will be who I will be," beyond human fashioning and control, in whom I find true rest.

Prayer: *O God, I find my rest in you. Amen.*

✣Episcopal priest and pastoral counselor, Christ Episcopal Church, Nashville, Tennessee.
[*]*The Heart of the World: A Spiritual Catechism* by Thomas Keating. Copyright © 1981 by Cistercian Abbey of Spencer, Inc. Reprinted by permission of The Crossroad Publishing Company.

Tuesday, October 12   Read Exodus 33:18-20.

After his success in persuading Yahweh neither to destroy nor abandon Israel, Moses is emboldened to request to see Yahweh's very glory. That no one may see God and live (v. 20), a frequent motif in the Hebrew scriptures, makes the granting of the request impossible. Why would Moses ask to see Yahweh's glory?

Although it is impossible to know Moses's mind, a review of events might offer us a clue. Moses has received the law from Yahweh at Sinai; he has confronted his people with their apostasy in the incident of the golden calf; he has argued that Yahweh must not forsake his people in spite of their transgression. Moses has experienced profound communion with Yahweh, followed by the threat of the loss of Yahweh's presence, and finally receives Yahweh's promise to go with the people of Israel to the promised land.

When we are deeply attached to someone and then experience the threat of disruption of that bond, even when the tie is restored, a certain anxiety may remain. We now know in a new way that we can lose the relationship. Perhaps the request for a more intimate relationship with Yahweh was Moses's way of attempting to anchor the relationship more firmly than by simply accepting Yahweh's promise of presence. Perhaps it was Moses's way of saying, "If you are truly going to be present to me, give me a token, a special favor, that I may know you truly mean what you say. Assure me I can count on you to be there for me."

In our anxiety to make sure that God is reliably there for us, we seek to see the divine glory. Yet Yahweh will be gracious and have compassion as Yahweh wills. The Holy One is a God to be trusted, but not secured.

Prayer: *In you, O Lord, I put my trust. Amen.*

Wednesday, October 13   Read Exodus 33:21-23.

Moses has been refused his request to see Yahweh's glory; yet, he is granted a knowledge of God superior to that of ordinary persons. Yahweh allows Moses to see his back, but not his face. This is an obscure, enigmatic passage, one that does not easily open itself for our understanding. It is as though a full view of God would be too much for Moses to bear. Yahweh instead gives Moses a partial view, a view of his back as his glory passes by.

Like Moses, none of us are given more than a partial view of divine glory. But these partial views, moments of unity when the glory of the Lord is revealed to us, render all other moments and views as shadowy and insubstantial. Until we have been granted a partial view of divine glory, it is as though we have not really been living until that point.

It is much like the experience of someone who has fallen in love and for whom the world takes on a magnificence that had been previously veiled. The vitality and beauty always beneath the surface is now allowed to shine forth in some of its splendor. This vision offers a window through which to see the glory that is at the heart of all things, but usually unrecognized.

Just as the lover must come to see that he or she does not possess the beloved and learn to accept what the beloved does indeed have to offer, so our partial views of the Holy One school us in detaching from the idols of our own desire and making space for the actual vision God grants us.

If the glory of the Lord is something we do not control, the idol by contrast promises a glory that will be at our disposal. The idol promises not a partial view, but a full view, a view that is ours for the keeping and as such seems to promise a view far superior to one of an invisible God.

Prayer: *O Lord, open my eyes to see your glory. Amen.*

Thursday, October 14　　　　　Read Psalm 99.

Psalm 99 is a poem to the Holy One of Israel. The psalm refers to two sacred objects by which Yahweh's presence was evidenced in the midst of Israel: the tent of meeting and the ark of the covenant. The tent of meeting was set up outside the Israelite camp. Moses would go there to encounter Yahweh, who would descend in a pillar of clouds. Those with difficult problems would go out to the tent, and Moses would bring these concerns before Yahweh.

The ark of the covenant, with its winged cherubim, was a depository for the tablets of the Decalogue. The Israelites imagined Yahweh invisibly throned on the ark. It went with the people when they moved and when they went into battle, the sign of Yahweh's presence among (and leading) the people.

If the tent of meeting was the symbol of Yahweh's transcendence, the ark of the covenant was the sign of Yahweh's abiding and immanent presence. Where do you go to encounter the Holy One? A place apart, like the tent of meeting, is a place removed from your usual rounds, a place where you can bring yourself before God.

I know it is important for me to take an intensive period each year to go apart to a monastery. Only in taking a significant period of time apart in a place apart can I remember who God is and who I am. Inevitably the time will disclose the idols I am worshiping. Then I will remember yet again the first commandment, to have one God.

When I go apart, as to a tent of meeting, I am more likely to perceive the Holy One enthroned as an abiding presence in my life. There I can turn away from idols to rest in the transcendent and abiding presence of the Holy One.

Prayer: *Holy, holy, holy Lord, God of power and might, heaven and earth are full of your glory. Amen. (Sanctus)*

Friday, October 15   Read 1 Thessalonians 1:1-10.

Paul writes to those in Thessalonica whom he converted to the gospel. They are largely "God-fearing" Greeks, pagans, and important women in the community. He gives thanks that they have "turned to God from idols, to serve a living and true God." What would it have been like for these persons to leave the service of an idol for a God who truly lives?

I believe that we may arrive at an approximate answer to this question when we think about what it is like for us to leave the service of one of our own idols. If I am in thrall to an idol, it is the source of my security, as I imagine it. I can hardly imagine living without it. In fact, beginning to imagine living without it will likely cause me great anxiety. If I should actually leave the idol's service, at least initially, I will likely feel guilty for doing so.

For example, as a way of being in the world, I might never ask anything for myself, yet feel I must always be accommodating, cheerful, cooperative, and giving to others. This never/always, black/white thinking is characteristic of idolatrous living. This way of being is my god; it is that to which I give my highest loyalty. If, however, I even think of saying to someone that I do not have something to give, then I may feel anxious because I am thinking of forsaking what I imagine to be the source of my security. The idol whispers to me, "This is who you are. How can you be otherwise?"

If I actually begin to behave in a limit-setting, non-accommodating fashion, I will probably at first feel guilty. I am no longer worshiping at my old shrine. The living God is not interested in the idol of my self-image. With practice and encouragement in my new way of being, I will come to know a new freedom in the service of the living God.

Prayer: *Set me free, O Lord, for your service. Amen.*

Saturday, October 16   Read Matthew 22:15-18.

In this reading we see how Jesus handles the malice of the Pharisees. The Pharisees first attempt to set Jesus up with some smooth words, pretending to appreciate his honesty, then they seek to entrap him with a question on the lawfulness of paying taxes to the Roman emperor. If Jesus says no then he appears to be subversive of the Roman state; if he says yes then he seems to collaborate with a foreign occupying force.

Jesus will grasp neither of the alternatives. Instead, he confronts the Pharisees with their malice and their true motive of trying to trap. We should note that in the face of this verbal attack Jesus neither retreats from his assailants nor retaliates in kind. Nor does he discuss the question on the terms in which the Pharisees present it. He first simply names the question for what it is: a malicious attack.

In our common life together as Christians there is a reluctance, if not an almost absolute inability, to name hatred by its proper name. Either we respond to malice with masochism, mistakenly believing that passively enduring it is somehow Christlike, or we retaliate with some act of hatred of our own. Of course, our own hatred may come in a form as cleverly disguised as that of the Pharisees!

Someone once described masochism as a safe way to hate, allowing someone to hurt you as a method of self-hate. Jesus does not allow the Pharisees to skewer him with their question, and he does not hate them in return. He simply points attention to their malicious intent and risks inflaming their hatred in unmasking them. In so doing he serves them notice that he will not be intimidated by their hatred.

Prayer: *O God, give us the strength to name hatred without fleeing or fighting. Amen.*

Sunday, October 17   Read Matthew 22:19-22.

Jesus now formulates on his own terms an answer to the Pharisees' question on the payment of taxes to the Roman emperor. He asks for a coin and serves his questioners notice that he, too, can ask questions. He asks whose face is on the coin, and when told, gives a reply which takes his questioners by surprise.

Jesus will not be drawn into a fight on the Pharisees' question. He leaves it to them to determine what belongs to Caesar and what belongs to God. If the question had been one which allowed for an easy answer, the Pharisees would never have posed it. Jesus offers no simple resolution.

In this century, one of the great idols is the nation-state. We know of too many horrors which have been justified under the rubric of national security or national honor. The state is not God. It is not immortal, even though it often pretends that it is. It is not omnipotent, although in many places its power appears unshakable. It is not omniscient, even when its citizens do not as yet know how to challenge its accepted dogma.

For the followers of Jesus, the state at best commands a secondary loyalty; at worst it is an idol that demands human sacrifice. Like the hatred of the Pharisees that Jesus names, courageous followers of Jesus in every age have named the hatred hidden by states that have pretended to be God.

When Moses came down from Mount Sinai to find Israel worshiping a golden calf, he took it, burned it, ground it to powder and made the people drink it (Exod. 32:19-20). When the state is made a golden calf, it will be reduced in the end to ashes and become a galling drink to those who have placed their faith in it. Only God is Holy.

Prayer: *Holy God, Holy and Mighty, Holy Immortal One, Have mercy upon us. (The Trisagion)*

God's Love: From Mountaintop to Valley

October 18-24, 1993   **Judith Freeman Clark**✢
Monday, October 4   Read Deuteronomy 34:1-3.

In the final chapter of Deuteronomy, God shows Moses the promised land, renewing the covenant with him. At the top of Mount Nebo, God brings Moses to what is surely the pinnacle of his long life.

It is an appealing image. Moses, the aging patriarch, surveying the land God promised to the tribes of Israel, his eyes sweeping from north to west, then southward and to the east. What a marvelous panorama, what joy for Moses to *see* that promised land! How humble he must have felt. God had selected Moses, had tested him and had been with him; and through Moses God had brought God's people to the place promised to them.

Mountaintop experiences are compelling—and rare. To see potential and promise stretching from horizon to horizon fills us with joy. However, because our lives are riddled with doubt, we seldom taste this joy. Standing on Mount Nebo, Moses could rejoice because he knew that *here* was a sign of God's grace to Moses and the Hebrews.

Like Moses, we strive to reach the peak of faith. We work toward a clarity of vision so we may see purpose and truth in our lives. And we hope that God may grant us a mountaintop experience. Like Moses, we may then glimpse the promised land and know God's love.

Prayer: *God, bring us to the mountaintop; help us see the blessings and opportunities that await us; show us the promised land. Amen.*

✢Writer; Episcopal laywoman; Newport, New Hampshire.

Tuesday, October 19   Read Deuteronomy 34:4-12.

In bringing Moses to Mount Nebo to show him the region promised to the Israelites, God withheld one thing. God denied Moses access to the promised land, saying: "I have let you see it with your own eyes, but you shall not cross over there."

Why did God refuse Moses the joy of walking on that fertile earth? And after so many years of service, did it seem to Moses that God was unfairly ignoring the covenant between them? Or did Moses understand God's intention in offering a distant glimpse of the promised land?

Moses' life was full of mountaintop experiences. His initial encounter with God was at Mount Horeb; Moses went to Mount Sinai and received the Ten Commandments from God. A recurrent theme in Moses' life, the mountaintop provides a metaphor for us as well.

Moses could be more receptive to God when he stood on the highest peak. And this is how it is for us: we see most clearly from the mountaintop. Our vision of God, our ability to hear God is acute when we are uplifted. Which may be why God grants us mountaintop experiences—they boost our spirits and, because of this, God knows we will hold on to what we see and hear. When we descend again to the valley, we can recall the mountaintop and be encouraged.

God repeatedly raised Moses up and brought him down again, but Moses' faith never wavered. He cherished the affirming message he received on the mountain—and never stopped proclaiming the power of God's love.

Prayer: *God, bring us to the place where we find your enduring love, and preserve your mercy within us as we again go down into life's dark valleys. Amen.*

Wednesday, October 20 Read Psalm 90:1-6.

This psalm, which is attributed as a prayer of Moses, begins by affirming the timeless, all-encompassing love of God. By contrast, the next verses describe the transitory quality of human existence. The illusory qualities of humankind are revealed with stunningly majestic imagery in verses 4-6.

Here in this psalm, Moses tries to convince us of the need to rely only on God. "You mortals" implies that we are immature and weak; the phrase "you have been our dwelling place in all generations" suggests God's mature, comforting properties. "You sweep them away....they are...like grass" describes our frailty and unreliability; the phrase "from everlasting to everlasting you are God" underscores the incontrovertible stability that God provides.

Perhaps Moses felt this psalm would be effective in presenting the polarity of God and humanity. In some ways, it is another example of the mountaintop metaphor about which we read earlier: God's everlasting, unshakable, and uplifting love contrasts sharply with our doubt-ridden, forlorn, and lowly mortality. God *is* the mountaintop; we are the valley.

Moses uses this contrast to remind us how futile it is to put trust in things created by men and women, since these things will pass away. This emphasis is heard in Moses' words

> You turn us back into dust . . . ;
> they are like a dream.

His thought is not to depress or frighten us; rather, he is intent on directing us to accept and affirm God's grandeur and eternal love.

Prayer: *Dear God, may we, like Moses, be able to acknowledge your blessed and healing timelessness. Amen.*

305

Thursday, October 21   Read Psalm 90:14-17.

Moses speaks for all humankind when he pleads with God to "satisfy us in the morning. . . / that we may rejoice and be glad all our days."

Who among us does not yearn to awaken each morning with a song of praise in his or her heart? Yet many of us start the day with a grim sense of obligation toward work, antipathy for family members, or dread of whatever the daily routine requires.

The value of Psalm 90 is that it voices admissions and entreaties we all would bring before God. In its candor, it brings us closer to God. In acknowledging that life isn't always comfortable, that we will spend time in "valley experiences," that we will have "years when we have seen evil" ("years of misery," TEV; "days of suffering," NEB), we take a step towards healing acceptance of what *is*. And by so doing we feel nearer to God.

"Make us glad as many days as you have afflicted us," does not represent bargaining. Instead, these words are Moses' admission of how critical God's love is and his request for balance in all that God lovingly provides. They are Moses' acceptance of the valley—and his expectation of the mountaintop.

God does for us what we cannot do for ourselves, something Moses knew and felt compelled to express. Moses understood that each of us can benefit from voicing our vulnerability. He knew the importance of differentiating between God's omniscience and our blindness. Most of all, Moses had the wisdom to encourage us to ask for help from the true source of strength.

Prayer: *God, hear us when we come to you in our need, and lift us up by your promise of rest, renewal, and salvation. Amen.*

Friday, October 22 Read 1 Thessalonians 2:1-8.

This letter of Paul, believed to be the earliest piece of writing in the New Testament, expresses a theme previously presented by Moses: God is the only source of comfort and strength, no matter how deep the valley, how great the tragedy, or how heavy the burden.

Paul had his "mountaintop" experience on the road to Damascus, then spent the rest of his life in the valley. Perhaps this is why he treats the theme differently: explaining how God assisted the Christians in their work, Paul does not suggest they had enjoyed a mountaintop experience. To the contrary, his words "we had already suffered and been shamefully mistreated at Philippi" refer to an ongoing valley experience. Nonetheless, each struggle served only to strengthen Paul's belief in God's power.

In Paul's earnest reminders, "we speak, not to please mortals, but to please God," we hear echoes of the early Christians' courage in the face of great trials. Paul's repeated assertions, "We never came with words of flattery or with a pretext for greed," plead for acceptance and understanding. That these early Christian men and women had experienced the worst is evident in Paul's impassioned words.

In their reliance on God, the Christians overcame persecution and emerged with a stronger faith. They left a valley believing that they had been approved by God to be entrusted with the gospel message. We are heirs to this trust. And, Paul tells us, that, no matter how weary or troubled we feel, God is with us and will see us through.

Prayer: *Remind us, God, that your love is incomprehensible, that your power over our lives is unalterable, and that your belief in our goodness defies human understanding. Amen.*

Saturday, October 23   Read Matthew 22:34-40.

Of all the Gospel writers, Matthew most carefully shows Jesus as the fulfillment of Old Testament prophecy. He likens Jesus to another, yet far greater Moses. When the Pharisees challenged Jesus to explain the truth about his teachings, Jesus answered them simply. He used no guile, no convoluted arguments, no clever expressions. Jesus' reply to the Pharisees was merely, "Love the Lord your God with all your heart, and with all your soul, and with all your mind." He summarized the Law and used the Pharisees' own logic and text to explain what God expected. He left the Pharisees with no logical point from which to argue further.

This parallels what sometimes happens inside us when we ask God for guidance, comfort, or support. We may approach God with an earnest request for wisdom, an urgent plea for immediate relief from suffering, a heartfelt cry for assistance. We want an explanation for what bothers us. Because we are confused or in pain, perhaps because we are having a "valley experience," we are overwhelmed. We distort everything around us—even God—and forget that in God's magnificent simplicity only one thing is required.

We may expect God will set us some hard task in exchange for guidance. We may assume we will be asked to pay a spiritual "fee" for God's comforting presence. We may even believe that in exchange for God's support, we will be expected to forfeit all human joys and pleasures. Like the Pharisees, we are often blind to God's divine truth and can scarcely believe that God requires only one things from us: *love* in exchange for being loved.

Prayer: *God, give me grace each day to see new opportunities to love you with all of my heart, and soul, and mind. Amen.*

Sunday, October 24 Read Matthew 22:41-46.

It is not easy to do Jesus' bidding: "Love your neighbor as yourself." In fact, virtually everything in life conspires against us as we strive to fulfill the terms of this second great commandment. Loving God is one thing—our relationship with God is, for the most part, internal, spiritual, contemplative. It may be turbulent and compelling, but it is also a relationship that brings us "mountaintop" experiences. It is more exciting, mystifying, and satisfying than a human relationship ever can be.

Jesus told the Pharisees (and he tells us), "On these two commandments hang all the law and prophet." It sounds simple. Just two expressions of divine law: love God; love your neighbor. And most of us believe we put good effort into the first law, especially at Christmas or Easter, or when we feel particularly thankful or relieved.

The second law is more challenging, perhaps because it carries with it an imperative that we are not always equipped to handle. Loving all people—no matter what their condition of health, their intellectual capability, or their social situation—is the real test of whether we truly love God. Do we have the will to love God? Are we amenable to putting our resources at God's disposal? If we are, we then are called to do the same for our neighbor.

Committing heart, soul, and mind means constant fidelity to God. It also means relating to other people. By translating our love for God into acts of peace, compassion, and kindness towards others, we can hope God will become a living presence in our daily lives.

Prayer: *God, as we search for ways to love you more completely, help us remember that your true desire is that we love one another. Grant us daily with opportunities to prove that love. Amen.*

TRUST AND OBEY

October 25-31, 1993   **John Ed Mathison**✢
Monday, October 25   Read Joshua 3:1-7.

Most of us have known great spiritual giants in the past about whom there is no question that the living God was with them. What we know about those people causes us to stand in awe at the power and presence of God in their lives.

Measuring ourselves against those people sometimes causes us to question God's presence in our lives. We usually evaluate other people by the high points in their lives, then evaluate ourselves by those times when we doubt God's power and God's presence.

This illustrates the situation that confronted Joshua. Moses had been a great leader. No one questioned God's presence and power in his life. Now God wanted to show Joshua that divine presence and power were just as available to him. God used this incident at the Jordan River "so that they may know that I will be with you as I was with Moses."

This week look for ways God is showing you how much God is with you and wants to empower you. Remember that you are a vital part of the history God is writing today!

Suggestion for prayer and meditation: *Pray for a few moments about the opportunities God will give you today. Focus on some ways in the past that God communicated the divine presence and power to you. Pray for the perceptiveness to be open to the ways God wants to communicate that power and presence to you today.*

Prayer: *Oh, God, I thank you for the powerful witness of your presence in the lives of people who have influenced me. May I be open for you to use me as an influence in the lives of others. Amen.*

✢Senior minister, Frazer Memorial United Methodist Church, Montgomery, Alabama.

Tuesday, October 26   Read Joshua 3:8-17.

The greatest joy in my life comes when I am obedient to God. The biggest problem I have is in wanting to do things my way rather than God's way. This daily struggle forces me into some tough decisions.

Joshua faced a tough decision. God commanded him to tell the priests to take the ark of the covenant into the Jordan River so that God might allow the people to pass through the Jordan. Joshua was probably intimidated because he remembered Moses and the Red Sea. Now God wanted him to be obedient in a similar situation.

Very often I think that God could do great things through other people but not me. We all would like to place the responsibility for God's mighty deeds with other people. God always has a way of coming back to me with the possibility and responsibility for obedience.

According to human logic, God's suggestion to Joshua was foolish. According to faith, it was an opportunity for obedience and miraculous works. Joshua chose to obey, and "the ark of the covenant of the LORD stood on dry ground in the middle of the Jordan, until the entire nation finished crossing over the Jordan."

Each day I have the opportunity either to reason things out by human logic or to act in faith in obedience to God's command. Today God is calling you and me to obedience. It is a call not to success but to obedience.

Suggestion for meditation: *Reflect on the events you have planned for today and see how God might use you for a special witness in these events.*
Prayer: *God, I thank you for your demonstration of power in the lives of other people. It is frightening to think that you might use me for something very special today. Give me the courage to obey. Amen.*

Wednesday, October 27   Read Psalm 107:1-7.

I was coaching a Little League baseball team. One little boy on my team had the most expensive baseball equipment, had read the best books on baseball, and knew all the baseball language. The only problem was that he could not play baseball. He could not catch. He could not hit. He could not run.

One day he was giving a lecture to his other teammates about how to hit. Finally one of the other boys looked at him and said, "Why don't you quit talking about hitting? We want to see you actually hit the ball one time!" Talking is one thing—delivering is something else. It is so easy to talk a good game, but credibility comes when what we say is backed up by what we do.

The psalmist discovered that God always delivers. There are a lot of beautiful words in the psalms about how great God is. But the bottom line for the psalmist was the fact that God always delivered!

Psalm 107 describes how God has delivered a troubled people. God found them wandering in the desert and led them by a straight way until they reached an inhabited town. Even more than that, however, God satisfied the hunger and thirsts of their souls.

Suggestion for meditation: *Reflect on ways that God has delivered you in the past. Like the psalmist, offer words of thanks for the very special ways God has delivered and led you.*

Prayer: *O God, it is easy for me to "talk the talk," but my greatest need is to "walk the walk." My desire today is to have my life-style consistent with what I profess as a Christian. Please help me make that happen. Amen.*

Thursday, October 28　　　　Read Psalm 107:33-43.

God's deliverance is both a mystery and a miracle. The mystery is that oftentimes we do not understand it because we see things from such a limited perspective. The miracle of God's deliverance goes far beyond our greatest comprehension.

Here, the psalmist stands in awe at the mighty acts of God. He notices that God can turn a river into a desert and a fruitful land into a salty waste, that God can turn a desert into a pool of water of parched land into a spring of water. God's works are awesome!

We can marvel at the mystery of the miracle of God's deliverance, but we are most wise when we submit to the plan God has for each of us. The psalmist's advice to each of us is:

> Let those who are wise give heed to these things,
> 　　and consider the steadfast love of the LORD.

Are we simply standing on the sidelines, watching God's work today, or are we making ourselves available for God to use us to bring about the Kingdom?

Suggestion for meditation: *Reflect today on ways in which God's awesome power has been demonstrated in your life. Reflect on ways in which you might be one of God's agents to bring about deliverance to other people.*

Prayer: *O God, it is an awesome thought to contemplate your majesty and your power. It is even more awesome to think that I am a part of your plan for a demonstration of that power and the deliverance of your people. It is through my recognition of my weakness that I accept your strength in carrying out your mission for me today. Amen.*

313

Friday, October 29   Read 1 Thessalonians 2:9-18.

Paul appeals to the people of Thessalonica to practice the Christian faith. Writing like a father who is concerned about his children, he encourages the people by pointing to his life and his friends.

The world today needs more models of the Christian faith. Young people have so few adults to whom they can look as a model or mentor. The church needs to be a place where models and mentors are evident.

But Paul also reminds the Thessalonians that the ultimate motivation for walking in the Christian faith rests in the power that comes from God and not from any person: Lead a life worthy of God, who calls you into his own kingdom and glory. Even the best models can be disappointing. God has never been a disappointment. God is always faithful and true to the divine word.

Today—indeed, on any day—who of us know how many people may be looking up to us? We need to ask ourselves what kind of model we are providing and if our life is motivated by the truth that comes from God.

Suggestion for meditation: *Reflect on some of the people who have had a very positive and meaningful influence on your life. Name some of your role models and mentors of the past. Reflect also on some of the people who might be looking to you as a role model. Think of specific ways in which you can be a good role model for others today.*

Prayer: *O God, please raise up strong role models for the world to see. May my local church become a center for developing people who live the Christian faith with integrity. May I, like Paul, lead a life worthy of you, who call me. Amen.*

Saturday, October 30   Read Matthew 23:1-7.

While it is good to emphasize the importance of improving the quality of ministry, it is also a danger for a pastor to become so professional in what he or she does that they become "professionals" rather than servants. Whether clergy or laity, in ministry to others we need to guard against making recognition from others our motivation rather than serviceto others in Christ's name.

It is imperative that we take time to pause occasionally and examine our motivation. Too often we reach out to others because we think they can do something for us. Motivation for ministry and service can easily become based on the kind of recognition we receive. Jesus warns that sometimes we can love the places of honor more than we love the people whom we are called to serve. We can easily become more interested in things than in people. We, likewise, can fall into the trap of loving things and using people, when the priority of Jesus was always to love people and to use things.

Suggestion for meditation: *Think about some way today that you can serve someone without their knowing that you have offered that service and with there being no way you can receive recognition for it. Also, be aware of what other people are doing for you without receiving any kind of recognition. Examine what you do today by the standard of whether it is pleasing to God or to people.*

Prayer: *Oh God, today may my ministry and Christian service be based on the motivation of love for you and not on a relationship where I expect some reciprocal action. May I remember that what I do for other people is exactly what I am doing for you. May my greatest desire be to hear you say, "Well done, good and faithful servant." Amen.*

Sunday, October 31   Read Matthew 23:8-12.

It is natural for people to desire compensation for something they do. This does not exclude people who serve in the church nor ordained clergy persons.

Jesus confronted a group of religious professionals who began to enjoy the special roles and titles given to them. Jesus reminded them of their role. The Christian is called not to receive accolades and places of prominence but to be a servant.

Serving is the bottom line for doing effective and meaningful ministry. The world oftentimes doesn't hear what we say because it has not seen us putting words into action. Many times when we reach out to people in need, our servanthood becomes a bridge over which the gospel of God's grace can come into the lives of people. People don't care how much we know until they know how much we care!

Will I look at my life today through a lens that allows me to see the needs of others? Am I ready and willing to serve in the name of Christ? Is my mind turned inward or focused outward? What is my motivation for the deeds of service that I do?

Suggestion for meditation: *Think about some ways in which you have seen other people demonstrate the work of a servant. Give thanks for these specific acts that have had a special influence on your life. Reflect on some specific ways in which you might show others how much you care.*

Prayer: *O Lord, help me this day to make Christian service my number one priority. May I measure the effectiveness of my relationships by the extent to which I am giving rather than receiving. Amen.*

WHAT DOES THE COVENANT DEMAND?

November 1-7, 1993   **Jorge A. González✛**
Monday, November 1   Read Joshua 24:1-3*a*, 14-15.

Choice

As Christians we are heirs to those covenant traditions which we share with the Israelites of the Old Testament and with the New Testament church. One of those is the story of the covenant renewal ceremony which took place at Shechem under the leadership of Joshua.

It was here that the successor to Moses challenged the Israelites saying, "Choose this day whom you will serve." Their options were clear: "The gods that your ancestors served beyond the river" (Euphrates); those they served "in Egypt"; "the gods of the Amorites in whose land you are living"; or "the LORD." Joshua unequivocally stated his own choice: "As for me and my household, we will serve the LORD."

This is the same kind of challenge we face. Whether we will render our loyalty to values and principles cherished in the traditions of our ancestors, or to those which emerged from the struggles of our own "Egyptian" bondage, or to those derived from our conditioning to the materialistic and secular culture "in whose land we are living." Will we join Joshua in his declaration of unconditional loyalty: "As for me and my household, we will serve the LORD"?

Prayer: *Lord, help me to see that whatever other loyalties might make demands upon my life, none can even begin to compare with the call to choose to serve you. Amen.*

✛Clergy member, North Georgia Conference of The United Methodist Church; Fuller E. Calloway Professor of Religion, Berry College, Rome, Georgia.

Tuesday, November 2   Read Joshua 24:16-18.

Commitment

The reply which the people gave to Joshua's challenge was immediate and unequivocal: "Far be it from us that we should forsake the LORD to serve other gods." Remember, this was a generation born in the wilderness, for only Joshua and Caleb were left of the males who had fled from Egypt under Moses' leadership (5:4). Yet these people spoke as if they themselves had experienced God's saving acts, as if they had witnessed the great signs through which God brought Israel out of bondage. Moreover, it is probable that the assembly at Shechem included other people for whom this was something akin to our own naturalization ceremonies. Here several groups of people, who had not been among those of the Exodus, became part of Israel.

Most citizens of the United States are so by birth. I came here as a refugee and became a citizen by deliberate choice and through a commitment made at a naturalization ceremony. Yet, on Thanksgiving Day I will participate fully in the festivities of this very American celebration. I will enjoy the turkey, dressing, cranberry sauce, and all the trimmings as if this day had been a long-observed tradition in my own family.

Similarly, the scriptures show that not all Israelites were descendants of those who came out of Egypt with Moses, but they all were incorporated into Israel through their commitment. In making this commitment, they claimed the Exodus tradition as their own. So it is also in the church. Ours is an open community in which persons of all races, cultures, languages, and traditions are incorporated through an act of commitment into the one Body of Christ.

Prayer: *Lord, inspire in me the commitment that may make me a faithful member of your covenant community, the church. Amen.*

Wednesday, November 3   Read Joshua 24:19-25.

Loyalty

Joshua confronted the Shechem assembly with the demand of the covenant for absolute, unconditional loyalty to the God of Israel. According to him, there was no room for a lukewarm commitment in this covenant relationship. Joshua declared: "The LORD...is a holy God." This was his way of saying that the Lord, "the Wholly Other," is separated by a chasm from the people of Israel, for they stand in the frailty of their humanity.

Given the power and the glory of God and the weakness inherent to the Israelites, Joshua tells them: "You cannot serve the LORD." Then he adds: "He is a jealous God; he will not forgive your transgressions or your sins." Such words sound strange to our ears, accustomed as we are to thinking always of God's forgiveness. Certainly God does forgive, but here the words of warning are not a general address to all sinners but a specific address to those who, having made a commitment to God, forget to be loyal to the vow taken.

The Bible frequently refers to the covenant in terms derived from a monogamous marriage relationship, and therefore betrayal of the covenant is equated with adultery (e.g., Hos. 2; 3:1). For Israel the worship of other gods was an attack upon the essence of the covenant. This was no "open marriage" but a binding together of God and Israel with an absolute loyalty.

This is the same undivided loyalty that God expects of us. No one forced us to enter into a covenant relationship with God; we chose freely to respond to the call to whatever is our avenue of ministry and service. But we have to do so with singleness of spirit and with absolute loyalty.

Prayer: *Lord, teach me to be loyal that I may truly serve you with all my heart, my soul, my strength, my mind. Amen.*

Thursday, November 4   Read Psalm 78:1-7.

Obedience

The Book of Psalms has been called "the hymnbook of the Second Temple." Compiled after the return from the Exile and the rebuilding of the Temple of Jerusalem, this magnificent collection of hymns, used in the Temple liturgy, embodied many ancient traditions. Just as our modern hymnals include works that span the centuries, many of which formed part of earlier collections, so it is with the Psalter.

Psalm 78 is identified as "A Maskil of Asaph." We do not know with certainty what this means. It has been suggested that a maskil is "an efficacious song," and it is probable that the term *Asaph* identifies this psalm as part of a collection belonging to a guild of Temple singers that originated in the time of David and was founded by a master singer by that name. If so, the references in this psalm to "things that we have heard and known, that our ancestors have told us" harken to a time rooted in the deep past, perhaps the time of Moses at Sinai, perhaps that of Joshua at Shechem.

The point about these ancient traditions of Israel is that the Lord "commanded our ancestors to teach to their children; that the next generation might know them, the children yet unborn, and rise up and tell them to their children, so that they should set their hope in God and not forget the works of God, but keep his commandments...." One generation to the next, and then again to the next, and on, and on...always teaching obedience to God and to the terms of the covenant. Here, also, is a call to our teaching the tradition and texts of God.

Prayer: *Thanks be to you, God, for all the past generations who have brought your witness to us. Help me to be faithful to this task for the sake of future generations. Amen.*

Friday, November 5   Read 1 Thessalonians 4:13-18.

Hope

The covenant community exists in hope. Not that kind of weak, wishy-washy hope that we have when we say things like "I hope it won't rain today." This kind of hope is marked by uncertainty and goes no further than the expression of a wish or desire. But Christian hope is something entirely different. Certainty is at its very root. Christian hope takes a stand in full confidence because it knows that the outcome is assured.

Such is the hope expressed in Paul's letter to the Thessalonian Christians. Theirs was a small community, an enclave within the larger society of the Macedonian capital. The pressures of the world around them, as well as the death of some of the members of the community, prompted some of the Christians in Thessalonica to begin to question the validity of their hope. Some thought, *Perhaps when the end of the present age comes, those who have died in the faith will not be able to witness it.* Others said; "What's the use? Evidently we have hoped in vain and Christ will never return." And still others were so obsessed with their expectation of the imminent end of the present age that they failed to assume any responsibilities for the here and now.

In response to this crisis Paul assures the Christians in Thessalonica of what is the very essence of their hope: the certain knowledge that death is not the final word but that the final word is Christ's, that the community of Christ's people, the church, is composed of all who throughout the ages have lived and died in the hope of the resurrection, and that by the power of Christ death holds no power over Christ's own.

Prayer: *Lord, awaken and strengthen my hope that I may march into the unknown future, both in this life and in the hereafter, with absolute trust in your love and in your power. Amen.*

321

Saturday, November 6   Read Matthew 25:1-12.

Preparedness

The parables of Jesus must be understood as parables; that is to say, they should neither be allegorized nor taken to be examples of proper behavior. In the parable which is our text for today, the action of the wise bridesmaids is not offered as a model of right behavior. Certainly the foolish five acted wrongly, but the wise ones were not much better with their selfish attitudes and their unwillingness to share.

Nor is this parable to be taken as an allegory, full of symbolic and hidden meanings attaching some significance to the number of bridesmaids, or to the lamps, the groom, or the oil. A true parable makes one single point. It is singularly focused to that end, and the purpose of the story is to illustrate this idea in a compelling fashion.

In this case, when first told by Jesus, the parable focused on being prepared for the imminent coming of the kingdom of God. Later, by the time the parable was incorporated into the Gospel of Matthew, it was seen by the early Christians as a call to be prepared for the prompt return of their risen Lord. To us, almost twenty centuries later, it still is a call to be prepared, to be ready, for the divine action which breaks with sudden impetus into our times, into our history, and continues to unfold the divine will in our midst.

As part of this covenant community which is the church, we are called upon to be prepared for whatever God chooses to call us to do. Whether it be to continue to serve through the actions of our life and witness or to glorify God at the end of time.

Prayer: *Teach me, Lord, to be prepared at all times to fulfill your will in my life as I strive to be faithful to the demands of your covenant. Amen.*

Sunday, November 7   Read Matthew 25:13.

Alertness

What does the covenant demand? It demands choice, commitment, loyalty, obedience, hope, and preparedness. It also demands alertness.

The single verse which we consider today probably was not an integral part of the parable in Matthew 25:1-12. By adding it there has been a slight, but important, shift in the focus of the parable. The thrust of the parable does not lie in the fact that the maidens went to sleep at their post, for both the wise and the foolish maidens did that. The message of the parable is to be prepared at all times for what is to come. But because the maids did go to sleep while waiting for the groom, the author of the Gospel placed this story immediately after a series of passages, all of which call the Christian to be watchful and alert to the unexpected arrival of the end. The admonition to "keep awake" would have to be addressed to the wise as well as to the foolish maids, for they all went to sleep.

However, in bringing the story together with those that speak of watchfulness, the Gospel writer has pointed to a true fact. It is not enough to be prepared; one must also be alert and watchful. Of what value is a sentry who is armed and equipped to sound the alarm if he goes to sleep at his post? What good is it for a driver to have his car equipped with safety features if he goes to sleep at the wheel?

Those of us who have responded to the call to be in service as part of the covenant community of God must be alert at all times. We must be ready to face the challenges that come, empowered by the presence of Christ in our lives.

Prayer: *Lord, it was you who called me. I say, "I am here, my God and my Savior, waiting and willing to do your will." Keep me ever watchful and alert, ready to respond to your will. Amen.*

Watching and waiting are not isolated and discrete acts, but rather reflect the whole spiritual endeavor. They are spirituality in the concrete, because spirituality is, first and continuously, listening or attentiveness to God's spirit within us.

Paul demands watchfulness! Keeping awake and going to sleep are metaphors of watchfulness or lack of it. We can perceive God's activity in the world and within ourselves only if we are watchful. Indeed, it is this attitude that allows us to recognize and embrace the God who comes.

Waiting is not a passive, hopeless state determined by events totally out of our hands. "A waiting person is someone who is present to the moment, who believes that this moment is *the moment*."* A waiting person knows that the actions and decisions of the present moment are determinative of what will happen in the age to come.

Waiting gives rise to patience, hope, trust, presence, action. Watching helps us recognize and embrace the surprise, the mystery. Watching and waiting change us and teach us to know God. They help us fully understand God's ways. Nothing happens in our individual lives as Christians or in our communal life as the church without our watching, listening, preparing, waiting, and praying for something to happen.

Prayer: *God of mystery, grant me a watchful, discerning heart. Help me to be attentive, always, to your spirit within me. Amen.*

✢Council Director, Iowa Annual Conference of The United Methodist Church, Des Moines, Iowa.
*Henri J. M. Nouwen, "A Spirituality of Waiting." (*Weavings*, Vol. II, No. 1, 1987), p. 9.

Tuesday, November 9   Read 1 Thessalonians 5:4-6.

Waiting and watching are not things we do very well. Most of us consider waiting a waste of time. Watching is tedious or boring. We stay busy, self-sufficient, and aloof. A full life, we think, is a life full of our activity.

Yet God created us with the potential to watch and wait, to be "advent" people. Paul reminds us that we are all children of the light and children of the day. Children of the light are faithful, watchful, and hopeful. Children of the day are attentive to what is coming because we have experienced God's realm; we already belong to the day.

God created us with a "watching and waiting" song within our souls. The psalmist gives expression to our song: My soul waits for the LORD / More than those who watch for the morning (Psalm 130:5-6).

We want to nurture this song. We desire a waiting attitude, a watching eye, a yearning heart. We long for attentiveness to what is coming.

Waiting people affirm that what they are waiting for has already begun in their lives. "The secret of waiting is the faith that seed has been planted, that something has begun."[*] We are advent people when we long for union with God, when we hunger for the touch of God in our lives, when we listen to the "watching and waiting" song within us, when we affirm that we are children of the light.

Prayer: *O God, I am yours, a child of the Light. Help me live this and every day in your presence, aware that you have already begun a great thing in my life. Amen.*

---

[*]Henri J. M. Nouwen, "A Spirituality of Waiting." (*Weavings*, Vol. II. No. 1, 1987), p. 9.

Wednesday, November 10 Read Psalm 123.

Our lives as Christians are the result of God's unwavering love for us and our constant, unwavering focus on God. For the psalmist, God's mercy is available to those who maintain a constant, unwavering focus on the Lord.

To you I lift up my eyes;
  O you who are enthroned in the heavens!
As the eyes of the servants
    look to the hand of their master,
as the eyes of a maid
  to the hand of her mistress,
so our eyes look to the LORD our God,
  until he has mercy upon us.

Watching and waiting people are attentive. Their focus is always on God. They know their very lives are discovered and nourished by "paying attention" to God. They are attentive to and act upon the Spirit speaking within them. They lift up their eyes to God.

Although God initiates the journey, our journeys also include our intentional decisions to pay more attention to God within us and around us. We learn how to focus our attention on God by practicing certain "means of grace" which we call disciplines. Spiritual disciplines develop our attentiveness to God's acts of grace in all aspects of life. They help open our field of spiritual perception to God's acts of grace and calling which are yet to come.

Prayer: *O God of mercy, I lift up my eyes to you. Grant me the courage and desire to keep you as the focus of my life. Amen.*

Thursday, November 11   Read Judges 4:1-7.

Deborah was a prophetess during the period of judges in Israel. Her favorable oracles aroused Barak to go into battle against the army of the Canaanite King Jabin. She successfully prophesied that God would give the Canaanite army into Barak's hand.

Deborah sat under a palm and waited for God's word for the embattled and oppressed Israelites. Many of us have a sacred place where we regularly watch and wait for God's word or seek God's presence. An important sacred space for me is the North Dakota prairie where I grew up. I am overwhelmed by the presence of God whenever I return to those windswept hillsides.

Attentiveness to God is contingent upon positioning ourselves, physically and spiritually, to hear God. It is difficult to wait and watch for God's activity within us and in the world if we are not in position to hear and see. For us, positioning is the need to find a place and a time to regularly and patiently wait upon the Lord. It is going to prayer, even when we do not feel like praying. It is actively placing ourselves in a "position" to see Jesus when he walks by. Positioning includes how we sit, move, and breathe. It includes our reading, writing, and reflections on the scriptures.

Deborah was able to hear God's word for Barak and the Israelites because she was positioned, waiting to hear. Positioning is the first step in developing a personal discipline of attentiveness to God's yearning for us.

Suggestion for prayer: *Reflect on your sacred space. What are the ways you position yourself to listen to God? Pray for grace and strength to be ready to hear and respond to God's voice within.*

327

Friday, November 12   Read Matthew 25:14-30.

The parable of the talents is a parable of watchfulness, a parable, like many in Matthew, of the need to be ready for the unpredictable coming of the Lord. But it is also about stewardship in light of the unexpected return of the owner.

Stewardship begins with understanding our own dependence on God. Just as the master in the parable entrusted his property to three servants, all that we are and have is God's entrusted gift to us. If we rush headlong into life, consuming and controlling all in our path, we soon appropriate as real the illusion that we are dependent only on our own resources. We discover the depth of our dependence on God by listening to God.

Stewardship requires an active, faithful use of our gifts in the present moment. Dependence on God does not lead to passivity, but to a heightened awareness of God's claim upon our lives and the freedom to act. Faithful stewards care for God's gifts precisely because they know the gifts are God's.

The unfaithful servant in the parable was punished for two reasons. He did not fully understand his utter dependence on God. And, he failed to actively use what had been entrusted to him to expand the master's household.

We live in an environmentally aware age. This growing awareness is evidence of the Holy Spirit's activity. Increasingly, we are aware of our dependence on the gift and promises of God's creation. Increasingly, we are actively present to the perils and opportunities of this moment. Increasingly, we know that how we use the gifts of creation will determine the very future of the planet. We will be faithful stewards only if we watch diligently and actively, fully aware that all we are and have is a gift from God.

Prayer: *My Lord, let me receive each day as a precious gift. My Lord, let me live each day in faithfulness and fidelity to you. Amen.*

Saturday, November 13   Read Psalm 123.

Psalm 123 is a supplication for mercy. The psalmist reminds us that an important element of watching and waiting is longing for God's mercy and justice.

Jesus held in balance a life of prayer and a life of active ministry. He found it necessary to spend time and energy in prayer, listening to God. It is not surprising that the giants of the Christian faith have followed in Jesus' footsteps. Jesus always went from prayer to perform acts of healing, mercy, compassion, or justice. And he moved from acts of justice, mercy, or healing back to prayer.

What we learn from this rhythm in Jesus' life is that justice, mercy, healing, and compassion are rooted in attentiveness to God. The psalmist affirms the relatedness between waiting upon the Lord and the experience of God's mercy: "So our eyes look to the LORD our God, / until he has mercy upon us."

Today we live in a small world. We cannot escape the hurts and hungers of our sisters and brothers. But we do become somewhat callous to television pictures, news reports, and staggering statistics. So our eyes are no longer filled with God and the pain of our sisters and brothers. We become blind to what is about us. Solidarity with humanity, compassion, and justice are difficult to maintain.

Until we discover ourselves in solidarity with humankind, we will not discover ourselves in solidarity with Christ. By moving Godward, we must move toward neighbor, toward mercy and justice for persons and for the planet, toward social holiness, toward God's purpose for all humankind.

Prayer: *Have mercy on me, O Lord. Keep me in harmony with you and with your people. Amen.*

Sunday, November 14   Read 1 Thessalonians 5:1-11.

Paul admonishes the young Thessalonian congregation to be ready for the surprise—the day of the Lord, which will come unexpectedly. Paul is interested here not in describing or defending the difficulty that precedes the end time (the apocalypse), but only in the surprise itself and in the appropriate attitude and acts necessary for perceiving the surprise.

When four or five years old, our middle son loved to help me pop popcorn. He would wait motionless, eagerly and expectantly watching for the first kernel to pop. Stuart had waited and watched for that first pop many, many times. Yet each time he was delightfully surprised. His surprise was possible because he watched each time with the right attitude—hopefully and faithfully. This is the attitude Paul urges us to have in our preparation for the day of the Lord.

Waiting and watching people are full of hope and faith. Their watching is sustained by a trust that the possibilities will be fulfilled according to God's promises. Stuart was hopeful and expectant because he had grown to trust that the kernel would explode into a fluffy, white popped corn.

The church at Thessalonica was of mixed Jewish and Gentile membership. It was struggling and unstable. Paul discusses the "end time" to make a single point—the uncertainty and suddenness of the end requires the proper qualities of life in the here and now. Those qualities are faith, love, and hope. These qualities are to be worn like armor. They are to be practiced each day. For the surprise—the day of the Lord—is experienced each day that we live with faith, full of hope, and loving each other.

Prayer: *Lord Jesus, help me live each day full of faith, love, and hope. Give me the right attitude for perceiving this day as the day of the Lord. Amen.*

OF SHEEP AND SHEPHERDS

November 15-21, 1993   **Randolph M. Cross**✠

Monday, November 15   Read Psalm 100.

"We are [God's] people, and the sheep of [God's] pasture."

There may not be any more tender or important feeling than to feel as though I belong—that someone claims me. I am not talking about ownership, like a possession. I mean the sense of having a place, or being known and cared for by another. Now and then, our three year old will introduce our five year old to someone very proudly, "This is my brother!" You can feel behind the words a "belonging" spirit.

The psalmist writes with joy and enthusiasm in the psalm —"Make the noise, worship the Lord, come singing"—and *know* that the Lord is God! Tied to that joyful noisy knowledge is the equally joyful knowledge—"and *we* belong to God—we are God's sheep."

In the "eternal belonging," we can know steadfast love and faithfulness—we can know we will never be cut loose or left alone. We are God's. In that relationship, we can boldly and noisily worship—gratitude takes over as our motivation. All of *our* acts of love and creating places of belonging and peace for our world are new stanzas of the same song sung for generations—a song of love and thanks for the chance to belong and be claimed by God, who made us.

How will you sing your song of belonging today?

Suggestion for prayer: *Pray that God will guide your ways of responding to God's love in powerful acts and words today.*

✠Pastor, Faith United Methodist church, Fargo, North Dakota.

Tuesday, November 16   Read Ezekiel 34:11-16.

We are *so* used to *good* shepherds in our faith stories! Even Jesus called himself the Good Shepherd, who lays down his life for the sheep. One of the favorite parables is of the kind of shepherd who looks for the one lost sheep and celebrates when it is found. We are so "good shepherd" oriented that we may say "so what?" to Ezekiel's prophecy of God as the True Shepherd. I mean, what other kind of shepherd would God be, to seek out, rescue, gather, feed, and make to lie down all those who have been lost or strayed away, or who have been injured or weakened?

What we may have trouble imagining is what the sheep in Ezekiel's prophecy have had to endure up to this point. Those who were the very shepherds of Israel (the leaders of the nation) worked so effectively for years "fleecing the sheep"—living off the fat and wool of the sheep or Israel without once caring for them. The "shepherds" only fed themselves, devouring the life and health of the society— and *now,* God says, this will cease.

What we overhear must have been incredible good news for the common people—"I myself will be the shepherd of my sheep" God says. Finally, there will be peace and freedom and hope of wholeness under God's gentle, life-sustaining rule. How good it is to know that *God* is in charge from now on!

Have you ever felt burdened, or "devoured," or set upon by another who has charge over you? Do you long to rest under the care of one you can trust to care for you? Listen to Ezekiel's good news today—it was written for you. We can claim hope for justice and peace to come by God's hand. Be aware, however; God may send us to bring about that change!

Suggestion for prayer: *Pray for freedom and healing for those who live under another's uncaring hand.*

Wednesday, November 17   Read Ezekiel 34:20-24.

I grew up in a family of seven brothers and sisters. What Ezekiel writes of God's words in today's scripture describes very well life in a large family: "You pushed with flank and shoulder, and butted at all the weak with your horns... " In our family, at least, we learned early to stand our ground, even against each other! What some would call stubbornness, we simply called character, and without it, you were lost.

The difference between our family and today's scripture, however, is that our family acted out strong spirits and wills in the midst of loving relationships; you were allowed to "push" and "butt," but never in order to wound or break the "weaker" sheep, that is, sister or brother. In the time Ezekiel was written, however, there were certain privileged and powerful persons in the society who could only be called "fat sheep." They did not act out of love, but greed; and their methods of gaining wealth and power were oppressive.

When any of the seven of us children would act like "fat sheep," Mom or Dad would say "That's enough of that!" And so God speaks the same words: "The system is going to change, greedy ones—and you will be judged by your behavior and oppression!" (AP) Those must have been unwelcome words for the "fat sheep."

Perhaps we need to ask ourselves today if we appear and act more like the "fat" or the "lean" sheep; and I do not mean simply the shape of our bodies. How quick we are to "push" and "butt" to get our own way in the world, at the expense of another. "Leanness" isn't a matter of health—it's a matter of holiness and love.

Suggestion for meditation: *Where do I act like a "fat sheep" in my world? From whom do I need to ask forgiveness?*

Thursday, November 18   Read Ephesians 1:15-19.

My mother and father are wise people. Wisdom is a nice complement, a measured, even, thoughtful approach to the world. It calls up images of insight and judgment, of Solomon in his palace, and of Deborah under the sacred oak. Everybody should be wise—the world would be a gentle and perceptive place in which to live if that were so. The spirit of wisdom (v. 17) is what the writer of Ephesians prays to God to be a gift for his friends.

Did you notice what else is prayed for? That's right—the spirit of God's revelation! It is the prayer for the gift of the striking disclosure of God's very self and will for the world! If wisdom is a slow stroll, then revelation is a dance—an active, surprising, at times overwhelming view of the very person of God. Not to divide things too strictly, but it appears that wisdom is a head activity, revelation a heart work.

What a nice mixture of empowering gifts to pray for others to receive as they come to know God! The writer lays out what is to be accomplished through those gifts: enlightenment of heart, knowledge of hope and the inheritance that awaits the saints, and a sense of the "immeasurable greatness of power." How wonderful it would be for others to pray that we might receive these gifts from God!

Yet, those gifts are not to be taken lightly. To receive the gift of revelation and to go through the changes that it brings means that we are to become different people. When we are filled with hope and enlightened hearts, we touch the sense of that greatness of the power of God's love alive in us, then our work and life must be at God's disposal.

Suggestion for prayer: *Pray for revelation from God, and for the willingness to accept the work that follows.*

Friday, November 19   Read Ephesians 1:20-23.

Who's in charge of your church? the pastor? the trustees? the patriarch (or matriarch) who approves all plans for the future? Each congregation has its decision making group, although often it is *not* the elected persons of committees. Who's in charge? Who has authority and power? Many times the pain that exists in any church is caused by the very struggle for that power and "in-charge-ness."

It seems appropriate that every time the church gathers, we should recite these verses from Ephesians: Simply put, God has placed *Christ* over all things and made him the head for the church, *which is his body*. Scripturally speaking, *Christ* is in charge! Scripturally speaking as well, we are but the hands and feet and lungs and shoulders of Christ.

When our congregations or denominations seem to go askew, it very well may be that we have "decided" that the Body of Christ may make its own decisions and plans and strategies for ministry without considering the *Living Christ* as the head who must give direction to the Body.

By wisdom and revelation we come to understand Christ's direction. Those gifts must be received with two conditions: we must be willing to listen, we must be willing to abide by what we honestly believe we have received from the One in charge. It is a sure thing that our ministry as congregation and individuals will change and blossom under Christ's leadership and direction, as we are led into a powerful witness and presence of God's love in the world.

Suggestion for prayer: *Pray to recognize the leadership of Jesus Christ for the church. Image how differently the church will live with Christ in charge.*

Saturday, November 20   Read Matthew 25:31-40.

We began this week in celebration of being the sheep of God's pasture; we received both the blessing and judgment in Ezekiel as God "takes charge" of the flock from those who would oppress it. Yet, we are "sheep" who (according to Ephesians) are to receive the gifts of wisdom and revelation under the reign of the Living Christ.

In Matthew 25, we complete the circle and return to celebrate as Jesus offers the image of persons separated out for blessing because they *acted* in particular simple ways of love: feeding, welcoming, clothing, caring, visiting. Can it be that all we need to do to inherit the kingdom of God is to accomplish these small tasks? Great! No problem.

However—are you a sheep? Are *we* sheep? Do we even perform such simple tasks in our lives? Remember, it is for the benefit of the "least ones" that we must act in this way. Or is it possible that we can neglect these deeds for these least ones, whether for busyness or self-centeredness sake? There are so many hungry, thirsty, naked, sick, estranged, and lonely people in our neighborhood—not to mention in our world—that, indeed, to claim an easy entry through works into God's kingdom is almost a laugh, if it were not so bitterly sad.

What Jesus teaches is *not* a "works salvation," however. We can thank God for the gift of grace that justifies and brings eternal life without our working to try to save our own souls. What Christ *does* teach, though, is about *commitment* to the task of the faithful life, lived out in acts that prove our attentiveness to the will of God.

Suggestion for prayer: *Pray for an openness to joyful tasks of love under God's direction.*

Sunday, November 21   Read Matthew 25:31-33, 41-46.

And then, there are the goats. Jesus' painful promise is that when "Judgment Day" rolls around, there will be those who are not just left out, but banished from the presence of God. Their crime? They did not care in the least, in even the simplest ways, for those who were in simple, basic, life-necessary need. "They"—the goats—did not see the Son of Man in the lives of those needy persons, and so they held their love from those who could use it the most. Jesus says in so many words, "When you are that way, you are acting that way toward me—and that is reprehensible."

What a scary, foreboding prophecy! What a wonderful effective text for preachers to use to weave guilt and fear into their congregation, if they so choose: you are going to hell, and you don't even know it. Yet.

Where *is* the good news in this scripture? Isn't there anything to bring hope to us? Well, yes, there is. However your faith may lead you to believe concerning judgment, grace, and salvation, one thing is certain: Jesus' story is yet to occur. "The Son of Man" has not yet come in his glory, and has not "separated people one from another." We sheep and goats are still all mixed up and living together in our world, and the least members of our family—the whole human family—are still waiting to be fed and welcomed and clothed and loved in concrete ways. The good news is that there is still time to love one another, even in simple fundamental acts of caring. The message we cannot ignore, is that we, the followers of Christ, need to get to work—today, now.

Suggestion for prayer: *First, begin to identify in your mind the very obvious persons and places needing your love. Pray for the strength and energy to begin today to act in ways to share love.*

WAITING FOR GOD'S PROMISES

November 22-28, 1993   **Harry Y. Pak✠**
Monday, November 22   Read Isaiah 64:1-5b.

"Life is difficult."[*] With these words M. Scott Peck succinctly sums up the human condition. Thus there is a yearning in the human heart to transform the difficult present into a brighter future. The same yearning is reflected in our Isaiah passage.

In this activist culture we assume that the transformation would come through human efforts. The prophet, however, is convinced that God would have to bring it about because human efforts have proven futile. So he pleads and waits for God to come down.

Waiting provides a relevant theme for the Advent season which we are about to usher in. While waiting, Isaiah's people looked for spectacular signs of God's appearing, such as mountains quaking and fire kindling brushwood causing water to boil. At the first Christmas, too, people waited for the Messiah's coming in splendor and might. Thus, except for a few shepherds, they missed the cry of a baby coming from a Bethlehem stable. In search for the spectacular, it is easy to overlook the ordinary events through which God appears.

Prayer: *O God, may the coming Advent season be a time of expectant waiting for your coming, especially through common, ordinary events of life. Amen.*

✠Senior Pastor, Claremont United Methodist Church, Claremont, California.
[*]M. Scott Peck, *The Road Less Traveled* (New York: Simon & Schuster, 1978), p. 15.

Tuesday, November 23   Read Isaiah 64:5*c*-7;
Luke 3:1-18.

While waiting for God to come down, Isaiah becomes introspective. He becomes aware that "we have sinned," causing him to repent. Repentance is an appropriate theme for Advent, the season of waiting, which we usher in this Sunday. While waiting, we, too, need to repent.

But what does it mean to repent? At First United Methodist Church in Honolulu, where I used to pastor, there is an annual lectureship of some importance. In conjunction with the lectures a reception is held at the parsonage to honor the lecturers. My wife and I would spend some time cleaning the house. Invariably, we were left with excess clutter. In desperation we would designate a bedroom to dump all the unsightly things. But during the reception, we could never completely relax knowing that the house was not altogether in orderand in our minds was, *What if the guests want a tour of the house?* This is an analogy of how *not* to repent.

By contrast, Isaiah completely bares his outer and inner life before God. This is true repentance. True repentance is what John the Baptist urges us, too, in preparation for the coming of the Messiah. The preparation John insists we make is the cleansing of the whole life by repenting.

It may be that precisely this call to repentance can prompt us to clean up the inner clutter of our lives, especially as we prepare for Advent and Christmas. There is joy born of true repentance. This feeling of joy is not unlike the joy of a patient, who, after major cancer surgery, is told that all the malignancy has been removed.

Prayer: *O God, may the coming Advent, the time of waiting, be a time of repenting, in order that we may find the true joy of Christmas. Amen.*

339

Wednesday, November 24   Read Psalm 80:1-7, 17-19.

On our liturgical calendar the season of waiting, Advent, inevitably turns to the season of fulfillment, Christmastide. In actual life, however, it does not often happen that way. What if the season of waiting seems interminable? This is the predicament the psalmist expresses in our text.

The psalmist prays but God is silent and indifferent. Even worse, God seems to be cruel and heartless. So to the prayer for bread, tears are offered. In their thirst, they are given more tears. They are humiliated before their enemies who deride them and taunt them. Still the psalmist does not lose hope. Still he pleads for God to come to save: "Restore us, O God of hosts, / let your face shine, that we may be saved!"

Reginald Fuller gives this passage a Christological interpretation, since, he says, passages referring to the earthly king of Israel may be transferred to the messianic King. Thus, the phrases "man of thy right hand" and "son of man," become references to Christ and the passage becomes a petition for God to intervene by sending the Messiah.[*]

Let us take this psalm to heart, then our waiting will be expectant, even if the fulfillment does not neatly follow the liturgical calendar. Terry Anderson, a former hostage in Iran, is an example of such expectant waiting. As a hostage he waited, often in solitary confinement, six years for his release. He was tortured physically and mentally. At times he was on the verge of despair. But he never gave up. His faith and stubbornness kept him going. Helpless though he felt in the present, his faith made his waiting for his future hope expectant.

Prayer: *O God, may our waiting be faith-filled and expectant, no matter how dark the present circumstances may be. Amen.*

---

[*]Reginald H. Fuller, *Preaching the Lectionary* (Collegeville, MN: Liturgical Press, 1984), p. 202.

Thursday, November 25   Read 1 Corinthians 1:3-9.

What is the meaning of Advent, the season of waiting, for us Christians for whom Christmas has happened already. Are we simply to play-act as we wait for another Christmas? Today's Epistle reading answers this question.

Paul wrote after Jesus was born, lived, taught, faced the cross, resurrected, and ascended. He explains the meaning of waiting in this post resurrection era as he deals with a problem he faced in the Corinthian church. Leaders of the church boasted of their advanced knowledge of the gospel, their eloquence, and the variety of their spiritual gifts. While offering thanksgiving for these gifts, Paul immediately sets them in the context of the future, of the things yet to come. He reminds the Corinthians that in spite of all their present knowledge, God still has more truths to disclose. God has sent God's son into the world that first Christmas. But Christ will come again to complete what the first coming had started.

Paul reminds us, too, that even as we give thanks for the gifts we already possess, we wait for Christ's coming again to complete our Christian life. But the second coming need not be the far off end-time event. It can be any time when our lives are touched again and renewed by the Holy Spirit. Thus, Advent is the season of thanksgiving that Christ has already come *and* the season of anticipating Christ's coming again to complete what he has begun.

Prayer: *O God, may we come more and more to a spirit of thanksgiving for Christ's coming and a sense of anticipation for Christ's coming again. Amen.*

Friday, November 26   Read Matthew 13:24-30.

The three parables of Jesus, which constitute the texts for the next three meditations, all deal with future fulfillment of what is now only an unpromising beginning. They are appropriate texts for Advent, the time of waiting and preparing.

One day, as I was pulling into the church parking lot, I caught a glimpse of a familiar figure going into the church office. He had come three times that week before asking for help. I immediately concluded that he had come again to ask for more help. When I entered the office, our church secretary was beaming. She explained that this man, who, I thought, had come to ask for more help, had come instead to give a $30.00 donation to the church. This experience taught me not to hastily judge another person.

The parable of wheat and tares addresses this issue. Among other things it deals with the difficulty of distinguishing the good from the bad. God allows the bad to live side by side with the good until the harvest time. This is a message of promise as well as warning. Here, the analogy of seeds to human life breaks down. Weeds cannot possibly grow up to produce a crop of wheat. But human beings can be changed! Even if everyone else may consider us weeds, God, who knows us inside and outside, sees the potential in us for bearing good fruit. That is the promise. But we must conscientiously seek to cultivate our lives to produce good fruit. That is the warning. The season of Advent is a time to cultivate our lives.

Prayer: *O God, may our lives measure up to the promise and in due season produce good fruit. Amen.*

Saturday, November 27   Read Matthew 13:31-32.

The parable of the mustard seed, which is today's scripture, has reminded me of the days when I was a seminary intern serving as one of the campus ministers at the University of California, Berkeley. I was leading a Bible study of just four participants, including me. In the meantime, our mandate was to serve some thirty thousand students with the saving word which the gospel provides.

A similar experience must have faced the first followers of Jesus. As they tried to quantitatively assess their ministry as Jesus' disciples, the result seemed meager. This parable was an answer to this discouraged band of disciples.

It is also an answer to our times of discouragement in discipleship. The mustard seed was one of the smallest of all seeds. But when it was fully grown it often reached a height of eight to ten feet, and the birds could perch on its branches to find shade. So we ought not to be discouraged by small beginnings. What is important is all the potential stored in that small beginning.

But the growth is not ours to dictate. God, in God's own time, will bring about growth and harvest. In the meantime, we need to wait—a relevant thought for Advent.

Our waiting, however, is not passive waiting. Before the seed can be planted the ground needs to be prepared. The plnater must make sure the seed is provided with the most fertile place to germinate and grow. Then, and only then, we wait, expectantly.

Prayer: *O God, having done our best to prepare the soil and plant the seed of the gospel, help us to wait, patiently and expectantly, trusting in your power to bring forth growth. Amen.*

Sunday, November 28   Read Matthew 13:33-35.

In today's scripture, Jesus draws a very familiar picture of Palestinian home life. It is the picture of a housekeeper mixing into the dough of a new baking a tiny amount of yeast and waiting until the whole dough is leavened.

A small amount of yeast can leaven the whole mass of meal and change its quality. Just so, what really counts in Christian influence in the world is not the quantitative size but the indwelling dynamic force.

There is a further lesson. Once the yeast is put into the dough, the yeast does its work silently, almost imperceptibly. Like yeast, the kingdom of God too, expands silently and imperceptibly. The growth of the kingdom is dynamic, yet silent. This contrasts with our cult of noise in which we think the desired results will come if we can only shout long enough and loudly enough.

Translating this truth into our Christian life, as far as numbers are concerned, faithful Christians are few. We know all too well what it means to find no one else at our work or in our class in school who seeks to witness to Christian concern for moral values, honesty at work, or peace with one another, and among nations. We are but a small minority—but we are the yeast in the world. As we quietly witness to our faith, there is in us a hidden dynamic to revitalize others.

The kingdom of God works like the yeast. There is a silent yet steady indwelling of the present by God's future. So even as we wait, in this Advent season, the future God has in store for us is already permeating this present world.

Prayer: *O God, trusting in the promise of silent but dynamic force hidden behind the yeast, help us to recommit ourselves to witness for our faith. Amen.*

COURAGE, CONVICTION AND CONVERSION

November 29–December 5, 1993 **Sr. Barbara Jean, SHN✠**
Monday, November 29   Read Isaiah 40:1-2.

In this symphonic overture the prophet sought to link the release of the Jewish captives of Babylon with those of the great Exodus story. Such typology shows a conviction that God's relationship with the people Israel could be counted on as consistent and enduring. And, as always, such love is God's initiative rather than humanity's. The people are urged to respond to God's love because they have become reluctant to leave Babylon, as if they preferred estrangement to union.

The words used in this passage are passionate. They are reminiscent of the love relationship and bridal imagery used by the writer of the Song of Songs or the prophet Hosea. So, too, is the theme of God's continual longing for a people who prove unfaithful and yet always have the possibility of reconciliation held out to them.

The emphatic double command to "comfort" reaches far beyond our common understanding of consolation. It is a divine imperative to the prophet to move the people of God from their real physical trouble caused by separation, into the actual, tangible joy of reconciliation. The reunion is symbolized by their restoration to the holy city of Jerusalem.

What God speaks is no dreamer's fancy, but concrete fact in the form of a real, black-and-white Persian legal document and a bodily return to Zion.

Suggestion for meditation: *Through what adversity has God brought you into a deeper relationship? How have you recognized God's hand touching your life?*

✠An Episcopal religious of the Sisterhood of the Holy Nativity, Fond du Lac, Wisconsin.

Tuesday, November 30   Read Isaiah 40:1-11.

Linked are a series of commands: Comfort-Speak-Pre-pare-Cry-Behold. They form a procession of activity which leads toward the recognition of the Glory of God in our midst. The social and political milieu of Deutero-Isaiah's prophecy pointed toward the messianic hope, the restoration of Israel. But its religious significance goes far beyond simply time and space events. Here was the proclamation of a worldwide experience of the revelation of God, with the potential for establishing the kingdom of God.

First and foremost, religion is the relationship between God and humanity. Much of that relationship is of an inward or spiritual nature—but the "proof of the pudding" comes when that relationship can be recognized by the external realities of history, visible to all. Such facts were enumerated as the end of warfare, the leveling out of the way Israel would "walk," and ultimately the total provision by God for their eternal well-being.

Glory becomes the operative word for this salvation history. It symbolized not only God's victory over Israel's adversaries, but also God's very presence. Israel was to anticipate a majestic experience of God's presence, and all were to participate in this revelation.

The people were to participate by preparing the "Way" for God to come. The hindrances which blocked the coming were more than physical ones, they were also moral ones. So the prophet's message spoke also to the need for people to strive with all diligence to straighten out their lives.

Prayer: *O Lord, how would you have me prepare for the greater revelation of your presence in my world? What are the things that hinder your coming more deeply into my life? Give us grace that we may quicken our hearts and prepare the way. Amen.*

Wednesday, December 1   Read Mark 1:1.

"The beginning of the Gospel of Jesus Christ, the Son of God."

Already, in the very first verse of the very first chapter, the author of this Gospel spells out his entire theology. The only Evangelist to use the word *Gospel* in the title of his work, Mark speaks urgently and clearly. His intent is manifold: to bring conviction, courage and conversion to those whom he addresses.

This writing of the Gospel is dated about 70 A.D. Its significance lies in the historical events of the day. Jerusalem has been destroyed and both Jew and Christian have been beaten down. In those early days there was little to distinguish the followers of Christ from those loyal to Judaism. The Temple and Law of Moses was still important to them. So, one must read Mark's Gospel against the backdrop of this tragic event.

The significance of the opening sentence must also be viewed in its critical, historical setting. Mark is a deliberate theologian and begins with a theological certainty—Jesus Christ, the Son of God. He leaves no doubt about the authority or position of Jesus. In this way, Mark leaves no doubt that Jesus is not merely the preacher of the gospel, but is himself the Gospel—the Good News.

The intent of Mark is to present the Christ as deliberately and succinctly as possible. The best way to read the Gospel, therefore, is from start to finish, without stopping. Even Mark's vocabulary and the telling of Jesus' story cries out with the urgency of the message. Jerusalem has fallen and the people are in peril. They must learn quickly from whence comes their salvation.

Prayer: *Quickly come, Lord Jesus, and save us for your mercy's sake. Amen.*

347

Thursday, December 2   Read Psalm 85.

This Psalm picks up many of the themes of the Deutero-Isaiah passage: "salvation is at hand," "glory may dwell in the land," etc. It is a veritable compendium of theological terms for the eschatological event—the coming of the Lord. If Isaiah 40 is a symphonic overture for such an event, then this psalm is a recapitulation, in poetic form, of the same.

There appear to be three clear divisions to the psalm: the return of the captives from exile; a prayer for the restoration of God's people; a divine message. The release from bondage refers to a past event and points toward a paid debt. Restoration moves toward a present condition, with a plea to God to remove God's justifiable anger. The last, a divine message, depicts a state of righteousness and peace wherein Yahweh dwells once more among his people.

Theologically, the bondage or captivity of a people alludes to the enslavement to sin. In this selection of readings it becomes obvious that Jesus is the divine message, the dwelling of God upon earth, who frees us from such captivity. The offenses of all the people of God will be forgiven rather than merely canceled out. They are paid for by Christ, and we are restored to fellowship with God.

Yet, there remains a responsibility on our part to accept God's gift, and to turn from ungodliness to righteousness. We will continue to fall into sin, to be bound by our pride and self-will, if we don't pay attention to the life God calls us to. Rather than wrathful retribution, we will incur the just consequences for our actions. We must, therefore "harken to what the Lord God will say concerning us" and accept the peace God offers.

Suggestion for meditation: *In what way do you remain in bondage? How is God calling you into freedom?*

Friday, December 3   Read 2 Peter 3:12.

"Waiting for and hastening the coming of the day of God."

"The day of God." What is meant by this striking expression? Can it mean that He is not here with us now, but will only come in some future moment? Certainly not! God is not bound by time and space. We are. By the "day of God" must then be meant, a day which will be fully His and that we will recognize it as such. It will be a day when God will take first place in our lives. Such is implied by verse eleven: "what sort of persons ought you to be in lives of holiness and godliness?" Our holiness, our godliness becomes, then, the criterion for Kingdom living.

References to straight paths and smoothed out places are all imagery which describe "the day of God." His glory will be revealed in that great day, and all that stood in the way, all obstacles to His glory will be removed. God, in his moral attributes, will be conspicuously present in the world—thus the day of God is also known as the day of judgment.

Another translation of the word "hastening" (speudo, in Greek) may read "to desire with earnestness." This beautifully describes the godly who wait for the coming of the day of God with an eager longing. They await that time when all things created will be valued at their true worth; when human life, and all that belongs to it, will be seen in the light of the Infinite and Eternal Realities. Again, we meet up with an abbreviated theology of the eschatological event.

"Waiting for and desiring the day of God" are Peter's account of the way a Christian should live. Does this description apply to you?

Prayer: *Hasten, O Father, the coming of your Kingdom in me. Amen.*

349

Saturday, December 4   Read 2 Peter 3:13-15.

The expectation of the coming of the Lord affects a Christian in thought, word, and deed. First and foremost it reminds us of what human life really is and what that life really means. As with the assertion in the Isaiah passage, the coming of God will bring with it both a reason to dread and a reason to rejoice. The dread comes from that which is old and imperfect being burned away. All that we have known and become accustomed to will be dissolved in the fire. But a new heaven and a new earth await us . . . and that is cause for great rejoicing.

Being zealous to be found by God without spot or blemish points us to our sense of responsibility. We have a moral obligation to pursue the perfection for which we were created, not only for ourselves, but for the sake of the Kingdom. Peace comes as a result of this pursuit after perfection. Moral consistency—to know that right differs from wrong, practically speaking, is to know that we are responsible for what we do or what we neglect to do. This necessarily implies that some One exists to whom this responsibility is due—namely God.

Who of us can realize such potential? None of us is without some sort of spot or blemish, yet we always have before us the certainty of hope in our baptismal covenant. We have died with Christ, through the waters of baptism, that we might live with him in his Eternal Glory. The prophet Isaiah recognized the magnitude of God's mercy in that Christ will not only forgive iniquity, but will also tenderly carry us into the glory of the kingdom of God.

Suggestion for meditation: *The waters of salvation flowed from the Red Sea, the River Jordan, and baptismal font, weaving each of us into a marvelous tapestry of the people of God.*

Sunday, December 5   Read Mark 1:108.

John the Baptist, the Precursor of the Messiah, is a secondary figure, yet an extremely important one. Every good Jew knew that a forerunner must come before the Messiah, as it had been written and told in prophesy. Mark did not dare present Jesus as a merely historical figure, in a vacuum, but rather as one to whom all of history had been leading. The typology again is consistent.

The preaching of the Baptist echoes that of the Prophets of the Old Covenant, yet with a twist. He pronounces also the Spirit of God who will be poured out upon the people when the "Coming One" comes. The work of the Baptist demanded high qualities: courage, conviction and conversion—just the qualities the Gospel writer intended his readers to understand. In the great forerunner those qualities take on substance and allow him to stand as the exemplar of them.

And like responsibility is given us who follow Christ. All of us who claim any allegiance, who know any truth of the Gospel, owe it to others. We stand with the Baptist in proclamation, having those around us to whom we ought to point out the Lamb of God, if indeed we have found Him ourselves.

None of this story is new or different from what has been proclaimed for thousands of generations. God created us and holds us in love. We have wandered far from that love through pride and self-will. We have become enslaved by the pride of life, yet God stands ever ready to draw us back. Through the Exodus and the exile, through the destruction of Jerusalem, and through our own personal bondage or catastrophes, God is always there. He, Himself, paid the debt for our transgressions, and in Him we are free indeed.

Prayer: *God grant us courage and conviction to follow you, the one, true Lord. Amen.*

MESSENGERS OF THE LIGHT

December 6-12, 1993   **Anne Broyles**✝

Monday, December 6   Read John 1:1-8.

In the beginning was the Word.

As a child, I gazed at these words from the Gospel of John each week as I sat in church. Ornately carved on the pulpit, these words of a Word which existed before time began gave me great comfort. I could not imagine a world before my own short lifetime; yet, here was evidence that ages and ages ago, before even my great-great-great-grandmother lived, the Word coexisted with God and co-created the world.

And then God sent Jesus, the Word, as a love letter to all people. The Word became flesh that we might know God in a new way. As I grew up and learned the stories of the man Jesus, I felt God's love expressed through the life of Jesus, whose power affected not only me but brought light to all humanity.

Before he began his earthly ministry, "There was a man, sent by God, whose name was John." John was the intermediary by which many persons came to understand that God's Light was coming to earth in human form.

Just as God sent John, there have been countless others who have preached the good news of Jesus Christ. Whom do you know who points you to the Light that "shines in the darkness"? How have you received the personally addressed love letter from God whose name is Jesus Christ?

Prayer: *Gracious God, in this Advent season, open our hearts that we might hear your message and feel your Light from whatever messenger you send to us. Amen.*

✝Co-pastor of Malibu United Methodist Church; writer; retreat leader; Malibu, California.

Tuesday, December 7   Read John 1:19-28.

John was clear about his life and purpose. He was not the Christ, not Elijah, but, rather, "the voice of one crying out in the wilderness, 'Make straight the way of the Lord.' " As he received earnest seekers in the waters of the Jordan River, John sought to prepare the world for Christ's coming.

Humbly, John answered those who questioned his identity. He had no need to be the focus of attention but continually reminded his questioners of the One to come. Content with his role as the precursor of Christ, John knew that, as the farmer must first prepare the soil before the seeds may find nourishment in the earth, his call to repentance and baptizing prepared hearts for the reception of Jesus Christ and the new message of God's Light.

Each Sunday, a quiet man hands out bulletins as people arrive for worship. Week after week, year after year, this man has been for visitors and members alike in my congregation the introduction to our time of worship together. This man's gentle smile helps each worshipper prepare to receive the spirit of Christ in our time together.

So John's message of repentance helped its hearers prepare for a new message of love and forgiveness. "God's love can help you begin again," he reminded those people on the shores of the Jordan, "so turn your lives around" (AP).

Because John was so clear about who he was and what his call was, he effectively participated in Jesus' ministry. We, too, must discern the role we are to play in the bringing about of God's reign on earth. How are we called to share the good news of Jesus Christ?

Prayer: *God of love, help me know how I can be of service to you. Give me humility to accept my role and boldness to share your message of love. Amen.*

Wednesday, December 8   Read Psalm 126.

The Hebrew people told and retold their story as God's people—slavery and deliverance, exile and return, sadness and joy. The psalmist understood that God had been with the Hebrews in all the hills and valleys of their journey. "When the Lord restored the fortunes of Zion...our mouth was filled with laughter, and our tongue with shouts of joy."

Their joy included thankfulness to God, who again and again provided sustenance and a new beginning for them. Others were caught by this contagious joy and said, "The Lord has done great things for them." It was clear that the Hebrew God was a great God who cared for God's people in new and surprising ways.

How often does someone look at us and say, "God has done great things for them"? Do we acknowledge the ways God is working in our lives? When something positive happens to us, do we thank God? Do we find ourselves marveling at all of the "coincidences" that occur, or do we give God the glory for "God-incidences" that change our lives?

Our attitude as we face life's hills and valleys can have an effect on others who may be actively looking for signs of God in their midst. A young man who narrowly escapes death in a car accident sighs, "Thank God, I was wearing my seat belt. I mean, I really thank *God!*" And the casual newspaper reader may stop and remember his or her own reasons to give thanks.

We can be messengers of God's Light when we share with others the specific blessings we feel God has given to us.

Suggestion for meditation: *Make a list of God's blessings in your life. What holds you back from sharing this good news with others? How can you say, with the psalmist, "God has done great things for me; I am glad"?*

Thursday, December 9   Read Isaiah 61:1-4.

At the synagogue in Nazareth Jesus stood up to read this passage from Isaiah, then said, "Today this scripture has been fulfilled in your hearing" (Luke 4:21). Jesus was giving notice that his ministry would challenge the status quo, as Isaiah challenged the existing systems of his day.

"The Lord has anointed me...." Jesus understood his call to ministry and the implications of being anointed by God. God's call means reaching out, as Isaiah shows us, to the afflicted, the brokenhearted, the captives, those who mourn.

We reach out so that together we can build up ancient ruins, raise up former devastation, and repair ruined cities. When the Los Angeles riots occurred in April of 1992, many areas of the city were literally ruined, devastated. A coalition of people joined together to clean up and rebuild in the midst of ashes and broken windows.

Some of those who helped clean up Los Angeles were from the neighborhoods hardest hit by the riots. They were the afflicted, the brokenhearted, those who feel captive in a society that does not often acknowledge the depths of their economic despair. Others from outside the hard-hit area came to help, called to work side by side with people with whom they had previously felt little in common.

Reading Isaiah, we realize that proclaiming the year of the Lord's favor requires more than cleaning up after angry rioters. It means listening to the anger that caused the riots, looking at the criminal justice system which was called into question, putting money and energy into economic reform so that all people may receive God's message of Light.

Suggestion for meditation: *What places today need rebuilding?*
Prayer: *Wherever we live, whatever our situation, let us feel your call and eagerly respond, O God.*

Friday, December 10   Read Isaiah 61:8-11.

God sets before us a vision of a world where justice prevails for all people. The faithful are rewarded by an everlasting covenant with the Lord. It is clear to everyone "that they are a people the LORD has blessed." So blessed, the faithful ones rejoice at being clothed with "garments of salvation and "the robe of righteousness."

How do we live in faith-filled joyfulness?

Guided meditation: Picture a seed buried underneath the soil. Slowly, surely, the roots begin to wisp out, stretching in an intricate network. Then, as the sun and rain work together for the good of this seed, a stalk reaches upward until it breaks through the soil and seeks the sun's blessing.

The seed stalk grows tall and strong. What does it look like? Visualize your plant. Is it a sunflower? a zinnia? a sapling? How are *you* like this plant?

Think of your own life. You are the seed, rooted in good, rich earth and reaching toward the blue sky. In what are you rooted? Toward what do you grow? What actions do you take in your life to nurture your growth?

Isaiah tells us that righteousness and praise are natural consequences for those who love God and work to bring about God's reign. How are praise and righteousness taking root in your life?

Focus on the image of your plant, strong and sturdy as *you* are, growing toward the sun as you want to grow toward God. And give thanks that "as the earth brings forth its shoots, and as a garden causes what is sown in it to spring up, so the Lord God will cause righteousness and praise."

Prayer: *God, you nurture all my growth. Let me grow closer to you and let my life be full of praise and righteousness. Amen.*

Saturday, December 11   Read 1 Thessalonians 5:16-22.

The task of being God's messengers of light can seem overwhelming, especially on days when we see many manifestations of darkness and despair. But Paul gives us some practical advice for how to share God's good news. "Rejoice always, pray constantly, give thanks in all circumstances."

Many times it is hard to rejoice. A loved one is ill; war rages; bigotry and prejudice run strong in our community. But our rejoicing runs deeper than the events of any one day; we rejoice because we know that *whatever happens,* God is with us, loving us more than we will ever know.

In a world that includes pain and suffering, we know we need to be in constant prayer to be strengthened to work for the good. Indeed, Paul reminds us, "Hold fast what is good; abstain from every form of evil."

Constant prayer happens when we endeavor to bring God to every situation we encounter. "Give me your patience, Creator, with this child." "Be with me as I make this decision, O God." "Healer of every ill, bless the persons inside the ambulance whose sirens I hear."

Our prayers do not have to be long, or even prayed on our knees. We can encourage ourselves to pray constantly—at home, traveling, in meetings, at the grocery store, playing tennis. Our prayer life must be equal to the task of keeping up with whatever we are doing.

We have an active God who *chose* Isaiah, *brought back* the Hebrew people, *sent* John, and *calls* us. We are pulled into God's activity but can only sustain our commitment if we are connected to God's power through prayer.

Suggestion for meditation: *How can I serve God more fully through an active life? How can I connect to God more constantly through my prayer life?*

Sunday, December 12   Read 1 Thessalonians 5:23-24.

Paul often ends his letters with encouragement and praise for the people to whom he writes. To the followers at Thessalonica, he writes that they are not alone. They have a friend like Paul to nurture and guide them; and God, who is faithful, will keep them holy and give them divine peace.

When we serve as messengers of God's light, we work in partnership with each other under the guidance of the One who is always faithful. In some way, we feel the presence of John as he shared his message of repentance. We hear Isaiah's voice reminding us of what it means to live as one called by God. We say with the psalmist, "The LORD has done great things for us" (Psalm 126:3). We remember the practical wisdom of Paul and apply it to our own situations.

There is indeed a "great cloud of witnesses" cheering us on, providing support. When I speak out for equality of all peoples, I have behind me people like Martin Luther King, Jr., Fannie Lou Hamer, and Abraham Lincoln. When I lift up concern for the poor and oppressed, I am backed by people like Dorothy Day, Mother Teresa, and Oscar Romero. When I work for peace and proclaim reverence for life, ones like Albert Schweitzer provide me with strength and encouragement.

Most importantly, I am constantly undergirded by the life and example of Jesus Christ. He is with me every step of the way as I learn what it means to be a messenger of God's light.

"God who calls you is faithful." With God's help, I can move forward, clear about what my role is and ready to work for God's reign in my home, my neighborhood, my world.

Prayer: *God of light, I know you are with me in all I do. Guide me to serve in your name and spirit that your light will shine strong in the darkness, your love become the world's strength. Amen.*

GOD'S REVERSALS

December 13-19, 1993
Monday, December 13

Jo Carr✢
Read 2 Samuel 7:1-11, 16.

Coming to dwell with us

What a series of reversals!

David was the one who followed the sheep: now he leads the nation. David is the one who wants to build God a house: now God says "never mind that; I'm going to build *you* a house (dynasty)." The Lord God Almighty, who traveled with Moses and the nomads wherever they wandered, declines the offer of a stay-put cedar house, in order to be with the humble and homeless, whenever and wherever they gather together. Interesting, that…and even more so, as we reflect on the child born in a Bethlehem manger, who was heir of David's throne and last-and-greatest of his house… and who was also Son of God, coming to dwell, to pitch his tent with us!

So, as Father Andrew Greeley says, God "draws straight, with crooked lines." And even so, God comes to us in dramatic reversals and draws us close.

Thanks be to God!

Prayer: *It's true, God, that I can* read *all that, and* say *all that, and still be reluctant to* accept *it . . . that you, who created the stars of this December night, should care about and come to me.*
It is *true. Thanks be to thee. Amen.*

✢United Methodist minister and author; Pampa, Texas.

Tuesday, December 14　　　Read Psalms 89:1-4.

Christ the King

There is a Catholic high school in my hometown named Christ the King. Like high schools everywhere, it has bumper stickers. And like bumper stickers everywhere, they occasionally get tattered. One day I saw one that had lost its last letter. It said simply, "CHRIST THE KIN."

Yes!! *That's* it! This descendant of David who will always be King, this one of the dynasty that will last forever, this one sired by the Most High, this Christ the *King,* is also the one who came to pitch his tent among us, Christ the *Kin.*

What a reversal that is! And what it means is that he has our frame of reference. He knows about the kind of stuff we go through, knows about birth and homelessness, taxes, crowds, loneliness, being misunderstood, "sat upon/spat upon"—even knows about death.

He has experienced feast days and fasting, friends and friendlessness, joy and contentment, and concerns and small pleasures. We *can* relate to him, because he knows wherefrom we speak.

Thanks, thanks be to God for the great reversal: for coming to us in such a humble-ordinary way: as the Son, as the one, as Christ the Kin.

Prayer: *Dear God, may I appropriate that truth and make it my own, that Christ comes to us as one who knows us this Christmas season. Amen.*

Wednesday, December 15   Read Luke 1:26-28.

Who, me?

I suppose it started out like an ordinary day: chores to do, water to fetch from the village well...and the daydreaming of a young woman betrothed. And then out of nowhere appears God's angel, saying, "Hey, Mary!" or "Praises, the one God gazes upon!" or *"Ave, Maria!"*

Wow! No wonder she was astonished...greatly troubled ...mind-boggled at the kind of greeting this might be! What's more, there's that next line, more mind-boggling than the rest: "The Lord is with you!"

She may have thought, *The Lord is with this naive young village maid engaged to a carpenter? With* me *carrier of water jugs, apprentice at cooking and doer of the family wash? The Lord is with ordinary hometown* me?

And we say it, too, astonished ourselves that it be so. Hmm. I wonder if Mary went around the rest of her life with those five words weaving in and out of all her thinking: *TheLordiswithyoutheLordiswithyoutheLordiswithyoutheLord iswithyou...*

Prayer: *Lord, our God, may we, too—I, too—be haunted and hallowed like that, preoccupied with the ultimate reversal implied by those five words—"The Lord is with you!" Amen.*

Thursday, December 16   Read Luke 1:39-50.

Something to sing about

Troubled Mary, still wondering about what God had done (and what Joseph would do?), hurried across the Judean hills to share her wonderment with her cousin Elizabeth…Elizabeth, whose *own* child confirmed Mary's puzzlement…and Elizabeth said, "Blessed are you!" which, perhaps, helped Mary see that since her child is from God there is no need to worry because God will be with her.

And Mary, perhaps able to relax for the first time since Gabriel, then broke into song:

> My soul exalts…
> My spirit exults…

O joy! God's great reversal, God's holy folly of choosing young Mary from Nazareth (read "Nowheresville") to bear the Messiah, is something to sing about! How that choice exalts the name of God, who can use a maid of low estate (and a stable, a manger, a house in the back of the carpenter's shop) for the nurture of God's only Son!

Let us, with Mary, *exalt* God's name, *exult* in God's wondrous reversals, and sing "Joy! Joy!"

> Joy to the world! the Lord is come!
> Let earth receive her King;
> let every heart prepare him room,
>   and heaven and nature sing…*

Prayer: *Let me, today, Lord, exalt your holy name, and exult in the ways you reach out to us this Advent season. And let me share the joy with all I meet! Amen.*

---

*From the hymn "Joy to the World" by Isaac Watts.

Friday, December 17   Read Luke 1:50-55.

> For the Mighty One has done
>   great things for me,
> and holy is his name.
> His mercy is for those who fear him
>   from generation to generation.

Scholars and hymnists call Mary's song the Magnificat. It is a prayer of thanksgiving and a hymn of praise. And perhaps it is also a prophecy of what's to come, made by a politically savvy young woman? Or, maybe (more likely?), it is her remembering of history, as Israelites were called to do, recounting how God took a slave people...how God pulls off these outrageous reversals...showing mercy to the humble, and routing "the arrogant of heart" (NJB)....deflating the powerful, and exalting the powerless...giving feasts to the hungry, and sending away empty-handed the only ones who could have afforded the prices on the menu at the Christmas feast!

How *odd* of God! Yet, how repeatedly *like* God!

Suggestion for meditation: *Are there reversals that I need to make? At this holy season, are there reversals I need to make that have to do with "the Christmas feast"? Like this tradition we embrace of giving primarily to the much-gifted? Or this habit we have of spending the "season of waiting" in a great deal of rushing about?*

Prayer: *God, guide me! Empower me to make some creative reversals! Amen.*

Saturday, December 18   Read Luke 1:26-28.

Favored ones

What does it mean in *my* everydayness, to say, "The Lord is with me!"? That I don't have to face my hard stuff alone?

I think of Mary and Joseph, facing the untimely pregnancy, the away-from-home childbirth, the sudden and unplanned trip to Egypt, the long return trip home, the challenges of child-rearing—and God with them in all of that. Is that what it means for me, too?

Does it mean that the Lord is with me in my "low estate" (1:48, KJV) as he was for Mary? What a reversal! That this best-of-all-blessings of God's presence is not something I have to qualify for by becoming mature enough, or educated enough, or spiritual enough, or even *good* enough ...but that God chooses to be with me out of love! In my head, I accept that. What a freeing and life-changing truth when I can accept it in my heart!

We sing, this season, of Emmanuel. That word translates "God-with-us." Yes, and that makes us *all* "favored ones."

> Come, thou long expected Jesus,
> born to set thy people free;
> from our fears and sins release us,
> let us find our rest in thee.*

A blessing for me to absorb and to share: *The Lord "bless, preserve, and keep you; the Lord mercifully with his favor look upon you, and fill you with all spiritual benediction and grace."***

---

*From "Come Thou Long Expected Jesus" by Charles Wesley.
**From "The Celebration and Blessing of a Marriage," *The Book of Common Prayer* (1977).

Sunday, December 19   Read Romans 16:25-27.

Emmanuel! God-with-us!

The final doxology of Paul's most formal book may have been tacked on by some later editor who wanted a fitting closure to the "complete works" of Paul. And it, too, speaks of a reversal, of a mystery now revealed! It speaks of God glorified in the life of that barn-born baby, village-raised rabbi, Jesus: the Christ!

Praises! Sing and shout and celebrate, this Christmas season because the Lord is with us! Ever since the hidden mystery was revealed in a manger...ever since some shepherds came to see the source of the bright starshine and went away telling everybody who would listen what had been made known to them—that God-is-with-us!

> All this took place to fulfill what had been spoken by
> the Lord through the prophet:
> "Look, the virgin
>   shall conceive and bear a son,
> and they shall name him
>   Emmanuel,"
> which means, "God is with us."
>   —Matthew 1:22-23

Emmanuel! *That's* the finale, the doxology, the hymn of hymns. God has chosen to dwell with ordinary me. Praise be to God!

Suggestion for meditation: *Reflect for a time on this greatest gift. Compose your own prayer of thanksgiving . . . and* sing *it! Amen!*

FOR MINE EYES HAVE SEEN THY SALVATION

December 20-26, 1993 **J. Barrie Shepherd**✛
Monday, December 20 Read Luke 2:29-32.

The lectionary readings for this week leap ahead to Christmas Day and then beyond. They focus our meditations upon the joy and gladness, the sheer celebration of the Christ event, then turn to examine its inner meaning in the light of all history.

Yet something in me digs in its heels at this move. I don't want to skip over this fourth and last week of the Advent season. The inner rhythm of my own spirit tells me, *Hold on; we're not there yet. Don't spoil everything now by losing patience and rushing on ahead.*

Anticipation, after all, is much of the secret of this holy season. In it we learn, once again, to wait, and to hope, and to "keep a good lookout." In an age that has come to demand instant gratification, this is a most valuable lesson to review at least once a year.

My own memories of Christmas as a child whisper to me that getting there was more than half the fun. I don't much remember the actual presents I looked forward to so fervently, but, deeply embedded in my subconscious, there lies not just the vivid memory but also the tantalizingly real presence of those magical, hope-brimmed days of waiting filled with secrets, scents, and sweet mysterious smiles.

Prayer: *Lord, preserve me from foolish nostalgia; yet permit me to know once again the childlike joy of truly waiting for Christmas. Amen.*

✛Minister of The First Presbyterian Church in the City of New York; poet, author.

Tuesday, December 21   Read Psalm 111.

As this week moves along, the readings seem to catch the reader up into a mounting chorus of praise. From psalmist to prophet and to Simeon and Anna, the song of delight in the glory of God's salvation rings forth in true exaltation.

I am reminded of a renowned preacher and a professor of mine at Edinburgh who spoke of the Book of Psalms as being like a smoldering volcano of praise whose fires are forever threatening to burst forth, even in the most desolate-seeming passages, so that by the time the collection reaches its climax in the last forty psalms or so, the eruption is in full flow, blazing forth into the clear, unadulterated praise of God.

So it is with these Christmas lections. They lead along the ancient paths of the joyful acknowledgment of divine glory. This is a grateful praise we are called to join: "I will give thanks to the LORD with my whole heart." The best of our praising arises from gratitude. There can be a tendency in religious circles to regard the praise of God as a way of seeking favor with the deity, like the kind of obsequious flattery used to gain advantage with despotic rulers in times gone by.

The praise I read in the scriptures has no such calculating tone. It is absolutely emptied of self-interest and is filled instead with a completely selfless exhilaration at the sheer wonder and majesty of God's amazing grace.

The greatest word of praise in the whole Bible, of course, is one few of us have the freedom or the faith to utter very often. But—blessings be!—this time of year we get the chance to stand up and sing it forth at the very top of our lung power. The word is *Hallelujah*; and thanks to good Mr. Handel, we can stand up and bellow it unashamedly.

Prayer: *Lord, catch me up into your praise. Let me become an* Hallelujah *to your glory. Amen.*

Wednesday, December 22   Read Isaiah 61:10–62:3.

This reading is filled with the imagery of decoration and garlanding. It expresses the joy of God's salvation in terms of festal garments, crowns, royal diadems, and robes.

Part of our Christmas preparation is an act of bedecking, as we place greenery about our churches and homes. Despite the custom's roots in pre-Christian times, there is, still, a beauty in it and a meaning that lies deeper than a simple urge to decorate.

> We bring the outside in
> this chill and waning season,
> cut boughs and branches, strands
> of light and living green and deck
> them all about the walls and ledges
> of our houses, make believe we fashion
> an enchanted forest glade to frame
> our festive celebrations.
> Evergreens, we call them,
> though they bleed and die,
> so soon, in over-heated rooms.
> Yet that dying lends a fragrance
> and a grace, foretells, if we
> will heed, another time and space,
> where tree and thorns, no longer green,
> fulfill their cruel, necessary function
> in the bright evergreening
> of our wintered race.*

Prayer: *Clothe me with the garments of salvation, O God, and cover me with the robe of your righteousness, even the humble swaddling bands of the babe in the manger. Amen.*

---

*"Hanging the Greens," by J. Barrie Shepherd. Copyright © 1985 Christian Century Foundation. Reprinted by permission from the December 11, 1985 issue of *The Christian Century*.

Thursday, December 23   Read Psalm 98.

The new song of God's praise mounts higher and higher as the full orchestra of creation, seas, floods, and hills joins in this mighty hymn to God's glory. How utterly tame and predictable, how contrived even the very best of our attempts at worship appear in the light of these ecstatic scenes! What must it be like to actually hear the hills "sing together with joy before the Lord"? (TEV)

We tend to skip over the last few lines of this psalm—at least I do. Joy in the Lord's coming is something I can relate to, if somewhat distantly; but the news that the Lord is coming to judge the earth is not a thought I choose to linger on.

Strange, how the biblical writers always seem to conceive of God's judgment as a joyful thing! The whole idea makes *me* just a bit uneasy. Oh yes, I realize that in Christ my condemnation has been set aside—and yet…and yet.…

Might it be that the biblical writers looked forward eagerly to God's judgment because they knew that it will be completely just, that the poor and downtrodden, whom these writers tend to represent, have good things in store?

He will judge the world with righteousness,
    and the peoples with equity.

But as for those of us who are *not* all that poor, or downtrodden, those of us who, in any divine and perfectly just rearrangement of the affairs of the world might have less than the best to look forward to.…Well, we know we *ought* to look forward to it—but we are not all that sure.

Prayer: *Teach me again, good Lord, that your judgment will only condemn what is evil and will delight in mercy and fulfill itself in grace. Amen.*

Friday, December 24　　　　　　Read Galatians 4:4-7.

"The fullness of time." What a rich, evocative expression! It conjures up for me a picture of a golden goblet into which a clear stream of crystal water runs until, at last, it brims over, across the gilded rim and down the gleaming sides to spill across whatever lies below.

Can time really be like that? A vast container into which event follows event in a seemingly endless and meaningless stream and then…fullness is reached; and the whole thing spills forth in completely new and unpredictable directions.

Our Christmas Eve service seems like that: carols and readings; candlelight and holly berry; ancient narratives; lively ideas; lilting, lovely melodies. And then, just at midnight, *silence*. Nothing more to be said, or sung. Silence is the only fitting response—silence, and an enormous expectation.

The time is once again full-filled. Twelve chimes on the tower bell. Pitch darkness in the sanctuary. And finally one candle flame, then two, the seven-branched candelabra, and hand reaching toward hand along and across the pews until time's fullness becomes also the fullness of light.

No glaring kilowatt display this, but the soft, fragile golden light of several hundred hand-lit, hand-held candles, each hand forming its own lampshade, its own manger for this little glimmer-gleam, newborn into its care and keeping this December midnight hour—in the fullness of time.

Finally, so softly you can barely hear it, a whisper from the organ, "Silent Night" stealing across oaken rows to touch the heart, moisten the eyes, maybe even liberate the lives that crowd into this fullness of both holy place and time.

Prayer: *Lord Christ, come to my silent emptiness this holy night. Fill it full, far beyond time, toward the fringes of eternity. Amen.*

Saturday, December 25 (Christmas)
Read Isaiah 52:7-10.

George Frederick Handel does more than set us free to bellow *Hallelujah!* He takes passage after passage of immortal scripture and sets it to almost equally immortal melody, lending a new dimension of delight to our history of salvation.

This Isaiah passage, for example, can never be the same after one has heard a soprano soloist singing its words into one of the loveliest arias in the *Messiah.* In the mind's eye, one may even catch a glimpse of the speeding sandals of those messengers racing across the mountains to bear the great glad news of grace to the waiting, anxious city of this world.

For many, indeed, this season is not complete until we have listened to or sung the music of Handel's greatest oratorio. I first fell in love with the *Messiah* as an eighteen year old, spending my first winter in the Royal Air Force at a bomber base high on the Lincolnshire wolds.

On December nights, a group from the base would trudge those snowy hills to rehearse for the Christmas *Messiah* at the village church nearby. We sang our hearts out in that frigid ancient chancel, warmed up over cocoa and cakes at a choir member's home, then tramped back under the stars, singing all the way—and startling quite a few sheep on the journey!

Music, of all sorts, is such an integral part of this festival of Christ's birth, because it echoes the angels' song, of course, but also because music speaks *to* us and *for* us on a level far deeper than words alone. Is it too much to hope that—since all communication will be perfected in the end—music will prove to be the language of heaven?

Prayer: *Sing to my soul this holy day, Lord God, the worn, yet wondrous melodies of love. Amen.*

Sunday, December 26   Read John 1:1-10.

It's as if John were saying, "Now hold everything, folks. This wasn't *really* the beginning. I mean these stories of his birth are all very nice, with their angels, shepherds, manger, and the rest; but this whole thing actually began long before, before time was even thought of!"

"In the beginning," John begins—as if he were starting Genesis all over again—"In the beginning, when all that Genesis stuff was starting to take place, the Word was there already; in fact, the Word was what the whole thing was about."

This infant Jesus, whom people rhapsodize about, embodied far more than any cute and cuddly newborn, cowshed babe. In him was gathered, somehow comprised (yet not compromised) in human form, the power of our creation and redemption. In him invisible has become visible, intangible is now fully and most amazingly tangible, the secret to the mystery we have grappled with across the ages is once and for all revealed at the heart of a human life.

This life we know and cherish, the light that shines upon us in the darkness, lends meaning, purpose, destination, even destiny to our days. All this we have from him; all this came to us, comes to us still, in him.

How to hold on to this in the wintry days ahead? How to keep in mind—soul and life as well—that the meaning of our days, the solution to our problems, the light for all our darkness, do not emanate from a bank book or discount store, a flash of entertainment, or a futile, fleeting passion?

The light still shines; the Word still speaks. All we have to do is listen and look up.

Prayer: *Speak your Word to me, and then through me; and thus let your light shine. Amen.*

In Love and Mercy, God-with-us

December 27-31, 1993
Monday, December 27

George Donigian[+]
Read Psalm 72:1-14.

Psalm 72 contains much hope for justice and may be read even with a sense of messianic expectancy. Images of the rule and prosperity of the king strike us as reminders of an agrarian society in which environmental pollutants were unknown, a society in which digital clocks and computer logs did not disrupt rhythms of life, a tribal society ignorant of global concerns and global economics.

Despite a bucolic vision, the psalmist makes readers aware that the idylls of the king are possible only through the mercy of God and only as the king does the work of justice. The strength of the psalm lies not in the words of dominion but in the words of deliverance (vv. 12-14). The needy are delivered; the poor and the weak receive mercy and are saved from violence and oppression. The oppressed are precious in the sight of the king.

How unlike many modern political scenarios is this vision! One imagines scenes at which the psalm might be read aloud. I imagine that someone like Hophni (one of Eli's sons) might read only verses 1-11. A Nathan might read the fullness of those first verses and then help the king recognize God's demand for justice in verses 12-14. How might a prophet of today read this passage?

Suggestion for prayer: *Today and during this week, pray to hear the cries of the needy and to seek ways to work for and with Jesus Christ to deliver those in need.*

[+]Editor, Children's Department, Division of Church School Publications, General Board of Discipleship of The United Methodist Church; clergy member of the Virginia Annual Conference.

Tuesday, December 28   Read Isaiah 60:1-3.

The imperative mode speaks today as it did when the prophet first uttered the words: "Arise, shine; for your light has come, and the glory of the LORD has risen upon you."

Arise and *shine* evoke images of energy, joy, and light. Though the words are addressed to Zion, Isaiah does not limit this proclamation of salvation to a particular area. In any place, those in need or those who are oppressed are also weary and living in despair and mourning. The oppression of despair penetrates all human categories and definitions of class and caste. That is why Isaiah 60 has been such an important part of Advent traditions. To all who are oppressed, the meaning of the words penetrates to the core of our being, revealing our need and our desire for grace and mercy. Arise, shine; and see the revelation of the Lord!

In my inner city neighborhood, people go through their daily routines, with behavior patterns weighted down by economic and social burdens. They are little different from any other people—the burden of despair squashes hope among all people. Yet, Isaiah's joyful ingathering goes beyond all boundaries, even the boundaries of time. He communicates the vitality of salvation to people enervated and despairing of hope. The glory of the Lord has risen upon you. Arise, shine!

Prayer: *O Christ, True Light of God, make my soul worthy to behold joyfully the light of your glory, and to rest in the hope of the good things to come in the mansions of the just until that time of your glorious coming. Have mercy upon all your creation and upon me, a sinner. Amen.**

---

*A prayer by the Armenian Saint Nerses Shnorhali (the gracious one); from oral tradition.

Wednesday, December 29   Read Isaiah 60:4-6.

"Lift up your eyes and look around," commands Isaiah. There follows a description of the nations coming to Zion. They bring home the exiles, and the nations also bring tributes and wealth to the king.

Though the words indicate a physical act, the biblical witness helps us understand that perception involves more than eyesight. These verses about seeing evoke two biblical passages, images of mercy and of justice. The first is Psalm 72, in which the kings of Tarshish, Sheba, and Seba bring gifts to Israel's king. Then comes the promise that all nations serve the king because he has delivered the oppressed. The king serves the cause of the Lord and is just.

After the seventy returned from their mission, Jesus rejoiced in prayer and said to the disciples, "Blessed are the eyes that see what you see" (Luke 10:23). Then Jesus tells the disciples that many prophets and kings desired to see what the disciples have seen, but did not receive that gift.

Lift up your eyes and look around in your own prayer and devotion. What do you perceive to be the needs in your community? in the nations? in God's creation? What of God's spirit has become radiant in you?

To move from Advent to Christmas to Epiphany is to go from the condition of need to the radiant joy of salvation. Radiant joy is not the sated aftereffect of a Christmas feast. Radiant joy lives and grows as we serve God, moving beyond private concerns into the radiant concern for God's creatures; our joy in our salvation becomes a part of all those we meet.

Prayer: *God, elevate our spirits that we may rejoice in the perceptions your Spirit gives. Elevate our lives that we may plunge into the depths of servanthood and do your deeds of justice and mercy. Amen.*

375

Thursday, December 30   Read Ephesians 3:1-6.

To read Ephesians 3 is to get caught up in a vigorous rambling that addresses the mission-oriented devotion of the Christian life. Given the relative freedom of my life, I do not often think of myself as a prisoner of Christ Jesus. I remember Martin Luther's comment that the Christian is subject to no one and yet, servant to all. But does that a prisoner make?

The image of prisoner for the sake of Christ in a society that persecuted Christians must have brought hope to those who heard the letter read and comfort to those suffering Christians who identified with the suffering Christ.

"Prisoner for Christ Jesus for the sake of the Gentiles" moves beyond the early understanding of Christianity as a sect to the beginning of Christianity as a religion for all peoples. Advent focuses upon the particular messianic expectation of Israel. Christmas expands the fulfillment of that messianic hope in Jesus Christ. Yet the Christmas celebration is incomplete if we remain beside the manger in the stable. The twelve days of Christmas push us away from the straw to the vigorous life of discipleship, a life worthy of captivity.

Discipleship pushes us to engage in the deeds of justice, mercy, and love, which form our ministry and mission. We become advocates for needy children who have no one to speak for them. We shelter homeless persons who have no place to rest their heads. We speak out for political prisoners and victims of oppression that their voices may be heard. Such are some of the deeds of justice, mercy, and love that become the prisoners for Christ Jesus "for the sake of the Gentiles."

Prayer: *Holy are you, compassionate God. Let your compassion radiate in our spirits that all may know we are prisoners for Christ. Amen.*

Friday, December 31   Read Ephesians 3:7-12.

The cycle of Advent–Christmas–Epiphany provides us with an awareness of the boundless, unsearchable riches of Christ. We move from expectation and hope to the manifestation of God's power and light in Jesus Christ. We become aware of an innocent strength emanating from a stable, and we radiate awe in the incarnation. Such knowledge celebrates our awareness of God's intent for all the world, the gracious gift of salvation for all people. That good news of salvation underlies all our worship.

For the sake of this good news, each of us is called to be a servant. Ephesians 3 connects our servanthood with the church and "through the church the wisdom of God in its rich variety might be made known." Here we bump into the problem of the church: service can be voided by church traditions, and congregational rituals may eliminate servanthood because the institutional needs must be met.

We are connected to God's rich variety, which incarnates itself in the many servants who are the church visible and invisible, and we are servants according to the gift of God's grace. We dare to remind those within and without the church that the people and the God who brought Christmas also bring Epiphany, servanthood, Emmanuel, God-with-us. That good news prolongs the first joys of Christmas and carries that joy deeper into Epiphany's celebration of the Word become flesh that lived among us.

Thanks be to God.

Prayer: *At night, in the day—at all times we pray, loving Creator. Accept our prayers and worship, O Lord, and grant us your mercy that we, servants according to your gifts, may scale the heights and plumb the depths of your rich grace. Amen.*

The Revised Common Lectionary 1993
(*Disciplines* Edition)

January 1-3
Jeremiah 31:7-14
Psalm 147:12-20
Ephesians 1:3-6, 15-18
John 1:1-18

January 4-10
Isaiah 42:1-9
Psalm 29
Acts 10:34-43
Matthew 3:13-17

January 11-17
Isaiah 49:1-7
Psalm 40:1-11
1 Corinthians 1:1-9
John 1:29-42

January 18-24
Isaiah 9:1-4
Psalm 27:1, 4-9
1 Corinthians 1:10-18
Matthew 4:12-23

January 25-31
Micah 6:1-8
Psalm 15
1 Corinthians 1:18-31
Matthew 5:1-12

February 1-7
Isaiah 58:1-12
Psalm 112:1-10
1 Corinthians 2:1-12
Matthew 5:13-16

February 8-14
Deuteronomy 30:15-20
Psalm 119:1-8
1 Corinthians 3:1-9
Matthew 5:17-26

February 15-21
Exodus 24:12-18
Psalm 99
2 Peter 1:16-21
Matthew 17:1-9

February 22-28
First Sunday in Lent
Genesis 2:15-17; 3:1-7
Psalm 32
Romans 5:12-19
Matthew 4:1-11
  Ash Wednesday
  Joel 2:1-2, 12-17
    (or Isaiah 58:1-12)
  Psalm 51:1-17
  2 Corinthians 5:20*b*-6:10
  Matthew 6:1-6, 16-21

March 1-7
Genesis 12:1-4*a*
Psalm 121
Romans 4:1-5, 13-17
John 3:1-17

March 8-14
Exodus 17:1-7
Psalm 95
Romans 5:1-11
John 4:5-42

March 15-21
1 Samuel 16:1-13
Psalm 23
Ephesians 5:8-14
John 9:1-41

March 22-28
Ezekiel 37:1-14
Psalm 130
Romans 8:6-11
John 11:1-45

March 29–April 4
Passion/Palm Sunday
Matthew 21:1-11
Psalm 118:1-2, 19-29
Isaiah 50:4-9*a*
Psalm 31:9-16
Philippians 2:5-11
Matthew 26:14–27:66

April 5-11
Easter
Acts 10:34-43
Psalm 118:1-2, 14-24
Colossians 3:1-4
John 20:1-18
  (or Matthew 28:1-10)
Holy Week
(selected lections)
Monday:
Isaiah 42:1-9
Hebrews 9:11-15
Tuesday:
Isaiah 49:1-7
John 12:20-36
Wednesday:
John 13:21-32
Maundy Thursday:
Psalm 116:12-19
John 13:1-17, 34
Good Friday:
Psalm 22
John 19:1-30
Holy Saturday:
Job 14:11-14
John 19:38-42

April 12-18
Acts 2:14*a*, 22-32
Psalm 16
1 Peter 1:3-9
John 20:19-31

April 19-25
Acts 2:14*a*, 36-41
Psalm 116:1-2, 12-19
1 Peter 1:17-23
Luke 24:13-35

April 26–May 2
Acts 2:42-47
Psalm 23
1 Peter 2:19-25
John 10:1-10

May 3-9
Acts 7:55-60
Psalm 31:1-5, 15-16
1 Peter 2:2-10
John 14:1-14

May 10-16
Acts 17:22-31
Psalm 66:8-10
1 Peter 3:13-22
John 14:15-21

May 17-23
Acts 1:6-14
Psalm 68:1-10, 32-35
1 Peter 4:12-13; 5:6-11
John 17:1-11

May 24-30
Pentecost
Acts 2:1-21
Psalm 104:1*a*, 24-34, 35*b*
1 Corinthians 12:3*b*-13
John 7:37-39

May 31–June 6
Trinity
Genesis 1:1-2:4*a*
Psalm 8
2 Corinthians 13:11-13
Matthew 28:16-20

June 7-13
Genesis 18:1-15
Psalm 116:1-2, 12-19
Romans 5:6-11
Matthew 9:35-10:8 (9-23)

June 14-20
Genesis 21:8-21
Psalm 86:1-10, 16-17
Romans 6:1*b*-11
Matthew 10:24-39

June 21-27
Genesis 22:1-14
Psalm 13
Romans 6:12-23
Matthew 10:40-42

June 28–July 4
Genesis 24:34-38,
  42-49, 58-67
Psalm 45:10-17
Romans 7:15-25*a*
Matthew 11:16-19, 25-30

July 5-11
Genesis 25:19-34
Psalm 119:105-112
Romans 8:1-11
Matthew 13:1-9, 18-23

July 12-18
Genesis 28:10-19a
Psalm 139:1-12, 23-24
Romans 8:12-25
Matthew 13:24-30, 36-43

July 19-25
Genesis 29:15-28
Psalm 105:1-11, 45b
Romans 8:26-39
Matthew 13:31-33, 44-52

July 26–August 1
Genesis 32:22-31
Psalm 17:1-9, 15
Romans 9:1-5
Matthew 14:13-21

August 2-8
Genesis 37:1-4, 12-28
Psalm 105:1-6, 16-22, 45b
Romans 10:5-15
Matthew 14:22-23

August 9-15
Genesis 45:1-15
Psalm 133
Romans 11:1-2a, 29-32
Matthew 15:(10-20) 21-28

August 16-22
Exodus 1:8–2:10
Psalm 124
Romans 12:1-8
Matthew 16:13-20

August 23-29
Exodus 3:1-15
Psalm 105:1-6, 23-26, 45b
Romans 12:9-21
Matthew 16:21-28

August 30–September 5
Exodus 12:1-14
Psalm 149
Romans 13:8-14
Matthew 18:15-20

September 6-12
Exodus 14:19-31
Exodus 15:1b-11, 20-21
Romans 14:1-12
Matthew 18:21-35

September 13-19
Exodus 16:2-15
Psalm 105:1-6, 37-45
Philippians 1:21-30
Matthew 20:1-16

September 20-26
Exodus 17:1-7
Psalm 78:1-4, 12-16
Philippians 2:1-13
Matthew 21:23-32

September 27–October 3
Exodus 20:1-20
Psalm 19
Philippians 3:4*b*-14
Matthew 21:33-43

October 4-10
Exodus 32:1-14
Psalm 106:1-6, 19-23
Philippians 4:1-9
Matthew 22:1-14

October 11-17
Exodus 33:12-23
Psalm 99
1 Thessalonians 1:1-10
Matthew 22:15-22

October 18-24
Deuteronomy 34:1-12
Psalm 90:1-6, 14-17
1 Thessalonians 2:1-8
Matthew 22:34-46

October 25-31
Joshua 3:7-17
Psalm 107:1-7, 33-43
1 Thessalonians 2:9-13
Matthew 23:1-12

November 1-7
Joshua 24:1-3*a*, 14-25
Psalm 78:1-7
1 Thessalonians 4:13-18
Matthew 25:1-13

All Saints Day
Revelation 7:9-17
Psalm 34:1-10
1 John 3:1-3
Matthew 5:1-12

November 8-14
Judges 4:1-7
Psalm 123
1 Thessalonians 5:1-11
Matthew 25:14-30

November 15-21
Ezekiel 34:11-16, 20-24
Psalm 100
Ephesians 1:15-23
Matthew 25:31-46

November 22-28
First Sunday in Advent
Isaiah 64:1-9
Psalm 80:1-7, 17-19
1 Corinthians 1:3-9
Matthew 13:24-37

November 29–December 5
Second Sunday in Advent
Isaiah 40:1-11
Psalm 85:1-2, 8-13
2 Peter 3:8-15*a*
Mark 1:1-8

December 6-12
Third Sunday in Advent
Isaiah 61:1-4, 8-11
Psalm 126
1 Thessalonians 5:16-24
John 1:6-8, 19-28

December 13-19
Fourth Sunday in Advent
2 Samuel 7:1-11, 16
Luke 1:47-55
   (or Psalm 89:1-4, 19-24)
Romans 16:25-27
Luke 1:26-28

December 20-26
Isaiah 61:10–62:3
Psalm 111
Galatians 4:4-7
Luke 2:22-40
  Christmas Day
  Isaiah 52:7-10
  Psalm 98
  Hebrews 1:1-12
  John 1:1-14

December 27–
    January 2, 1994
  (Epiphany readings)
Isaiah 60:1-6
Psalm 72:1-14
Ephesians 3:1-12
Matthew 2:1-12

Gracious God, help me share my life and faith....
And let me be open to others as they share the ways
they experience your power. May we know the
unity to which you call us. *Amen.*

Disciplines 1991
(a prayer by Anne Broyles)